Home Plans for the 80's

Home plans for the 80's

Murray Armor and
Michael Furnell

PRISM PRESS

First published in 1983 by

PRISM PRESS
Stable Court
Chalmington
Dorchester, Dorset DT2 OHB

ISBN 0 907061 39 7 Hardback
ISBN 0 907061 40 0 Paperback

Published simultaneously in South Africa by
BOK BOOKS INTERNATIONAL 1982
Durban North – Republic of South Africa

Distributed by:
U.S.A. — Network Inc, P.O. Box 2246, Berkeley,
California 94702
Australia — Doubleday Australia Pty Ltd, 14 Mars
Road, Lane Cove, N.S.W. 2066
New Zealand — Roulston Greene Ltd, P.O. Box 33-
850, Takapuna, Auckland 9

Printed by Purnell and Sons (Book Production) Ltd.,
Paulton, Bristol.

Contents

ACKNOWLEDGEMENTS

Drawings by Derrick Spence.
Designed by: Bob Cooke
              Steve Rich
              Jane Willis
Design pages co-ordinator: Tim Woods
Architectural consultant: Jeff Brabban
With many others whose work has been acknowledged
in the text or privately.

Introduction

Having a new home built to a design that you yourself have chosen is one of the most popular ambitions in the world, and for thousands of people every year it is a dream which comes true. Individual building plots are easier to come by in the eighties than they have been for twenty years. The Banks and Building Societies are in competition to lend money for new houses, and are much more flexible in the ways in which they will do this. The recession in the building industry means that both builders and sub-contractors are enthusiastic about working for private clients. If you have always wanted to build to your very own design, now is the time to do it.

To take advantage of this and build on your own land you will have to make many decisions, and you will have to plan and manage the whole thing in a very careful way. Making the right decision depends on your analysis of many different factors, but the aim of everyone building for themselves is the same. Invariably your new home has to be *a very good investment*, and *exactly the home you want to live in* and building it has to be a cheerful and stress-free business.

Achieving these aims is not difficult, but the whole business has to be handled properly, and this needs a very clear understanding of how the system works, and of the options open to you.

Home Plans for the Eighties is set out in a way to give you all the information that you will need to make the right decisions, and to make your own dreams come true. The options explained and the advice given are based on day-to-day experience with thousands of people who have built on their own land. All the designs shown have been built, often with modifications to suit individual clients. Some of them have been built literally hundreds of times.

Later in this book you will find details of how the plans can be obtained, and details are given of other services which you will find useful. At the very end is a list of organisations and firms that can give specialised help in many ways, and a catalogue of books, periodicals and leaflets for further reading. We hope all of this will be useful to the readers for whom this book was written — those who dream of a new home and intend to make their dreams come true.

A new home— The essentials

So you are looking at designs for a new home. If you are just looking, dreaming dreams perhaps, or looking for ideas to help you to choose what sort of house you should buy from a builder, then this is a book to be dipped into wherever it interests you, and it has lots to say. On the other hand, if you are really hoping to build on your own land, then you have got to read it in a very different way. You have to sort out the dreams from reality, and to do this you have to look hard at three essentials.

First of all, you need to consider designs in relation to your financial situation. You know what you can afford to spend, and now you have to work out what you can build within your budget.

Secondly you have to think about your dream house as an investment, and to make sure that what you will pay for it will be more than covered by its market value. You will want it to increase in value in step with house values generally, and hopefully ahead of them.

Thirdly, you have to think about your home being exactly the building that you want to live in, suiting your own life-style, with the appearance and the atmosphere that you want.

If you have already got a site, or there is a site which you are thinking of buying, then you can look at all of this in relation to that site. You will be able to identify a narrow range of options, and then make firm decisions. If you have not got a site, and are reading this book to help you to know what is both possible and practicable when you look at building plots for sale, then it is even more important to understand the basis of the decisions which you will have to make in due course.

Sad to say, many of the decisions will be made for you by others. The planners will decide whether your new home can be built at all, and if they agree then they must approve every detail of its appearance and materials. The Building Regulations will often control where you put the building on the site, and will determine many details of its construction. The cost of services — water, gas, electricity and road access — and involvement with other legal obligations can be a major factor in choosing a design. All of these constraints and legal requirements are dealt with on pages 64 to 72 and it is vital to realise the importance of all of them.

The cost of a new home is dealt with on pages 2 to 8. Here you will find repeated references to 'costs per sq.ft' and this is a concept that has just got to be understood if you are to get anywhere. Average cost per sq.ft. multiplied by the number of sq.ft. in a design, gives a very rough indication of total cost. This can be related to your budget costs, and doing this is the essential first step in deciding what you can afford, and what is out of the question.

The whole business of design, and how best to analyse your own requirements, is discussed on pages 9 to 14. This deals with design concepts — with changing styles in design, with styles that will date and those that are less likely to, and with the relationship between design features and costs. Other specialist chapters deal with the materials and the fittings which give the home its feel and character.

The 200 pages of home plans include designs to meet almost every situation in a wide variety of styles and materials. Plans are available for all of them as they are illustrated, and they can also be supplied with modifications and alterations within the original design concept. These standard plans are also of great use in deciding what features you may want in a design that has been specially drawn to suit your own particular requirements. However before you consider a special design of your own remember that all of the standard homes have been built and all of their designs were drawn to be cost effective. They are all capable of being built in a straightforward way using standard building industry techniques. Twenty designs on pages 171 to 190 are by Prestoplan Limited, and are specifically for timber frame construction. Timber frames are discussed at length in a later chapter, and if required most of our 200 designs can be built in this way.

Finally, the chapter 'Making it all happen' is concerned with just that, and describes how a design on our pages can become a real home. This usually takes between 6 months and a year; 2 to 4 months obtaining planning consent and dealing with legal matters, and 4 to 6 months building. Sometimes things move more quickly, but rarely does a new house built on a fixed price basis take longer — and you *must* deal in fixed prices in this age of inflation. All the advice in the book is written lightly, because you simply must read it all if you want to build, and a more formal style would not encourage you to do so! It is based on experience with over 2000 new homes built on the owner's own sites. All of them got their dream homes — as does virtually everyone who actually makes a start. If you decide to build for yourself then your planning of the project involves so many others —Building Society Managers, the Bank, Planners, Building Inspectors, builders, the N.H.B.C., Inspecting Architects and so on — that they all have a vested interest in seeing the job through. Once you wind up the machine it starts rolling and will carry on right to the end. And at the end you will not only have your dream home, you will also have had a lot of fun. Good Luck.

What will it cost?

Long before you are able to consider the actual cost of the particular house or bungalow that you want to build you will need to know the approximate cost of the sort of home that you have in mind. This is essential to enable you to know the size of property which you can afford, and the sort of designs which you should consider. These figures which you need are expressed in costs per sq.ft. This requires some further explanation.

For most technical and legal purposes the floor area of a building is not the overall area, but is the 'area enclosed by the internal faces of the external walls'. It is at least 10% less than the area obtained by multiplying together the outside measurements, which is called the plinth area. The diagram explains this. In this book all areas are the strict legal areas, but in some publications it is the overall areas, or plinth areas that are quoted. Obviously costs per sq. ft. of plinth areas are significantly less, so that care must be taken in comparing figures from different sources. For a two storey building the areas of the two floors are added together.

Any general figures for costs per sq.ft. depend on three factors. These are:
   What you build
   How you build
   Where and when you build
How these factors affect your costs is dealt with on the following pages.

SIZE RELATED TO HOUSING TYPE

Up to 700 sq. ft. — Holiday chalets and 1/2 bedroomed old people's bungalows only.

700 to 800 sq. ft. — Smallest possible 3 bedroom semi-detached houses. Small 2 bedroom bungalows.

800 to 900 sq. ft. — Small 3 bedroom bungalows with integral lounge/dining rooms and compact kitchen. 2 bedroom bungalows with larger kitchens or a separate dining room. Most estate built 3 bedroom semi-detached houses.

Around 1000 sq. ft. — Large 3 bedroom semi-detached houses. 3 bedroom detached houses. Small 4 bedroom houses. 4 bedroom bungalows with integral lounge/dining room. 3 bedroom bungalows with separate dining room or large kitchen. Luxury two bedroom bungalows.

Around 1300 sq. ft. — 3 or 4 bedroom detached houses and bungalows with the possibility of a small study, or second bathroom, or a utility room.

Around 1600 sq. ft. — 4 bedroom houses, or bungalows with 2 bathrooms, large lounges, small studies, utility rooms.

Around 2000 sq. ft. — Large 4/5 bedroom houses and bungalows.

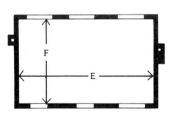

FIRST FLOOR

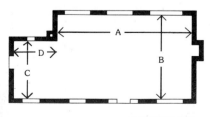

GROUND FLOOR

The area of a dwelling is the total floor area enclosed by the internal faces of the external wall.

(A × B) + (C × D) + (E × F) = total area for the plan above, which is for the house on the right.

This large detached house with Georgian windows is 2000 sq. ft.

This three bedroom bungalow is 840 sq ft. plus the garage.

This four bedroom farmhouse is 1508 sq. ft.

WHAT YOU BUILD

The costs per sq.ft. for both bungalows and houses are much the same provided that the buildings have straight-forward foundations, and that you can avoid expensive roofing materials.

The key element in costs is the roof — how it is built and how it is tiled. Any arrangement to put rooms in the roof, as in dormer bungalows, or in many traditional style house designs, inevitably adds to costs. The most cost effective roofs are built from factory made trussed rafters. These are wholly supported by external walls, and although they provide useful attic space for storage and water tanks they do not provide any room for living accommodation. A dormer bungalow with rooms in the roof needs traditional purlin construction,

and in most circumstances this costs significantly more than a trussed rafter roof.

Dormer bungalows are unpopular with the planners and generally out of fashion, but gable window features in two storey designs are very much part of today's cottage style. It is often possible to build these using trussed rafters. The diagrams explain this. Wherever possible all designs in this book use trussed rafters.

The span of the roof is an important cost factor, with the optimum distance about 25 ft. Any span over 30 ft. involves increased construction costs, and any spans under 20 ft. are disproportionately expensive. The pitch, or angle of the slope of the roof, affects the cost by increasing the area to be tiled, and above 35° this becomes significant. However, the most important

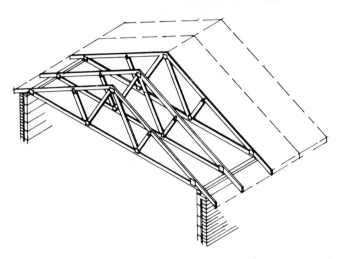

Trussed rafter roof — easily erected, cost effective, limited space for storage.

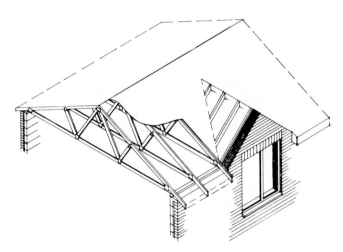

Gable feature in a trussed rafter roof requires that the window head is below the eaves.

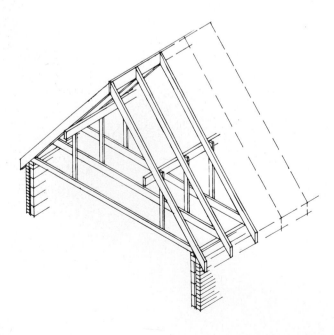

Traditional purlin roof — plenty of room but expensive to construct.

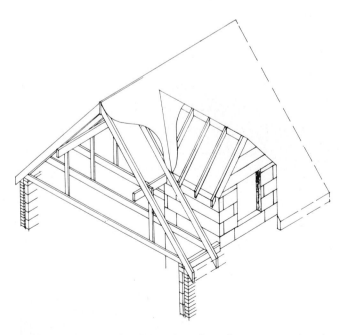

Gable window in a traditional roof can be set at any height.

factor in roof costs is the roofing material.

95% of all new roofs are tiled with concrete inter-locking tiles, and these are available in a wide variety of shapes and colours. Some are indistinguishable from natural clay tiles. In certain areas the planners may insist on other roofing materials, and these can add enormously to costs. Clay tiles, traditional plain tiles whether concrete or clay, and either real or artificial slates are all very significantly more expensive. Some of these materials require rafters to be set closely together to support their weight, and add 50% to the cost of the roof timbers. All this is discussed further in the chapter on roof tiles; at this stage the thing to remember is that any movement away from concrete inter-locking tiles will cost a lot of money. How much? One example. The 'Carlton' design shown below costs £2978 more to build when roofed with concrete plain tiles than when it is built with inter-locking concrete pantiles, and this is a 13% increase on the 1983 cost of building this bungalow.

Below the roof your costs will be determined by two things — the fixtures and fittings you choose, and the shape and materials of the shell. Fixtures and fittings — kitchens, bathrooms, doors, fireplaces, flooring etc — are up to you. Our average costs are based on fittings appropriate to the size of the dwelling — luxury kitchens in large homes, economy kitchens in small homes. The economies of scale when building large properties tend to be balanced by the more expensive fittings and fixtures put into them, so average costs do not vary much with size.

The Carlton bungalow, which costs £2978 more to roof using one concrete tile than another. This is considerably more than the extra cost of putting it on a reinforced raft foundations. Many clients are unnecessarily concerned at the cost of special foundations but ignore the greater expense of any special tiles required by the planners.

A house has a smaller roof than a bungalow for the same floor area. so the effect of expensive tiles on houses is less significant in terms of cost per sq. ft.

The cost of building the walls depends on a number of factors, and whether or not you use a timber frame is irrelevant compared with the cost of the outer skin. Our average costs are based on this being in wire-cut facing bricks, or in blocks for a rendered finish, or in a good quality artificial stone. Natural stone, especially with stone surrounds for windows, will add significantly to costs — although not as much as expensive roof materials. There are no general price guidelines for stone; everything depends on local prices and who you can get to lay it in a way that will do it justice. If everything else about a property is right, then building it in real stone is an investment as it should add significantly to the value of the property. The same is true of building in hand made bricks, but in practice those who build in real stone, or in hand made or reclaimed bricks, do so at the insistence of the planners, and rarely from choice. All of this is discussed at length later.

External joinery can be the usual painted softwood, or stained softwood which adds nothing to cost and a great deal to character, or hardwood. Hardwood windows, windowboards, door frames and doors add about £800 to the cost of a medium sized home. They should add far more than that to its value, and hardwood joinery is now the choice of the majority of those who build for themselves. Aluminium and plastic windows are principally used in the refurbishing of old buildings, and are not used to any significant extent in new housing. Their day may come, but it has not arrived yet. They are very expensive. All this is discussed elsewhere in the chapter on joinery.

The design of the superstructure of a building has an effect on costs that relates mainly to the way it affects the area of external walling involved. The diagram explains this. Ceiling spans over 14'6" bring problems for your architect, as do galleries, large stairwells, and projecting balconies, but these features are usually found in large houses where they have less effect on costs per square foot than in smaller properties.

Below the superstructure are the foundations, defined as the part of the building where you pour your money into the ground, never to be seen again. Do not worry about the 'best' foundations for any situation; Building Regulations are so strict and so concerned with the worst possible circumstances that any foundations approved at the Town Hall will be more than adequate for their purpose. All that you have to do is to make sure that the work is in accordance with the drawing. Fortunately the Building Inspector will also make this his concern, but he will not help you to meet the cost of his enthusiasms. Before you agree to any special foundation arrangements always make sure they are obligatory and not just a suggestion, and look at the full cost implications.

Most new houses are built on standard strip foundations with solid floors. This involves digging trenches under the walls, pouring a 9" layer of concrete in the bottom, building up from this to just above ground level, and then laying a concrete floor. There are alternatives for different sites but all of them cost money. These are shown opposite in order of descending cost.

2 small two bedroom bungalows and one had 30% more walling to be paid for than the other.

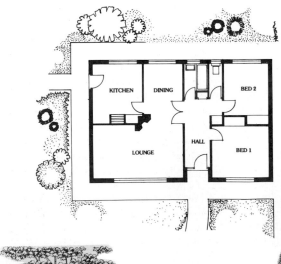

Piling. Building a modern home on deep piles driven into the ground can cost £3 a sq.ft. or more by the time you have paid for the test bore holes, engineer's designs and the work itself. It is a way of being able to build on very bad ground indeed, and is often cost effective when the land was cheap to start with, or when the value of the finished home will be high.

Underbuilding. Building a garage under the home, or building a home into a hillside to give a series of split levels, is definitely not cost effective and should be avoided if you are very concerned with cost and have acceptable alternatives. Developers and those concerned with the building industry often build in this way very cheaply, but will rarely tender competitive prices to do this for others. It is invariably cheaper to carve out a plateau from a hill, or to build one up and then to build from the level base. On the other hand, multilevel buildings do look very nice from outside. Whether they will suit your living pattern is another matter.

Raft Foundations. In mining areas or on soft land the authorities may require you to build on a raft, which is simply a slab of reinforced concrete that sits just under the surface taking the whole weight of the building. This is rarely as expensive as you fear it will be, and is unlikely to add more than £1 a sq.ft. to the costs —often less.

Trench Fill Foundations. This is a technique for filling your foundation trenches to the top with concrete, and avoiding foundation brickwork altogether. In rural areas where bricklayers' travelling costs are significant and where a concrete truck can get all around the foundations this approach may even save money.

Reinforced Strip Foundations. If the authorities are concerned about the ground on which you are building and are making noises about a raft, then ask if reinforced strip foundations might be acceptable. You will need a civil engineer to specify the reinforcing mesh to be put in the concrete, and to provide design calculations for this, but his fees plus the cost of the work may be significantly less than the alternative.

Suspended Floors. There are only two reasons for having suspended floors. Firstly if you like a suspended wooden floor, believing it to be kinder to your arthritis, or giving a better spring to the floor when you have disco parties, then go ahead and pay for it. It will cost less than £1 a sq.ft. The other reason for having it is that you may have more than 2'6" of fill to be put into your foundations between ground level and floor level. If this is the case the N.H.B.C. will insist on a suspended floor, and although the building regulations do not require it, it is a good thing anyway. It can be either a wooden floor or a reinforced concrete floor; the latter may be marginally cheaper.

Service Connections. Finally, the total cost of your new home will also depend on what you have to pay for service connections. The cost of getting water, gas and electricity to the site are really part of your site costs, but have to be considered carefully just the same. Most serviced plots have got these utilities conveniently to hand, and only connection fees and service trenches have to be considered. Isolated plots in the country are a different matter. Drainage is dealt with on pages 70 and 71. All our costs quoted allow for the average cost of making drain connections on serviced plots, or for the installation of a septic tank on isolated sites. Surprisingly, septic tanks cost very little more than a drain connection.

So much for the cost of what you build.

HOW YOU BUILD

There are two ways in which those building a new home on their own land arrange to have the building work done. The majority — perhaps 75% — engage a builder to take the whole job as a single contract, with an N.H.B.C. Certificate on the finished property at the end of it all. The others manage the job themselves using sub-contractors, and the popularity of this approach is growing. In Milton Keynes for instance, where the new town authority releases hundreds of serviced plots a year for sale to private individuals, most of them build in this way. There is rarely a middle road; the idea of having a builder to put up the shell and then taking the job on from there yourself is attractive, but it does not often happen. Building using sub-contractors gives very real cost savings, and also very real responsibilities, problems and panics to be dealt with. All this is discussed further in a later chapter, but as the cost saving can be 20% or more the approach that you adopt does affect your budget costs. If in doubt use a builder. The self-build movement is for those with abundant self-confidence.

WHERE AND WHEN YOU BUILD

We are all used to regional variations in the market values of homes in different parts of the country, and accept as a fact of life that a house in Surrey will cost twice as much as the same home in Humberside. Land prices account for much of this. What is more difficult to understand is that building costs will also vary, although not to the same extent. Why this should be so is an interesting subject for an argument over a pint of beer, but such debate will not detract from the fact that you will have to pay more to build on your own land in some areas than in others. Generally speaking it will cost up to £2 a sq.ft. over the average to build in a high cost housing area.

In rural areas costs are usually lower, but you may have to pay more than the average if the site is remote and the workmen's travelling costs are significant. This is particularly true in the South West and parts of West Wales. On the other hand, a surprisingly large number of those who build already have local contacts or are very good at making them, and find the bargains.

Any cost of building for yourself, and indeed the ease with which you can interest a builder in quoting for a job on your own land, depends on the state of trade in the building industry. At present it is very depressed, and builders are anxious to quote for any sort of work. In the 70's when the housing market was firmer, builders were less enthusiastic about one-off jobs. Whether these conditions will return is a mute point, but it is important always to look at up-to-date costs and to keep in mind the possibility of an upturn in home sales. If this happens it will be more difficult and more expensive to build on your own site, but also the value of the home you build will escalate quickly, and the differential between cost and value will improve.

One of the best ways of getting reliable up-to-date costs is to look at the figures quoted by the companies who provide a package service for individual sites. Both the firms concerned with traditional construction and those selling a timber-frame service will quote realistic prices, and if you make sure that these are for the finished job, including the services and the access, then they are an excellent guide to what you should expect to pay. Design & Materials Limited publish case histories giving the plans photos and the actual costs of a recently completed job every month, and these are available through Plan Sales Services to anyone sending a stamped addressed envelope. They are concerned with both the contract costs of those who employ builders, and the adventures of those who build using sub-contractors in all parts of the country. The costs shown here are based on an analysis of these case histories and on other real experience.

Spring 1983 national average costs for single and two storey homes to D & M standard designs, built on single sites by individual clients, on straight-forward foundations, including fittings and fixtures appropriate to the size of the property, central heating, double glazing, connection to drains or septic tank, garage, short length of drive, no landscaping.

When built by an established N.H.B.C. builder, working from his offices following an invitation to tender, formal contract.
— from £25 per sq. ft. (January 1983 contracts).

When built by a reputable small builder, N.H.B.C. registered, working from his home, usually himself a tradesman, following an informal approach and contract established by exchange of letters.
— £21 to £23 per sq. ft. (January 1983 contracts).

When built by a competant private individual on a direct labour basis, using sub-contractors, without providing any labour himself.
— £17 to £19 per sq. ft. (January 1983 completions), occasionally much less.

Self-build housing, individuals or housing associations, typically over 50% of the labour provided by the individual or the association.
— approximately £14 per sq. ft.

The average figures quoted remain remarkably consistent, irrespective of the size of the building. The more expensive fittings in larger properties are balanced by savings consequent on the economies of scale.

FACTORS WHICH WILL KEEP DOWN COSTS.

Use of concrete inter-locking tiles.
Cost effective walling materials.
Trussed rafter roofs with spans of between 24 ft. and 28 ft.
Care taken that any special design features are arranged in the most cost effective way.
Building on a level plinth.
Building using strip foundations and level floors.

FACTORS WHICH WILL INCREASE COSTS.

Unusually expensive fixtures and fittings.
Roofing material other than inter-locking concrete tiles, especially on steep pitches.
Natural stone or hand-made brick walling (but this may be a good investment).
Hardwood joinery (but this may be a good investment).
Building other than on a level site.
Complex designs which increase the area of external walling, and involve complex roof shapes.
Dormer roofs, especially dormer bungalows.
Special foundation arrangements.

Choosing a design

Having considered the size of home that will suit your finances, the constraints of your site, and bearing in mind the probable requirements of the planners, you can move to the business of choosing between designs. This involves the appearance and style of the building, and the number, size and arrangement of the rooms which it will contain.

The external appearance of homes built in Britain in the last sixty years has varied enormously, and until very recently there has been a marked distinction between the *avant garde* homes that are featured in the text books as being the influential designs of their decade, and what was actually being built. The architecturally significant homes of the thirties had flat roofs, architectural use of glass, rounded corners and a German name — the Bauhaus style. They were about as different from the mock Tudor homes that the developers were actually building as they could be. Then came the War, and after it both the theorists and the developers wanted a change. In the fifties and sixties, architects were seeking to express the essentials of function in bricks and mortar, stripping away unnecessary decoration and contrived features. At the same time the less aesthetically aware were opting for homes with simple (and cheap) shapes, and with low pitch roofs and picture windows (as in Hollywood films). Later in this period contrasting panels of timber and plastic became almost obligatory.

With the first oil crisis in 1972, came the concern for smaller windows and 'boxier designs'; the fashionable few built Georgian houses in Regency proportions, while the developers simply put Georgian windows into their same old boxes. Enter the Georgian style executive residence.

Meanwhile something was happening at the Town Hall. The reorganisation of local government in 1974 gave planners throughout the country a chance to see that they got their own way in the brand new authorities. In the old District Councils the planners had always been new boys, upstarts from the fifties, lacking the weight of those who had administered finance, housing or sewerage since the nineteenth century. In the new councils they could establish themselves — and they did. County design guides were produced, setting out clearly and unambiguously exactly what could expect to be approved, and what could not. Whether, as some maintained, it was never Parliament's intention that the Planning Acts should be used to exercise this sort of control is irrelevant; the design guides were published and have had a far reaching effect on our low density housing.

Perhaps it is fortunate that they were drawn up when there was no coherent establishment style for new homes, for in the absence of anything better they reached back to the early nineteenth century and everywhere looked for the essential features of the local

Rural Housing — 1960s.

Rural housing — 1980s.

9

cottages of that era. In Nottinghamshire, farm houses used to have gable roofs with steep pitches, so hipped roofs and low pitched roofs were forbidden. Essex cottages once had black boarded gables and dark stained joinery; these features became essential to speculators' developments in Basildon. Nowhere in 1830 had builders stuck panels of contrasting materials below windows to make their houses look pretty, and this fashion of the sixties came to an abrupt halt. Window design also changed as is discussed and illustrated in the chapter on joinery later. Even more far reaching, complex shapes and involved roof lines were introduced to give 'interest' to a design, sponsored by architects who had been urging simple shapes and functional structures only fifteen years before.

It was all fascinating, especially to the big developers who had to find whole ranges of new designs to replace their old ones that had lasted since the fifties. Look at a Wimpey estate of 1960, and a Wimpey estate today, and, if you prefer today's house designs, you will feel it

fortunate that those who bought the older homes have disguised them with such splendid front gardens.

Architects protested vigorously against the idea of any design guide at all, but mindful of a frightening fall-off in commissions due to the recession they hastily climbed on the band wagon and became pedantically involved in the minutæ of the regional styles. By 1980 the *avant garde* and popular taste had met up. Both were concerned that building shapes should be as complex as finances would permit, with careful use of natural looking material, and with small windows that were conveniently energy saving as well as being traditional. Within two years this led to contrived traditional features added as ornaments, and even to the re-emergence of pseudo Tudor styles and half-timbered houses with herringbone brick infill. Within one generation our whole approach to house styles had undergone a total revolution. We had arrived at the cottage style of the eighties.

What is the relevance of this history lesson to the

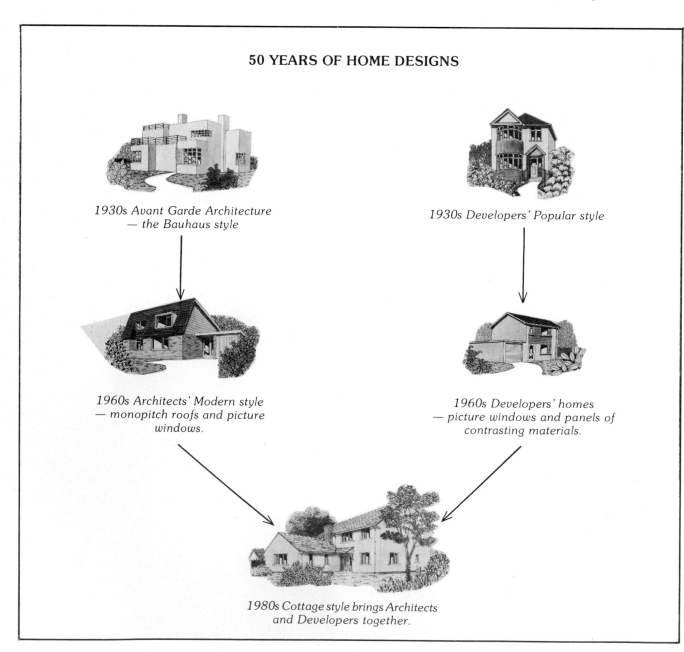

50 YEARS OF HOME DESIGNS

1930s Avant Garde Architecture — the Bauhaus style

1930s Developers' Popular style

1960s Architects' Modern style — monopitch roofs and picture windows.

1960s Developers' homes — picture windows and panels of contrasting materials.

1980s Cottage style brings Architects and Developers together.

reader who wants to build a new home today? For one thing, it must surely reassure him that today's style is likely to be with us for a long time. There is no alternative on the horizon, and there is widespread public disillusion with the modern architecture which it has replaced. Because it is traditional it suits our growing interest in conservation. All of this can only be a very good thing.

In all his drawings in this book Derrick Spence has shown homes in the styles that are likely to be generally acceptable to the planners in the sort of settings in which they are illustrated. However, you must remember that there are wide regional variations in planning policy, and particularly in the way in which bungalows are regarded. It is generally true that in most areas the planners would like to reduce the proportion of single storey homes that are approved. Planning authorities also differ in the extent to which accepted regional styles are insisted on in areas where there is a preponderance of existing buildings in other styles.

What will happen if you do not like the design guide recommendations for your new home? Except in conservation areas and other places of particular importance, the planners will often back down, or at least negotiate, on their imposition of many design features, and if they will not, formal planning appeals on these issues are often successful. On the other hand, a formal planning appeal is a lengthy process, and by the time you are discussing design details you are usually locked into a tight programme and cannot spare the time to appeal. Another consideration is that the cottage style is here to stay, and that if your home is to be the best possible investment, then like all other investments from Unit Trusts to jewellery, it should be a good fashionable example of its type.

The top end of the scale — a large farmhouse in Nottinghamshire built on a commanding site on a large arable farm. A building of this size is usually treated by the planners as an architectural unit on its own, and is less likely to have to conform to strict design guide standards.

Architect — Dennis E. Wilburn R.I.B.A.

So much for the external appearance of your home; now for the arrangement of the living space inside the building. If you wish you can simply leaf through the design pages and make a note of the plans which particularly appeal to you, but if you are actually choosing a new home let us urge you to find the time to analyse your wants before you get involved with individual designs. Start with the front door. Do you feel that front doors are important, and should be a key feature in the view of the front of the building as in a typical Georgian style house? Or are they not really important — as in many fifties style houses? Front doors lead into a hall. If you can build only 1500 sq.ft. within your budget, then do you want to use 150 of them on an imposing hall that is a room in its own right, with space for furniture, or do you want the minimum size hall and to use the area saved elsewhere? Or do you want

Do not get too involved with design details without having a clear idea of the atmosphere which you hope to give your new home.

a hall at all, and would you like a dining room in the centre of the house to give access to other rooms as in so many American designs?

A whole list of these different concepts of how we like to arrange the accommodation in our homes is shown opposite. Please answer the questions and establish your requirements in concept before considering the plans — it really is the right way round to do things. Whatever your requirements, today's cottage style, with

HOUSE/BUNGALOW LAYOUT
DESIGN CHECK LIST

Front Entrance

Do you think an impressive front entrance should be a key feature of the house?
Or just take its place in the front elevation?

Front Porch

Is this required? Is a storm porch required to draught-proof the hall when the door is opened?

Front Hall

Is it important that the hall should convey the whole feeling of the house as soon as you step inside? Or is it just a space between other rooms?
What furniture do you want in the hall? How essential is a cloaks cupboard?
Do you prefer a glazed or solid front door?

Lounge

Lounge or lounge/dining room? Is the feel to be of an enclosed room, with no more window than to provide a view, or is the preference for a large area of glazing with the room relating to the garden or patio outside? Are patio windows required?
Is a fireplace required? If not perhaps a dummy fireplace? If so, a feature fireplace or a classical small fireplace? If a feature fireplace, should this have a vertical feel, to the ceiling, or be a full wall feature, or have an extended mantel to provide shelving?
If you are having a lounge-dining room, is some form of room divider or natural break between the two parts of the room preferable?

Does the lounge/dining room need a door to the kitchen or just a hatch?
In general terms, do you like 'L' shaped lounge/dining rooms?

Dining Room

Maximum number to sit at table?
Door or hatch to kitchen?
Is a built-in sideboard acceptable to save space?

Kitchen

Will the family eat in the kitchen?
At a breakfast bar or table?
How many?
What major appliances are required in this room?
Is a structural larder required?
Is an Aga or similar solid fuel cooker required?

Utility Room

Need this be any more than a large porch?
What appliances are required in it?
What storage space?
A w.c. adjacent to the back door (useful in rural areas)?

Bathroom

One bathroom or two? If two, is one to be en suite with the master bedroom?
Fittings in bathrooms—bath? basin? w.c.? bidet? separate shower?
Airing cupboard in bathroom, or can it be elsewhere?

W.C.

Where?—in bathroom(s)? in cloakroom or hall? at back entrance?
Basins—in which w.c.'s?
Cloaks cupboard—in a cloakroom which is also a w.c., or would you save space by having hooks and rails actually in the cloakroom itself, not enclosed in a separate cupboard?

Bedrooms

How many double, how many single?
Is the master bedroom to be as generous as possible at the expense of the others?
Is provision to be made for built-in furniture?

Study

Is this to be significant room, or very small with just room for a desk and filing cabinet?
Does it need built-in shelving, or cupboards?
Will it double as an occasional bedroom, and thus require room for a divan?

Garage

Integral with the house with a communicating door to the utility room or kitchen, or separate?
How many cars?
Plus extra room for garden tools etc.?

Central Heating

What type of central heating system is envisaged?

Future

Is there any possibility of future extensions or alterations to suit changed family circumstances?

complex shapes and involved roof lines, makes special-arrangements and alterations a lot easier than they were when everything had to be accommodated in a more simple shape. Most things are possible if the site and your finances permit, and while you will have to accept the advice of your architect or designer about how you achieve your ambition, if you are paying the bill it is your prerogative to say exactly what your ambition is.

Naturally we hope you will find one of our plans that exactly suits your living pattern, your site, and the whim of the planning officer. However, it is not unlikely that you will want to make changes. The best way of advising us of these is given on page 282, but before sharpening your pencil you may find the following notes useful. They are based on a great deal of experience of dealing with clients' requests for alterations to standard plans.

POINTS TO BEAR IN MIND

 * Beware of adding windows to give more light and more views; you usually end up with nowhere to put your furniture.

 * Try to keep windows a minimum of 2'3" from the corners of the building. This ensures the strength of the structure. If you want a corner window you will have to pay for some way of reinforcing the corner walls.

 * Look at the way that the architect has put windows symmetrically in the building, and beware of damaging this symmetry. In general a ground floor window is balanced by a first floor window of the same width. Not essential, but think about it.

 * Regulations require that the main windows in a lounge, living room, dayroom, study and bedroom must be 12' from any boundary. Fire regulations limit the total area of doors and windows in all walls near to a boundary. You can have 60. sq ft. of

openings in a wall 3'3" from the boundary, but only 10 sq. ft. if you move in to 3'0". You need professional advice on this.

 * All rooms have to have opening lights to the windows up to a total of 5% of the floor area of the room. Patio doors count as windows if they also have trickle ventilators.

 * Bathrooms and lavatories can be built without any windows, as long as they have fan assisted ventilation via ducts in the roof, but even if you like this it is a bad re-sale feature.

 * Stairs are subject to dozens of regulations and cannot be moved about with impunity. Try to leave the stairs where they are. Above all try to avoid plans for two storey houses with no stairs at all. Every few years some authority or other builds council houses with this interesting feature, to the delight of the popular press.

 * A W.C. cannot open into a kitchen or living room. The W.C. should lead into a 'ventilated lobby' which is a hall, landing or utility room.

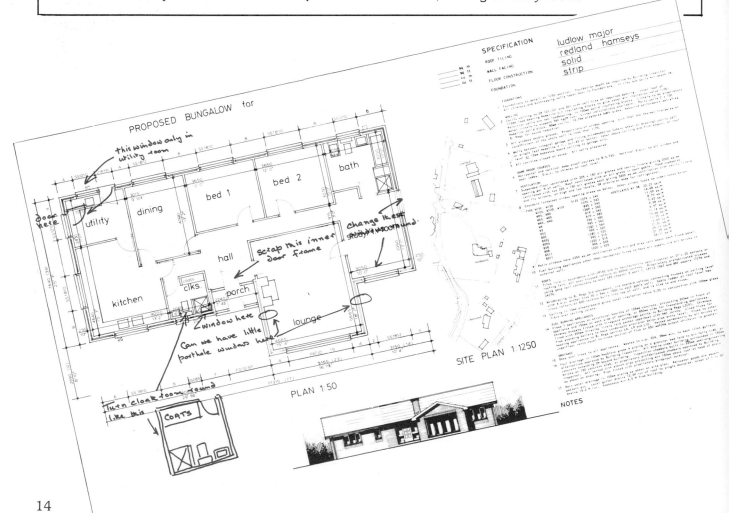

Garages

A garage for the car is part of our image of a dream home. This concept is so firmly rooted in our idea of what is right that it is worth looking at the argument against having a garage, as it is rarely realised how easily this can help a budget problem.

A garage usually accommodates a car and an assortment of garden tools. The car will not deteriorate if left standing in the open, although it will be colder to get into on a winter morning. The garden tools can go in a garden shed at the bottom of the garden, easily disguised with a vigorous evergreen climber. Thus the only reason for a garage is to conform to a dream image that is based on pride in one's automobile, and a desire to be seen to cherish it. However illogical this is, the great majority of people build a garage!

In spite of this you may wish to consider whether you would rather have two extra rooms instead of an integral garage, or perhaps a huge landscaped patio with a barbecue pit and pergola instead of a detached garage. Another option is to build the concrete slab for the garage foundation but to do no more until the new home is finished and you are sure you have the funds to build the home for the car. Until then the car will not come to any harm parked outside.

The pros and cons of detached versus integral garages are equally worth considering. If you have a narrow site you may not have much choice, but if this is not the case, then consider the factors in the box below.

As a compromise you may wish to consider a carport. If so, it is important that it is properly designed, with solid piers and a deep fascia so that it relates properly to the main building. This is never easy, and today's homes are less well suited to carports than the ranch style homes popular a few years ago.

* A detached garage can be positioned in relation to a house or bungalow so that the group of two buildings look better than a single dwelling with an integral garage. A link wall can add to this effect.

* A detached garage is cheaper to build than an integral garage, as it does not require complex foundations, a fireproof ceiling, or other expensive features.

* A detached garage can be built after the house or bungalow is built, or when it is approaching completion. If you are uncertain whether you can afford it you may find this useful.

* It is more expensive to put a water tap, electricity, or an outside W.C. into a detached garage than it it is into a integral garage.

* An integral garage provides somewhere to put a central heating boiler, or an extra freezer, and in many ways tends to be useful simply because it is part of the main building.

* An overwhelming advantage of an integral garage to the elderly or infirm is the opportunity to get in and out of the car 'out of the weather'.

Bricks

The new cottage style housing of the eighties has, in a way, rediscovered brick. Today's concern with houses that have complex shapes, with emphasis on architectural details, and with subtle use of colour and texture in materials has encouraged brickmakers to widen the range of bricks available, and given an opportunity for bricklayers to bring craft bricklaying back to house building. In the sixties and seventies brickwork in most housing was very dull, with bricks laid in the simplest possible way as a foil to contrasting panels of other materials. Brickwork features and special bricks were rarely used. Recently we have seen a brickwork revolution, and they are back in all their full range of shapes, colours and textures. This chapter is to help you in choosing both the brick and the style of brickwork for a new home.

Virtually every planning consent has a condition reading 'samples of walling material shall be submitted and approved before construction commences'. Whether you handle this yourself, or whether someone deals with this for you, the choice of the brick that you submit will normally be yours, and you will want advice on making your decision. If the planners decide to press alternatives on you, then it is even more important to know what you are discussing with them and where to go for further help.

As an alternative to this, in a particularly sensitive situation such as a conservation area, the planners may actually specify the bricks they require. You can argue, but are unlikely to win. In this case ask them to give you a sample !

Bricks are given trade names by manufacturers, such as Butterley Muirfield Mixture, where Butterley are the manufacturers, and Muirfield Mixture is one of their trade names. To the ordinary person this means nothing, but somewhere in the manufacturer's leaflet you should find a clue to which of a number of types the bricks belong. All bricks are available in a selection of colours and textures, but it is the type of brick that dictates the price. These prices vary enormously, and this is always a major consideration. The average 1000 sq.ft. bungalow needs about 7000 bricks, and the average 1600 sq.ft. house about 12,000. As brick prices can vary by £200 per thousand it is essential to know the cost of what you are discussing, and also to keep in mind that haulage costs form a significant part of the delivered price. However, price is not the only consideration.

All bricks made today have to meet very strict standards for both strength and durability and are suitable for all normal domestic uses. There are special standards for bricks that are to be used in special situations, such as cills, copings and some retaining walls. If plans for your new home have been professionally prepared then they will specify the type and class of brick that is to be used, and any divergence from this will quickly attract the attention of both the Building Inspector and the N.H.B.C. Inspector. Wirecut clay bricks are usually made to a special quality that suits them for any situation, and most of the wirecuts shown here are in this category.

BRICKS AND BRICKWORK

Having considered the different types of brick, it is important to appreciate the distinction between the colours which are available, and the textures. Two bricks of the same colour, but with different textures, can be very different in appearance. If you add another variable by using coloured mortar, the differences are emphasised. The colours of clay facing bricks are determined by the inherent colour of the fired clay, additions to the clay body to give through colours, surface effects given by the application of stained sands — which are rendered colour fast during firing — and variations in the firing conditions. Special textures may be given to the bricks in a wide variety of ways, or sometimes they are simply left smooth.

Such a variety of colours and textures is now available that it would be cumbersome to list them all here. A choice between them must be a personal judgement.

Finally, how on earth do you choose between them? One of the best ways is to find a builders' merchant with a brick library — a term for a display of representative bricks which are available. Usually these bricks are displayed in panels and choosing between them is easier than when looking at a single brick. Alternatively, write to the facing brick manufacturer for details of their clay facing bricks and delivered prices.

Choosing bricks from samples is always an interesting business. Make sure you view them in natural light if possible, and if you are looking at sample panels consider the effect of the mortar colour. Ideally confirm your choice by looking at a building in the brick which you want to use.

Butterley Jubilee Mixture.

Butterley Desford Old English Russett.

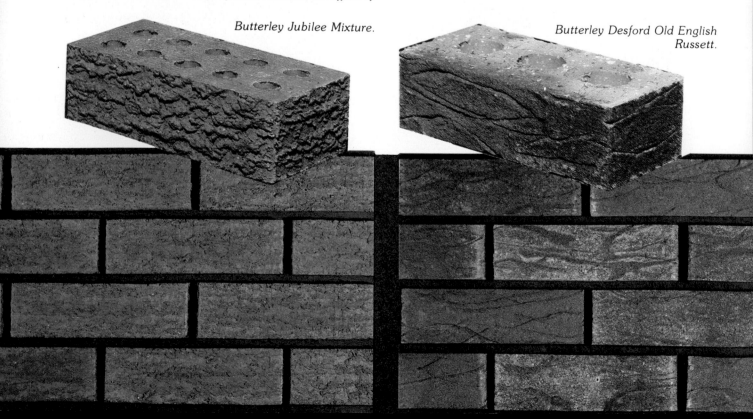

TYPES OF BRICKS

Fletton Bricks are also called LBC bricks, after the name of the only company which manufactures them. They are made from deposits of London clay, require little fuel to bake them, and as a result they are the cheapest clay bricks available. They are not very strong, but meet all requirements for building above damp course. There is a limited range of colours and textures. Fletton bricks are widely used in the Home Counties, and may be specifically required by planners in certain areas. Elsewhere they tend to be used in budget housing only. The price, ex works, for this type of brick is about £65 per thousand.

Wirecut Facing Bricks are made by a continuous extrusion process which enables the physical properties of the brick to be closely controlled, and are available to any standard required. A typical ex works price for Butterley Facing bricks is £130 per thousand for Jubilee Mixture. The range of colours and textures is very wide indeed, and these are the bricks usually used in new houses built by individuals on their own sites unless there are special considerations.

Stock Bricks are a traditional type of brick found in certain parts of the country. They have an irregular shape and the colour and surface texture is distinctive. They are available to any required specification.

Handmades are bricks which are literally made by hand. They have a distinctive appearance with a folded face known as the smile — see the photo below — and are always made from the very best of clays with super colours. Very much the thing for prestige housing, and if they cannot be used for the whole job within your budget, consider using them for internal feature walls. They need to be laid by a really good bricklayer to get the best effect. An average price is £212 per thousand.

Secondhand Bricks are widely used in certain areas of Cheshire, East Anglia and Sussex, where they may be required by the Planners. If you are buying secondhand bricks it is essential to get all you want for a job from the same source at the same time, otherwise they may not all match. It is unwise to make firm arrangements to buy secondhand bricks without consulting the builder or the bricklayer who is going to actually lay them. The cost of these bricks can vary enormously — and so can the quality.

Commons are bricks which are to be covered up by plaster or otherwise concealed, so that they do not need to have an attractive appearance. Always take advice on the suitability of Commons for the purpose to which you intend to put them. The cost of Common bricks is usually about £48 per thousand.

Class B Engineering Bricks are high quality bricks which are used for foundations, retaining walls and other situations where strength and resistance to water are important.

Concrete Bricks, Sandlime Bricks, Calcium Silicate Bricks, are rarely used for housing. The colours are usually artifical, and they are mainly used for commercial and industrial purposes. They are usually priced below clay bricks.

Butterley Sandringham Handmade.

Butterley Jacobean Blue-Red.

Butterley Desford Sand-stone bricks with plain tiles and mahogany joinery.

Butterley Golden Multiruf used for a new house at Weston Flavell, near North-ampton.

Butterley Blaby handmade bricks were used for this attractive feature walling.

BRICKWORK IS MORE THAN THE BRICK

A brick building takes its character from:
* The bricks.
* The bond or pattern in which they are laid.
* The colour of the mortar in the mortar joint.
* The use of brickwork features in the design.

The choice of bricks, and approval of brick features is something that will have to be settled with the planners, but the way in which the bricks are laid is largely going to depend on your builder or his bricklayer. Modern cottage style designs give many opportunities for the man who will lay your bricks to show off his craft skills, and if you take an interest in this you will be surprised how flattered he will be, and what a keen interest he will take in doing a good job for you. There are many patterns of brickwork, known as bonds, which were in general use until cavity walls arrived fifty years ago. The cavity requires that bricks are now laid in stretcher bond, which is dull, but the monotony of this can be relieved in various different ways. Brick pillars and landscaping features do not usually have a cavity, and the old bonds can be used. Soldier courses and other features can be used in cavity walls, and brick cills give a great deal of character to any building. Corbelled eaves at gable ends look well, and are a traditional feature in many parts of the country.

In addition to this, talk to the builder about the colour of the mortar. This normally depends on the sand used — most builder's merchants have a choice of grey, red or yellow sand, and each gives its own colour to the mortar made with it. Artificial colours are available for mixing with mortar if required, although great care should be taken with this. The mortar joint itself can be either recessed or flushed, or pointed in a variety of styles. Consideration of all of this is beyond the scope of this book, but what we do want to get across is the need to get the bricklayer interested in the job he is doing on your home, and the best way to start is to ask him to build a sample panel using the actual bricks that you are going to use. Give him half a chance and he will be demonstrating bonds and pointings until the pubs open, and then continue his lecture in the public bar. Once you have got your key building craftsman as interested as this, you can be pretty sure of getting the best job for miles around.

Brick features are back — what a good thing!

Above: 'Squint' bricks used to form the window cill. These particular ones are from Butterley's Caernarvon works.

BRICK FEATURES IN WALLING

Brick features in cavity walls have to conform to building regulations, and cannot be as uninhibited as when used in landscaping or for internal feature walls. The cavity must be left unobstructed, and a recognised bond used to maintain the strength of the panel. However, there are far more options than is often realised. Generally speaking any brickwork feature that is in the same brick as the main area of walling and which is properly proportioned in relation to the building as a whole will enhance the appearance of the property. If well done it will help to lift it right out of one class of building into another — and that means out of one level of investment up to another.

Blaby handmade golden russet bricks were used for the walling to this feature courtyard.

Choose bricks for landscape features with the same care that you use when you choose them for a fireplace. The Jacobean bricks used for this barbecue were ordered with a matching Royal Wedding plaque made by the brick manufacturer, and were chosen to complement the Catheralls paver bricks.

Fireplaces made with Butterley handmade bricks. The manufacturers will help with plans and kits for these indoor features.

The use of bricks for internal feature walls is increasing. They project their own character wherever they are used, so you must make sure that they will suit the furniture and the general decor, carpets and curtains that you will choose for the room. Besides feature fireplaces, internal brickwork is often used for halls, stairwells and kitchens. Usually hand made bricks are chosen.

Material for this chapter and all the photographs were provided by the Butterley Brick Company. Their bricks are available from works throughout the country, and Butterley freely give expert advice and help in choosing bricks for a new home. Contact them at Butterley Building Materials, Wellington Street, Ripley, Derby. Tel: 0773 43661.

Building in stone

A decision to build a new home in stone, or to have stone features as a significant element in the design, immediately involves you in making a whole list of decisions about the right stone to use, and the best way to use it. The right decisions will result in a house that is a show piece, and it is well worthwhile going to a great deal of trouble to look at all the options and to get the best advice.

First of all, any use of stone has to be in the local architectural style. Stone is used in different ways in different parts of the country, and invariably the way in which it is used reflects the characteristics of the local stone itself. Where it is easily worked to give a smooth finish, this finish to the walling is often an essential part of the character of local buildings, and the use of stone with a rough finish is incongruous. Some stone has a pronounced grain to it, rather like the grain in wood, and is always laid with the grain horizontal. In areas where this is traditional one can perhaps use other stone that is not typical of the area as long as it is laid with the long edge of every block horizontal. To do otherwise is to make the building stand out like a sore thumb, when the essence of any stone construction is that it should be seen to be a natural part of the landscape. Every area where stone is the traditional walling material has its own rules of this sort, and you will have to take care that you follow them. The planners themselves will give advice, as will your own architect or builder. Often the man who is selling you the stone will be the most help of all.

Stone is used in new buildings in two ways — as the walling material for the whole of the shell of the structure, or just for ornamental features. This latter use is now declining, and stone panels below windows, stone chimneys in brick bungalows, and stone gables are not nearly as common as they were in the 60's and 70's. On the other hand, the use of stone for the whole building is increasing as part of the general move to natural materials and traditional design. This often involves designing the building to suit the actual stone to be used. Yorkshire gritstone with a rocky face needs to be used in wide panels to give a massively solid feel to the structure, while Bath stone that is worked to a fine face can be used for narrow piers and delicate window surrounds. If your site is in a conservation area or if there are special design considerations then all of this has to be given very careful thought indeed.

Having considered the need for a design that suits the material, there are four aspects of any use of stone which have to be taken into account; the colour, the surface texture, the way it is laid, and the use of traditional features or 'dressings'. Each of these requires separate consideration.

Colour. Stone comes in a wide variety of colours, from warm Cotswold shades to the severe greys of the north. Often the choice of shade will be dictated by the planners, but if there is a choice it is important to guard against simply choosing the prettiest colour among the samples, and to consider the look of the building as a whole. This involves visualising the new home in its setting, and keeping in mind the colour of the roofing material that is to be used. Beware pinks and other non-traditional shades, and as a general rule keep very well clear of mixes of colours unless there is a local style that has quoins or window surrounds of a different shade to the rest of the walling. Mortar joints must always match the colour of the stone itself, and the brickwork technique of using a contrasting mortar to give a special effect should never be used.

Surface Finishes. The surface texture on stone walling can have as much effect on the overall appearance of the building as the colour. Faces vary from smooth to very rough and uneven, and all have special names — ashlar, tooled, chisel dressed, rough hewn etc, and different quarries and manufacturers have their own names for the different surfaces. Again, take local advice and make up your mind after looking at finished buildings rather than small samples. The same applies to different ways of pointing the mortar joints.

Features. Features in stonework such as quoins, window surrounds, and corbels once had a specific structural role in the building, but are now really ornamental. None of them are essential to ensure that the building will not fall down, but when used in the proper way they give a splendid air of 'being right' to a new house, and are definitely something to have if costs permit. The special blocks of stone used for features are called dressings or fittings, and a whole range of them are illustrated opposite. Again take local advice, and consult your supplier. Remember that dressings are often specially made and that the way in which they are described can vary. Order from a catalogue if at all possible.

Laying Stone. Building in stone is a very different business from laying bricks. Most stone used for new houses is either laid in a completely random way, or else used in irregular courses, and yet it has to be a coherent element in an integrated design. If a window has to be set at a certain height then the mason has to ensure that the pattern of stonework reaches this height as a natural break. The more irregular the pattern in which the stone is being used, the more important this is, because the effect of random walling depends on the regular use of large stones or jumpers. If these are missing near a window or doorway the whole wall will look wrong. If you are using coursed stone, remember traditional walling of this sort depends for its effect on

the courses being of different heights, and the balance between these courses is critical.

Achieving the right effect with natural stone is a job for a mason, who often has to cut or 'dress' the stone to size. Artificial stone is more easily laid, and is supplied in mixes of blocks to set proportions which suit the walling style required. Both quarries and artificial stone manufacturers have leaflets which show the styles of walling for which their stone is suitable.

Whoever is laying your stone will have a clear idea of the way that he is using it — make sure this matches your own ideas as well. Discuss the jointing and the different types of pointing, and jump in your car and go off for an hour with him to look at other stonework that he has built. It may be worthwhile getting him to spend half a day building you a panel of sample walling — indeed, the planners may ask for this. The home that he is to build for you will last hundreds of years; if you are building it in stone then do not grudge the time to make sure the use of the stone is exactly as your wish it.

Architectural feature stonework, or 'dressings' are part of traditional stone construction, and are available to match most types of walling stone. The illustration shows the whole building in Bradstone reconstituted stone, and the dressings used are as follows:

1–Plinth course. 2–Quoins. 3–Porch surround. 4–Traditional window surround without label moulding. 5–Label moulding used as string course. 6–Coping. 7–Traditional window surround with label moulding. 8–Kneelers. 9–Gable coping or water tabling. 10–Apex stone. 11–Traditional chimney coping. 12–Conventional chimney coping.

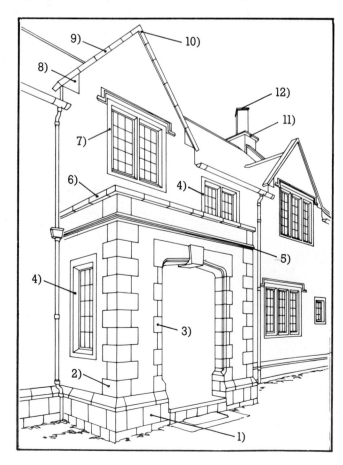

STONE LANDSCAPING

Stone built houses have a traditional feel to them, and invariably this is very important to their owners. It is most important not to detract from this atmosphere by using alien or aggressively modern materials for landscaping. Concrete paths, modern paving slabs or modern screen walling can easily spoil the appearance of a stone home, and all landscaping features should be given as much consideration as the design of the house itself. This involves careful thought about the scale of the features as well as about the materials.

Terraces and patios in particular should be large enough to give the house or bungalow a perspective, and to spread it visually. A small patio often looks like an outsize door mat, and gives a doll's house effect when it should help to make the whole building more impressive. The same is true of steps and balustrading, especially when they lead to a front entrance. All of this is a subject on its own. In this book we simply emphasise that it is an important subject, and that if you are building a new home in stone it is worthwhile making a modest investment to provide stone landscape features to give it the best possible setting. The market for stone in landscaping is very important to both quarries and artificial stone manufacturers, and they will all advise on matching landscaping material which they have available.

Reconstituted stone paving need not look 'new'. These photographs of Bradstone paving sets were taken at the Chelsea Flower Show.

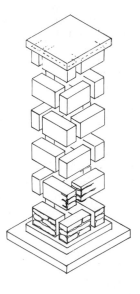

Sundials such as this are available in kit form. However easy they are to construct, it is essential to build them on a properly constructed foundation.

STONE AND YOUR BUDGET

All this mention of stone has so far avoided the question of cost. What does it cost to build in stone, and how will this suit your budget? The answer is that you have a very wide choice indeed, and, as with everything else, you will get the value that you pay for.

Building in natural stone is at the very top end of the market. The right house in hand dressed local stone, provided it is the right design and the right site, leads the field in value. For a four bedroomed detached house the cost will probably start at £5000 more than building in any other material, and it can be much more. Part of this is the cost of the stone itself, part is attributable to the high wastage of material when using real stone, and the rest to the premium cost of employing a stone mason. The results should be worth it, and it is certainly worthwhile obtaining the very best advice and workmen to make sure that you get what you are paying for.

With this level of costs it is not surprising that the majority of those who build in natural stone do so because this is a condition of their planning consents, and for no other reason. Most home builders who start off with an interest in using stone from a local quarry find that their budget will stretch to two extra rooms if they change their minds and use a reconstructed stone.

Reconstructed stone is defined in the relevant British Standard Specification as 'manufactured from cement and natural aggregates for use in a manner similar to natural building stone'. It comes in two categories — the material that looks like artificial stone, and the material where you can't be sure whether it is real or not. Both the way in which it is made and the costs are very different.

Split-faced stone is chipped out of slabs of coloured concrete using hydraulic chisels, and is often subsequently given a convex rocky face. It has a distinctive granular texture, is very consistent in colour, and has its own character which is generally very attractive in the right setting. The manufacturers do not claim that it simulates any particular sort of stone, and it really has to be considered as a material in its own right. In some parts of the country it is popular with both the planners and the public, and where it is appropriate for it to be used it is often cheaper than facing bricks. Quoins and jumper blocks are available to enable it to be laid in most of the traditional ways, and some manufacturers offer matching window cills and other features.

A far more sophisticated artificial stone is made by casting a mix of ground stone and cement in rubber moulds that were themselves moulded on real stone originals. This material is more expensive than split-faced stone, and because of the high capital costs involved and other commercial factors it is virtually the monopoly of one specialist company, Bradleys of Swindon. They have works in different parts of the country, and their trade name Bradstone is now generally (and incorrectly) used for any moulded stone.

The essential of the different types of Bradstone is that they are exact copies of particular types of natural stone, matching them in colour, texture, and in the size of the walling blocks. They are virtually indistinguishable from the real thing. Bradstone is designed to be used in exactly the same way as the natural stone which it simulates, and all the traditional dressings are available to match. It is widely acceptable to the planners in most situations where stone is appropriate, although it is not unusual for a planning consent to specify exactly the style and colour to be used, and even the works from

Above. Bradstone masonry block reproducing the appearance of traditional random rubble walling.

Left. Squared and pitched walling was developed for use in areas where the local stone is dressed to a pitched face.

Something of the subtlety of the shades in which Bradstone can be made is seen in the photograph above.

which it is to be obtained.

The cost of Bradstone as delivered is significantly less than the cost of natural stone as is seen in the table opposite. In addition to this there is not the wastage associated with natural stone, and the walling blocks do not require to be dressed and can be laid by a bricklayer provided he has relevant experience. This avoids the difficulty and high cost of finding a mason. Most of the stone houses in the photographs on these pages are built of Bradstone, and with the current emphasis on natural material for new houses this is the type of stone that will be of greatest interest to most readers of this book.

Another option in your choice of stone is to use reclaimed material from an old building. This is a practical proposition in some circumstances, but it is important to make a cynical appraisal of the old stone available before basing your whole budget on its use. The best person to advise you about this is almost certainly the mason who will be handling it for you, and he should be asked to confirm the proportion of the old stone that is sound, whether or not he is likely to get the total quantity that you require from the amount available, the cost of re-dressing it to give both the face and the bed (or thickness) that you require, and the labour cost of building your own home in this rather difficult material. After consideration of all of this the usual decision is that the old stone will be used for garden walling only! However, if you go ahead it is most important to work out exactly how much re-dressed stone you will require, with a 25% allowance for wastage, and to have this quantity dressed and stacked ready for use before you start building. In this way you will avoid the risk of running out of stone which cannot be matched from elsewhere.

BUILDING IN STONE — YOUR COST OPTIONS.

Typical costs of a square metre of walling stone, ex quarry or ex works, in January 1983.

Dressed stone, 4" on bed — material for building the outer skin of the walls
Cotswold stone, quarry in Wiltshire £60 plus.
Yorkstone, quarry at Ogley, from £18 to £33.
Forest of Dene stone, local quarries £20 plus.

Split faced artificial stone
Split faced reconstituted stone, pitch faced, £6.62 per square metre.

Moulded reconstituted stone
Bradstone, traditional walling £8.63 per square metre.

Photographs for this chapter were provided by E.H. Bradley Ltd, of Okus, Swindon, SN1 4JJ, manufacturers of Bradstone. Attractive colour leaflets for their full range of products are available from them at the address above, and their sales representatives will be pleased to call to advise on the use of their materials for a new home in any part of the country.

Tiles

The appearance of the roof of a building is an essential part of the character of the structure as a whole. As today's traditional style houses involve us in ever steeper roof pitches, so the area of roof which we see from the ground level increases and its importance as a feature increases with it. This has very important implications for those who are building a new home, and before you start looking at samples and colour charts it is worthwhile looking at the overall picture.

First of all, tiles and slate of all types which are used on new buildings today are made to standards that will ensure that they will last a lifetime or longer, and will keep out any extremes of weather provided they are fixed properly. No worries here. As far as anyone building a new home is concerned the criteria are costs, appearance and what the Planners say. A realistic view of this avoids confusion, the facts to be considered are as follows.

'Traditional' roofing materials are the ideal choice for traditional building. Unfortunately the market for them is so small that at times they are not widely available, and the price is usually very high, both of the materials and the labour to fix them. Because of this they are only used when cost is not an important consideration, or where the planners insist that traditional slates or clay tiles should be used. As with natural stone, the home builder on a fixed budget will find that using a traditional material for his roof will take him right out of one level of costs into another, and that if he can use concrete tiles instead, then the saving will pay for a larger home with an extra bedroom. As a result he invariably chooses concrete tiles.

Concrete tiles suffer from their name, which is a pity as a hundred years of expertise has gone into making sure that they look nothing like concrete! They are technically superior to most traditional tiles and slates, can be more securely fixed, and are used on lighter and more cost effective roof structures. Most of them lock together, which determines the spacing, and they are quickly and easily laid. Research over the years has led to standards which enable one manufacturer — Redland — to guarantee their performance for 100 years. They are used for over 95% of new housing, and modern tiles can match traditional tiles in appearance so perfectly that only an expert can tell the difference. All the photographs in this chapter are of concrete tiles.

Tiles and slates are also used for cladding walls, and tile hung walls are a most important feature of the domestic architecture of S.E.England and E.Anglia. All that is said about roofing tiles applies to wall tiles, and again concrete tiles have virtually taken over from traditional material.

For this reason the following pages are wholly concerned with concrete tiles, but in order to relate them to the clay tiles and the different sorts of slate which they match so closely, and so that the reader can understand what the Planners may talk about, it is first necessary to look at the range of traditional roofing materials. This is not an exhaustive list, and there are regional specialities which vary from Norfolk Reed to Westmorland Slate. However, if you think that you may use these materials you have a very special situation and need special advice!

Traditional tiling materials which you are likely to come up against are:

Clay Tiles. Generally of two types, small plain tiles about 8" x 5", and larger curved pantiles. Modern clay tiles are machine made and lack the irregularities of the old hand-made tiles, and old clay tile roofs also get a lot of character from the uneven rafters. Modern clay tiles are virtually indistinguishable from modern concrete tiles, but the Planners may insist on the traditional material in certain areas.

Welsh Slate. There is no real alternative to Welsh Slate, although asbestos cement slates are available which are just as thin and give a similar character to the roof. The concrete tile manufacturers make smooth flat tiles in a slate grey colour to give a roof something of the appearance of the natural slate, especially at a distance, but there is no serious comparison. If you want to build in parts of Wales you may have to use slate or asbestos slate, but discuss possible options with your architect or designer.

Stone Slates. The cost of using any form of stone slate is very high indeed. The genuine material is almost prohibitively expensive, and the various artificial stone slates merely very expensive. Both are heavy and require specially designed roofs. If you are lucky enough to have a site in an area where the Planners will insist on stone slate, such as parts of the Cotswolds or the Lake District, then the finished value of your house will balance the cost. If you do have any choice, then examine all the cost implications with care.

Secondhand Tiles and Slates. As with old hand-made bricks, there is a market in second-hand tiles and slates, and these are often advertised in magazines concerned with rural interests. This is something which always attracts those who are building in the country, and it can be a very good way of getting a genuinely traditional roof. It can also be a disaster.

If you want to use second-hand slates or tiles then get the best advice about the actual tiles that interest you, and if possible have a reputable tiling contractor buy and fix them for you. Above all make sure that you get enough sound tiles to finish the roof, as it is possible to find that you are short of a couple of hundred tiles which cannot be found anywhere else!

ROOF TILES — COSTS

To illustrate the tremendous variation in the cost of using different types of tiles and slates, and the implication of increasing the roof pitch, we look at the cost of a roof for our 'Blyth' house, on page 240. This is our most popular house design, and has been built with roof pitches varying from 22° to 40°. These are the roof and tiling costs in the Home Counties for this house as at January 1983, with the work carried out on a supply and fix basis, including roof trusses, under-slating felt, roof battens, all the tiles, but excluding the chimney and step flashings. The price differentials include allowances for the extra roof timbers for the heavier materials.

Standard Costs with Roof Pitch 35°

Concrete inter-locking tiles £3648
Traditional Welsh slate £8241
Asbestos cement slates £5338
Clay Pantiles £5557
Concrete plain tiles £6225
Artificial stone slates (diminishing
courses) £9208

The same roof tiled in concrete inter-locking tiles at 22° costs £3669 as special clips are required. When the pitch is increased to 40° the cost goes up to £4148.

Tiling in the Home Counties style. Plain tiles used for the vertical cladding, under a Regent tile roof.

Blyth Design House

CONCRETE TILES

Concrete tiles are available in a very wide range of styles and shades. As in all domestic architecture, recent years have seen a move away from formal geometric shapes and simple colours back to traditional tile shapes, subtle and mixed colours, and greater use of special feature tiles. The best way to choose tiles is on roofs, and the tile manufacturers representatives are always able to show you the sort of tile that interests you on the sort of roof that you intend to build. These descriptions of some of the more popular tiles from the Redland range are to help you identify what you will be seeing.

Many of today's concrete tiles have attractive mixed colours. The photographs on the left and centre are of mottled plain tiles, and on the right are of Grovebury double pantiles in a mottled shade.

Below. Redland Delta tiles, colour Tudor brown. These tiles are usually best suited to an urban situation.

Right. Regent tiles, colour farmhouse red, at Brentwood in Essex on a building in the traditional Essex farmhouse style.

Trough valley tiles used between two slopes of Grovebury double pantiles. You should get expert advice on whether to use a lead valley, or valley tiles.

Special valley tiles used with Redland plain tiles.

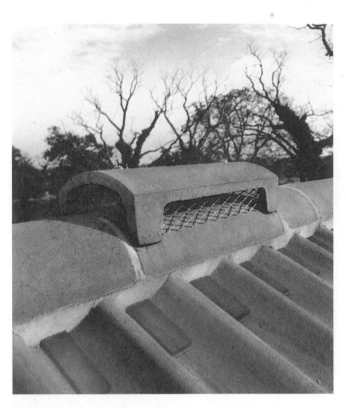

Below. The clean air acts are enabling mosses and lichens to establish themselves on roofs in suburban areas as well as deep in the country. This can be very attractive.

If you are taking an interest in the tiling on your new home you will have to learn the language. The top of the roof is the ridge, the valley between the two different planes of the roof is not surprisingly called the valley, and special tiles are used for both the ridge and the valley as seen in the photographs. You can also get special ventilation tiles and gas fire flue vents that fit on to the roof ridge. An alternative to valley tiles at low pitches may be a lead valley. If your architect has left you in any doubt about whether valley tiles or a lead valley should be used, then consult the tile manufacturer's representative.

The bottom edge of a roof is usually finished with a fascia board which carries the gutters. The soffit is the 'ceiling' under the overhang behind the fascia. The side edge of the roof is the verge. Until recently most verges were either hidden behind a barge board, or finished with mortar pointing, but now new cloaked verge tile systems give a maintenance free verge and are well worth considering.

Vertical tile hanging is usually handled by the same tiling contractor who deals with the roof. The choice of tile for vertical tile hanging is critical; it must be chosen at the time that you choose the roof tiles, and must complement the colour, style and texture of the roof tile.

Above left is a ridge tile flue vent. A flue from a small gas appliance can discharge through an inconspicuous vent of this sort, saving the cost of a chimney.

Some of the parts of a roof are illustrated below. Your verge, barge, and fascia must be in character with the rest of the building, and you should discuss this with all concerned.

Tiling a roof is not only physically demanding and dangerous: it is also a very exact science.

LAYING TILES

A roof of Redland tiles carries a 100 year guarantee on the tiles themselves, but they must be laid to manufacturer's recommendations. Roof tiling is skilled work, and the country is divided into four different exposure zones with different ways of fixing tiles in each zone to suit wind speeds and other factors.

The work of the roof tiler includes fastening under slating felt and the wooden battens to which the tiles are fixed. Here again the standards are precise, and have to be followed. Tiling work on a new home built on an individual site is best specified by reference to the manufacturer's recommendations, as these set standards that exceed statutory requirements and are very easily understood. The manufacturer's field staff will also keep in touch with work on site in their local areas, and will advise on any problems. The major manufacturers have Approved Roofing Contractor schemes — Redland have 350 approved contractors — and if you use them you will get a guarantee on both the tiles and the tiling work.

Material and photographs for this chapter were provided by Redland Roof Tiles Limited of Redland House, Reigate, Surrey. Their telephone number is 0732 42488 and the company is always pleased to give advice and supply literature to anyone interested in tiling a new home.

Windows

We expect rather a lot from windows. They must provide daylight, ventilation, a view of the outside world, and are an essential element in architectural style. They must be openable, yet keep out wind and rain. They must reduce unwanted noise. They must be safe to operate and must be easily cleaned. They must do all these things at an economic cost. The windows that you choose for a new home — or which the planners permit you to choose — will play a major part in the appearance and character of the building. Some idea of how important this is can be seen in these illustrations.

There is a bewildering range of window options in various materials. In this feature we look at the choice of windows with which you are most likely to be concerned if you are building on a plot of your own. Most building plots sold to individuals are in rural or suburban areas where planners are expecting designs to conform to the traditional local style. Window design is a matter where they impose their views very strongly, and most county design guides emphasise the need for windows which have what they call 'a vertical emphasis'. This requires that individual casements should be taller than they are wide, without any small top hung ventilators or horizontal dividing bars. Most of the plans in this book are illustrated with windows of this sort.

There are some parts of the country where there are not such strict rules, particularly in Wales and in the South West, and a wider choice of windows can be used

in most urban areas. It is always interesting to look at the sort of windows being installed in new housing under construction on individual plots near to where you hope to build, and ask at the planning office if you want specific advice on windows considered suitable in a particular situation.

When choosing windows for a new home you have first to consider the style that is appropriate, then the materials from which the windows will be made, the hinges and catches which you want them to have, and finally you must make sure that they are well made and will do a good job.

To start with design. As we have seen the planners will be much involved with your choice, and since April 1982 there has been another constraint. New building regulations concerned with insulation standards limit the windows in a new home to 12% of the wall area if single glazed, 24% if double glazed, and 36% if triple glazed. The effect of this is to ensure that virtually all new homes will be double glazed using sealed units — and the windows must be designed to suit them.

The main styles of windows for you to consider are shown overleaf. The notes reflect experience with those building for themselves rather than the views of either the architectural establishment or the manufacturers. Windows are available in all these styles in various finishes with a wide variety of fittings, and on a later page we look at these fittings in detail.

Picture window

Bay window

Sash window

Pivot window

Casement window

Casement Windows. Any windows with a vertical emphasis and no horizontal dividing bars. These are the fashionable windows for the eighties, usually double glazed and increasingly fitted with elaborate continental style hinges and sophisticated draught-proofing. They may be fitted with one central horizontal rail and called 'Town and Country windows'.

Ejma. Builders call this an Ejma style window, and they are to be found in most houses built between the twenties and the mid-seventies. Now rarely seen in new housing, simply because the small opening top light which spoils the symmetry is out of fashion and is unpopular with planners.

Landscape. Fixed bottom lights and opening top lights. Popular in the sixties and seventies when they went with ranch style homes with low pitch roofs.

Sash Windows. Traditional windows for period homes, and the only choice for a Georgian style house if cost is not a major consideration.

Georgian Windows. More properly called full-bar windows. The popularity of these windows in the late 1970's was the first evidence of the move away from picture windows back to a cottage style. Not now generally used in new housing as difficult to glaze using sealed units.

Pivot Windows. The popularity of these windows with architects is matched by their unpopularity with householders. Great for tearing curtains when opened roughly. Windows of the same shape are now available with other hinge systems which have overcome this difficulty.

Patio door

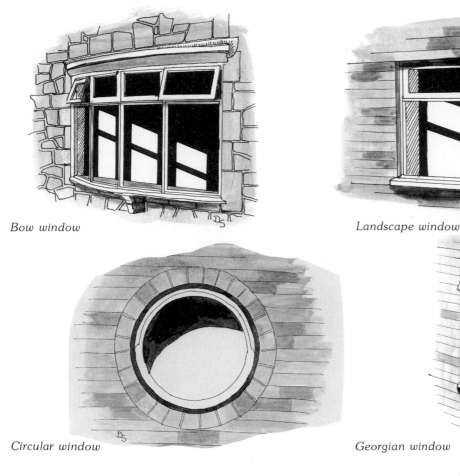

Bow window

Landscape window

Circular window

Georgian window

Picture Windows. Fashionable until recently, now criticised as providing goldfish bowl living. Problems with both Planners and Building Regulations.

Patio Doors. Architecturally impossible to integrate successfully into a traditionally styled home, but the convenience and householder appeal of patio doors outweighs all other considerations and they are here to stay. The way in which they provide a link between outdoors and indoors is the modern equivalent of the Victorian conservatory — and, like the conservatory, they have to be considered as features in their own right.

French Windows. The predecessors of patio doors, they are less convenient but more attractive. When fitted with full-bar glazing they can be very elegant indeed, also providing hundreds of window corners to be cleaned. Difficult to draught-proof successfully.

Bay Windows. A bay window is a splendid addition to any large room when considered from inside the house, but is difficult to incorporate into a modern exterior unless the shape of the building is already fairly complex or the structure is very large.

Bow Windows. Bow windows give character to a room from inside, but are difficult to fit into an overall design unless a number of bow windows are part of the whole design. As with bay windows, it is essential that the house is designed for these features, and that they are not 'stuck on' as an afterthought.

Circular Windows. Can be used to great effect to light a hall, or as features in a gable where they will also light the attic.

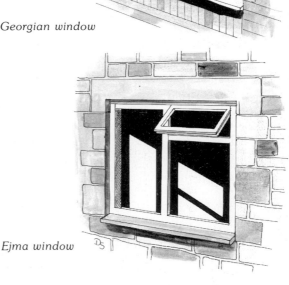

Ejma window

French window

The overwhelming majority of new homes are built with wooden joinery, and although aluminium and plastic windows are widely promoted they are very rarely used in new construction.

With wooden windows you have a choice of hardwood or softwood. Hardwood windows will add £500 to £1000 to the cost of a new home by the time you have paid for matching windowboards, but they also lift the property out of one value bracket straight into another. In this way they are a first class investment — if you can afford them. They give their own distinctive style to a property, which may take some getting used to as we intend to expect a view through a window to be surrounded by a white painted frame. However, contrary to some fears, they do not make a room seem dark.

Hardwood windows are rot-proof, and virtually maintenance free, requiring only a wipe with Sadolin or similar preservative every year. Most that are available in standard ranges are made in Luan or Philippines Mahogany, or else in slightly more expensive Brazilian Mahogany, and you may find that only a limited range of styles is available off-the-shelf. Don't worry — most joinery manufacturers will make windows to special order, although it may take some time.

Softwood windows are now made from timber that is preservative treated, and have an indefinite life, although those who have replaced windows in a house built in the fifties may find it difficult to accept this! They are increasingly available in Pre-dec or other

The section above shows a modern window frame with double glazing and a neoprene draught seal. Note the drip mouldings below the cill to help keep rain away from the surface of the wall below. On the right are three Ripper's windows in the same style, made from Philippines Mahogany, treated softwood for staining, and treated primed softwood for painting. Choose your window timber when you are considering the general design and appearance of your home, not as an afterthought.

special priming which gives the option of either painting or staining. Stained finishes are very popular with the planners and reduce maintenance costs. However, remember that this finish usually looks best under a stained roof fascia, and has to be considered in relation to the whole house style.

Painted windows are still the first choice for many home buyers, at least if you cannot afford hardwood. Remember that it is not the gloss of the top coat of paint that matters in the long run, but the way the timber was prepared and the quality of the priming coat.

FITTINGS

Until recently nearly all windows were fitted with butt hinges and cheap simple window stays and latches. We have now discovered that we have lagged far behind the rest of Europe in this, and at last we are catching up with new attractive fittings that are much more attractive. These really do make sense, and add very little to the total cost of a new home.

Firstly hinges. Remember that you intend to clean your windows, and that there is no reason why you should not clean the outside surface from inside the house. Lever type hinge systems make this possible, and usually incorporate friction pads of some sort to hold the window in any position required without having to secure it with a window stay. This sort of hinge can be used without any expensive machining of

the frame, and the extra cost over butt hinges is simply that of the lever hinges themselves, usually well under £5. The biggest advantage is that the last part of the movement when the window is shut is not a pivoting action, and all edges of the casement tighten into the frame together. This enables rubber draught seals to be fitted to the frame to the best advantage.

'Turn and tilt' hinges are more elaborate still, and enable a window to be opened from the top, the bottom, or at the side. This action is almost impossible to explain in words, but many readers will have met these windows on holiday abroad. Although they involve special machining of the window frames and are fairly expensive, there is no doubt they will grow in popularity.

Window catches need to fulfil three roles: to look attractive, to be as secure as possible, and to provide trickle ventilation. As with hinges, we have lagged far behind other countries in this, and are only just beginning to realise that an expensive window in an expensive home deserves more than a cheap and nasty latch. A good example of a modern latch is illustrated, incorporating a burglar-proof lock.

Trickle ventilators or night vents can be fitted to most windows by manufacturers as optional extras. They incorporate fly screens, but otherwise it is hard to know what they offer that a two position latch does not. They certainly do not improve the appearance of the joinery to which they are fitted, but there are situations in which they are useful.

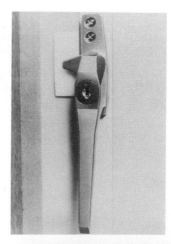

The modern hinge fitting on the left enables the housewife to clean the outside of the window from the inside of the room. It also incorporates a friction pad, so that the window stays at the point to which it has been opened and no window stay is required. A modern window latch incorporating a lock and a trickle ventilator set into a double glazing unit are also illustrated.

GLASS

Virtually everyone building a new home for themselves fits sealed double glazing units in their windows. Provided that the window frames were made to be double glazed the cost is not exorbitant, and is far less than the sort of double glazing costs quoted to those who want to improve the insulation of an existing house. There is little to choose between the units made by any of the leading manufacturers, but there is a wide variety of sorts of glass from which the units can be made.

Most double glazing units are made from 4mm float glass, which is adequate for sizes up to 4' x 3'. Above this size the glass thickness has to be increased and it is important to check that this is not overlooked.

Where any part of a glazed area is below 1' 6" from the floor, as in a patio door or special feature window, toughened glass should be used. This is now recommended under various Codes of Practice, but is not yet mandatory although no doubt it soon will be. The additional cost is minimal.

Patterned glass is used for double glazed units for bathrooms, and lavatories, and often for units in front door frames. It is available in a wide variety of patterns, and it is surprising how few home builders pay any attention to their wide range of options. Instead of leaving the choice to the builder you should visit a glass showroom and look at the huge range of designs; they

Two sealed insulated glazing units are shown below. The larger leaded light is triple glazed, and glazing of this sort is obligatory when the window area of the building comprises more than 36% of the wall surface area. The standard double glazing unit shown below is mandatory when the figure is 24%.

all cost the same, and double glazing units can be ordered to be made in most patterns of glass.

Tinted glass, or one of the various types of reflecting or thermal glass, is often specified for patio doors. It can be expensive, but it is very striking and the claims made by manufacturers are fully justified. If this interests you then remember that this sort of feature will give its own very distinctive character to the whole room, and this must suit your idea of the decor. Try to make your choice after seeing an actual example, and not from the brochures.

Leaded lights are becoming popular again, although not in their traditional form with individual pieces of glass held together with lead channels. Instead the leadwork effect is obtained by bonding strips of lead to the glass using a modern adhesive. This looks very effective.

Georgian wired-glass holds its shape even after it has shattered in a fire. It may be required in special situations, usually where there is an integral garage. It looks quite horrible, but is rarely required anywhere that this matters.

PATIO WINDOWS

Patio windows are an anachronism in a traditional cottage style home, but are certainly here to stay. The essential with a patio window is to relate it to a paved area outside that is large enough to balance the whole effect. The paved area should be at least half the wall area of the side of the house above it. If this is not possible then some other way of arranging the landscaping to do the same thing is most important.

Until recently the majority of patio windows were aluminium, usually fitted in hardwood frames. The popularity of hardwood joinery in recent years has led to the introduction of reasonably priced hardwood patio windows, and these are likely to become progressively more popular as a result of our concern with traditional materials. There are wide price ranges in patio windows, and, as with much else, you get what you pay for. The cheaper patio windows are made for replacing french windows in old houses, and are inappropriate to new homes. Choose from the middle or top of the range offered by a reputable manufacturer, and if the window does not run absolutely smoothly and is completely draught-proof then complain vigorously. The problem is invariably with the installation.

In an earlier chapter it was explained that a room must have windows that open to provide ventilation to a total of 5% of the floor area. Patio windows can contribute to this total only if there is a minimum of 15 sq. ins. of other ventilation provided, and if there is not another ordinary window in the room this means the patio window has to be fitted with a trickle ventilator. The design of these can vary from unobtrusive to very ugly; ask to see a sample and do not rely on a catalogue.

Timber patio doors have been in general use on the continent for a long time and are now becoming popular in Britain.

The photographs used in this feature were provided by Bowater Ripper Ltd., whose wide range of windows, patio doors, and other joinery is particularly appropriate to custom designed individual homes. They have very attractive literature on their products, obtainable from them at Castle Hedingham, Halstead, Essex C09 3EP., and they have stockists throughout the country.

Kitchens

How many times have you been in a friend's kitchen and wondered just why there was no work surface next to the cooker on which to place a saucepan? How many times have you inherited a kitchen when you have moved house and wondered why the waste bin was at the farthest point possible from the sink? How many times have you thought 'I could do better'? If you are building your own home you have an opportunity to do just that. For many couples, and most wives, this is the most challenging part of the whole business of building a new house or bungalow.

First of all, before considering either layouts or designs of kitchen units you will have to decide how big a kitchen you need. Kitchens in today's house designs range from the smallest practicable 'cooks' workshops' to traditional farmhouse kitchens to suit a lifestyle where everyone at home spends the whole day in the kitchen and the family only move into the parlour in the evening. Between the two is the functional kitchen that includes a small table and four chairs for informal family meals. Make sure that you get the size of kitchen that you need, and then you can set about furnishing it.

Next, what character are you going to give your kitchen? Your choice of fittings will determine this —the old world charm of oak, the farmhouse appeal of pine, the functional, clinical lines of white, the warmth of textures, the high-tech appeal of primary colours. Keep in mind the basic requirement that your kitchen has to complement the character of your house. In particular, if the kitchen is to be open plan with another room it must be complementary to the decor of that room; nothing looks worse than a classical lounge with a back drop of modern, brightly coloured kitchen units. Decide on a character for the kitchen, and stick to it.

This character must follow through all the details, and these are very important. Door handles, light fittings, pelmets, even the design of the bread board can either enhance or detract from the overall effect.

Once you know how big a kitchen you have to furnish, and the character that you wish to give to it, you can start considering how you plan the layout. As this planning involves shuffling the position of kitchen units, let us look at their general characteristics and think about your own preferences before getting down to details.

Farmhouse kitchen

'Cooks workshop' kitchen

Family kitchen

Decide what size and style of kitchen you need before considering the details of the layout.

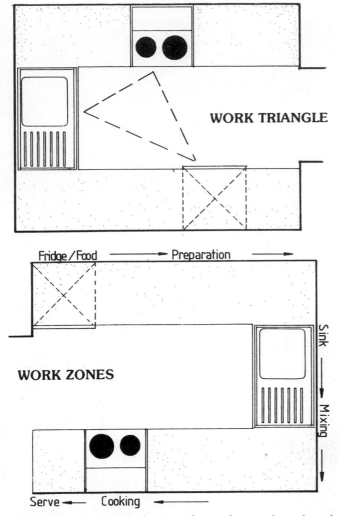

WORK TRIANGLE

Fridge / Food ———→ Preparation

WORK ZONES

Sink

Mixing

Serve ←— Cooking ←———

Typical kitchen plans showing the work triangle and work zones.

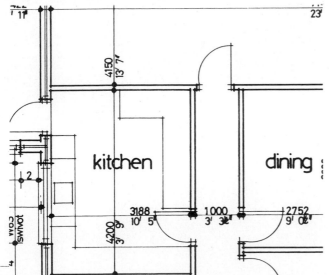

kitchen   dining

This kitchen plan is taken from a building regulation application drawing. The layout is purely notional, but you should stick to the sink position shown. Otherwise there are no mandatory building regulation requirements for kitchens, although the N.H.B.C. have storage and layout standards. All electrical work is to meet relevant safety regulations.

Don't try to put your ultimate kitchen layout on your Building Regulation plans — keep your options open!

POINTS TO CONSIDER

* The overall height of the units you intend to use. Most full height units — larders, oven housings etc. — are either 6' 4" or 7' 4" high. Wall units are usually chosen to suit them, and are either 2' 0" or 3' 0" high. This leaves a standard gap of 1' 6" between the top of the work surface and the bottom of a wall unit. Decide which height option you prefer — it is a very basic choice.

* Do you prefer full height doors in base units, that reach right up to the work surface, or do you like a line of drawers under the work surface? If you like full height doors but are worried about having enough room to store small items, then remember the possibility of a multi-drawer unit.

* What sort of work tops do you prefer — laminate, or ceramic tiles protected by a hardwood front edge?

* Do you want an orthodox stainless steel sink or a ceramic bowl set in your work top?

* Are you having a free standing cooker, or separate hob and oven units? Is a cooker hood important? Or are you installing one of the modern solid fuel cookers and designing your kitchen around it?

* Consider what other appliances you are planning for, and remember space for any appliances that you may need in the future. What else has to be kept in the kitchen? Fridge, freezer, dishwasher and washing machine are obvious. What about the ironing board, food mixer, childrens' dirty shoes and somewhere for the dog's basket? A wall unit 'for crockery' is one thing — how much storage you will need for *your* crockery is another.

Having considered all of this you can get down to the actual kitchen planning. There is no shortage of books on this subject, and many suppliers offer a design service although most housewives have their own strong views on the subject. Whatever your own opinions — and if you are planning your own home you should get the kitchen *you* want — remember that all kitchen design theory revolves around the work triangle. The three corners of this triangle are the fridge, sink and cooker; and the sides should total more than 12' 0" and less than 22' 0". This ensures that there is sufficient space around appliances and work surfaces, and avoids too much walking.

Once the work triangle is established the kitchen falls into natural 'zones', each with its own storage and work top space. The proportions of each zone should depend on your own lifestyle — large work surfaces and more storage space for the Cordon Bleu cooks among us, or alternative use of the same space for breakfast bar arrangements.

The kitchen photographs are of Moore's International kitchens. Moore's stockists will design kitchens for new homes. Literature and details of local agents is available from Moore's International Ltd., Aycliffe Industrial Estate, Newton Aycliff, Co. Durham.

Bathrooms

Modern bathrooms arrived when central heating enabled a whole house to be heated to a comfortable temperature. That was twenty-five years ago. Before then, the bathroom was the Cinderella of the home. It was often cold, and consequently neglected. When central heating made the bathroom as comfortable a room to enter as any other, the stage was set for a design revolution.

People realised that the bathroom had not only been neglected in general, but that over decades little change had taken place in the design of the basic requirements — the baths, washbasins, and W.Cs.

Manufacturers realised this too, and the demand for the bathroom to become a really live, integral part of the home encouraged great advances in the range of bathroom fittings, the way in which they worked, and their appearance. Bathroom technology and bathroom design was expected to equal the standards of modern kitchens and other rooms. The photographs show how effectively this has been done.

With the wide range of both functional and decorative bathroom fittings now available it is important to *plan* the bathroom in a new home, and not simply to buy a bathroom suite and then choose tiles to match. Look carefully at the best of what is on offer, and remember that the bathroom has only just come of age. Make your selection from the designs of the '80s rather than looking back to the styles used in older homes. The three basics of bath, basin and W.C. have now been joined by matching bidets, showers, sophisticated taps and mixers, co-ordinated surrounds, special tiling, soft floor covering and feature lighting. If a modern kitchen is chosen to be an attractive and efficient working area, a modern bathroom should be chosen to be a luxurious and efficient place to relax and be invigorated. This means considering the bathroom as an entity, and the best place to do this is in a supplier's showroom.

Baths are now available in many designs, shapes and sizes, and there is a continuing move away from iron baths to those in acrylic material which soak up far less heat and can be moulded into a wide range of interesting shapes. Corner baths offer one of the cheapest ways of providing a touch of super-luxury living to your home, as do the whirlpool baths which are now available.

Basins, whether on pedestals or built into vanity units, bidets, water closets and shower trays have not changed appreciably in design concept over the years, but what a change in design detail! One of the greatest improvements is in the way in which the taps and other controls are now co-ordinated into the design as a whole, and not stuck on as an afterthought.

It is taps and other 'water terminals' which are undergoing the biggest changes at the present time. Simple 'cold' and 'hot' taps are being overtaken by sophisticated mixer units with washerless controls. This means the end of dripping taps, no more stains from the drips, and does away with the chore of changing

New Status bath, tiara W.C. and basin from Ideal Standard.

50

washers. It also means that a single lever is all that has to be moved to obtain water at a pre-set temperature, with all that this offers to the elderly or to a mother bathing small children.

It is unfortunate that many bathroom displays at exhibitions in building centres seem to concentrate on layouts for large bathrooms, which is not very helpful to those looking for ideas for modern en suite bathrooms for new homes. This is because the largest market for the exhibitors is with those who are up-grading bath-rooms in older houses, and the displays are geared to this. Do not imagine from this that the best in design is essentially for the large bathroom — the compact installation had just as much to gain from modern trends and modern design, and there is plenty that is designed with space saving in mind.

Manufacturers of bathroom products keep up with the trends in colour, and even lead the fashion moves. One example is the introduction of three delicate shades, whisper pink, whisper blue, and whisper green by Ideal Standard. These were introduced at the same time as Pilkington launched two matching ranges of tiles called Tones and Echoes. White taps and shower controls from Ideal Standard complete this two company 'whisper tones' bathroom concept.

Below. The Linda Suite from Ideal Standard.

Above left. This Dualux basin mixer tap has a new colour finish which is becoming very popular.
Above right. Modern shower controls give constant water temperatures whatever the pressure. This is the Idealblend unit, which has ceramic disc seals which are unaffected by the hardest water.
Below. The photograph shows the new whisper tone tiles in a chevron and diamond pattern.

All the bathrooms illustrated here are by Ideal Standard, whose brochures are a useful source of ideas. Full details and a list of stockists can be obtained from Ideal Standard Ltd., P.O. Box 60, Hull HU5 4JE.

Insulation

There is no need to emphasise the importance of insulation in houses or bungalows to be built today; this is widely understood and many of those planning for a new home are in some ways almost too concerned with this. The features on the subject in every home interest magazine are mainly concerned with insulation in existing houses; since April 1982 all new homes have had to have new standards of built-in insulation, and these standards are so high that any additional expense on extra insulation is most unlikely to be cost effective.

The idea that you can have more than enough insulation often seems heretical to the housewife who is brain washed by a hundred features on the radio, or her husband who has read as many articles in D.I.Y. magazines, but there is a limit. This comes when no further expenditure is going to be cost effective, and when the level of insulation requires special precautions against condensation, or that you adopt an unusual lifestyle. We read of experimental houses that are so well insulated that they are kept warm with the heat from the electric light bulbs. All well and good — but how long do you think they take to warm up when children leave the door open? The 1982 insulation standards strike a balance between energy saving, ordinary living patterns, and worthwhile investment that should not be ignored lightly. If you decide to have any higher standards of insulation you should try to get first hand reports of what is involved, and should not rely on press features. Few low energy experimental homes are fun to live in, or are a long term unqualified success; their importance is as experiments.

Another point to keep in mind when considering all of this is that with the 1982 insulation levels no expenditure on insulation is likely to save as much money as turning the central heating thermostat down by two or three degrees. The most cost effective further investment is on thermal underwear, not on insulating the building.

Of course, all of this assumes that you also are concerned about having the best sort of central heating and central heating controls. This is dealt with in a separate chapter. As far as insulation is concerned, there are five separate areas of potential heat loss which you should recognise.

WALLS

In traditional construction the 1982 insulating standards are usually met by having an inner skin of 4" insulating blocks and additional insulation in the cavity. In a new home you can arrange this in any way you wish, and there are obvious advantages in using an insulating system that retains the cavity air space and which does not fill it completely. This is invariably done by increasing the cavity width to 3" and having a 1" slab of insulating material fastened against the inner skin with special wall ties. If you want even more insulation than is required to meet the standard you use a 2" slab of insulation. This arrangement gives the best of both worlds — insulation plus a clear cavity to keep out any threat of damp.

In timber frame construction the insulation is provided by a special quilt set into the frame, and invariably exceeds the required standard. This is dealt with at length in the chapter on timber frame homes. There are other ways of insulating walls in both traditional and timber frame homes, but they are not in general use in new construction.

DRAUGHT PROOFING

All windows and doors in modern homes should take advantage of the new sophisticated draught proofing seals which are now available, and ideally these should be built into the windows when they are manufactured, and not stuck on afterwards. Windows of this sort are usually called high performance windows. The specifications for all designs in this book are for High Performance windows.

ROOF

Mandatory standards are met by a 4" quilt of glass fibre. There are various other ways of providing the required insulation, but they are unusual. The quilt is usually laid between the ceiling ties and is available in either 24" or 16" widths to suit the usual rafter spacings.

This insulation is usually exposed to view in the roof space, and if you want to increase the thickness you can do so at any time. Another way of improving the level of roof insulation, which can only be arranged when the home is being built, is to specify foil backed plaster board. This provides significant extra insulation at very modest cost.

When the design involves a sloping ceiling just under the tiles, as in many purlin roof designs, the insulation specified between the plaster board and the tiles is most important, as it cannot be seen once it is installed. Make sure it is put there!

FLOORS

Current requirements for ordinary detached homes do not require normal floors to be insulated. If you want to stop heat loss down into the foundations this can be arranged quite easily, but you must make up your mind about this at an early stage so that details can be given in your Building Regulation application.

Solid floors are often insulated by having a layer of insulation below the concrete slab. This can be put below the full area of the building, or can be installed around the perimeter of the structure only.

Suspended floors used to be specially insulated by having a glass fibre quilt between the floor boards and the joists, but this is now being overtaken by the use of insulated flooring board. These can also be used on solid floors, and in some ways this is much easier than putting insulation under the floor slab.

Whichever way you may decide to install floor insulation it is essential to work to the material manufacturer's instructions to ensure that you avoid damp and condensation problems.

DOUBLE GLAZING

Heat goes out through windows, and double glazing is now virtually standard in all new homes. This is because it has become an accepted amenity; the actual regulations say that single glazing is acceptable provided it does not form more than 12% of an external wall; double glazing is acceptable up to 24%, and then triple glazing should be used. There is unlikely to be any advantage to be gained in moving to triple glazing other than to comply with the regulations. 'Double glazing' in new homes means sealed units fitted in windows which are designed for them. There are other approaches to this, but they are unusual and should be considered by inspecting a house in which they are fitted, and not by looking at catalogues or advertisements.

VENTILATION AND CONDENSATION

Modern homes with high standards of insulation and effective draught proofing offer more opportunities for condensation to be a nuisance than draughty buildings to earlier standards. Since 1982 new standards of roof ventilation have been obligatory which helps to offset this. However, it remains important to remember that your draughtproofing has done away with uncontrolled ventilation, and that you must provide controlled ventilation via your opening windows and extractor fans. This is particularly important in a new home that is still drying out. The N.H.B.C. has an excellent booklet about this.

Heating

The Bell 'Hole in the Wall' fireplace is perhaps the best known of all modern fireplace designs, and a back boiler can be fitted for limited central heating and domestic hot water.

This chapter is not a complete guide to heating a new home; it is a general introduction to the subject which can be followed up by reading the many excellent books which deal with the matter in detail.

While the actual choice of a fireplace or central heating system does not have to be made until a fairly late stage in the process of building a house or bungalow, basic decisions on what sort of appliances are to be installed have to be made at the design stage. This is because open fires and other sorts of heating equipment require different foundations and flues. Details of what is proposed have to be shown in building regulation applications, and it is very difficult indeed to change the specification once work has started.

Open fires, solid fuel boilers, and oil-fired boilers are

called Class One Appliances, and have to stand on hearths which are supported from the foundations. They require either chimneys or high performance flue pipes, and there are regulations which limit how these may be situated in relation to floor joists etc. Most gas fires and small gas boilers are Class Two Appliances, which do not require structural hearths, and can discharge flue gases via flue blocks. These can be built into a wall without a chimney breast, and can discharge via a ridge tile flue terminal, avoiding a chimney altogether.

An early decision has to be made about whether or not to have an open fire. This is a very personal choice, but there are a few inescapable facts. A home of up to about 900 sq.ft. can get full central heating from a back boiler behind most ordinary types of open fire, and a

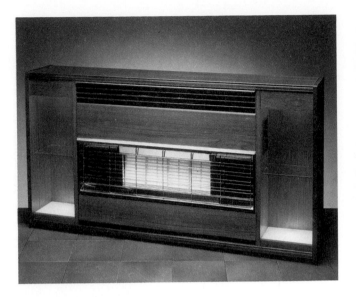

Above left. The Baxi Bermuda combined fire and boiler will provide full central heating for a three-bedroom home.
Above right. Modern solid fuel boilers are clean and unobtrusive. quite unlike the dirty monsters of grandma's day.
Left. Many modern gas boilers are wall mounted like this Glow Worm space-saver.

larger home of up to about 1500 sq.ft. can be heated from the back boilers of some special fires and most closed room heaters. Back boilers can also heat domestic hot water, and in this era of cheap automatic controls there is no reason why they should not do this together with a central heating boiler, so that the fire does the job when it is alight and the boiler takes over when the fire is not burning.

There are excellent gas fires with built in central heating boilers which can heat homes of up to about 1000 sq.ft. on their own. These have the added advantage that the 'back boiler' can work on its own without the fire being lit. They are deservedly popular and at current gas prices they probably give the best capital cost/running cost balance of any central heating installation.

If your home is too large for a central heating system from the fire in the lounge, or if you simply do not want a fire in the lounge, then you have to find somewhere to place a boiler or warm air heating unit or else consider electric heating.

All boilers these days are slimmed down and inconspicuous. Some gas boilers can be mounted on walls at a high level or be concealed in airing cupboards. Gas boilers do not require an oil tank or a coal bunker, and at current gas prices are more economical than oil — but gas prices are going up quickly. Oil boilers need a tank, which involves finding somewhere to put it. Solid fuel boilers are nearly as automatic as any others these days, but the fuel has to be stored, put into the hopper, and the ashes taken away. However, coal has a price advantage which is likely to remain.

Wood burning appliances are now very popular in rural areas where the householder can be sure of a reliable supply of logs. Many of these fires, boilers and kitchen stoves will also burn coal or coke, and are advertised as multi-fuel boilers. They have to be used strictly in accordance with the manufacturer's recommendations to avoid the risk of trouble from tar condensate in the chimney, but are very popular with those who have used them. D & M tell us that they are used by about a quarter of all their clients who build in the country.

A decision whether to have radiators or a warm air system is very much a matter of choice, with warm air definitely out of fashion these days. This can affect the resale potential of a house. There are some very attractive modern radiators about, and you should also look at skirting radiators. Some of these are very neat and inconspicuous, and are competitively priced.

Modern wood burning and multi-fuel appliances are now very sophisticated, and very attractive. The fire above is a Jetmaster, and the stove is by Franco-Belge.

Electric central heating comes in many forms — under floor heating, ceiling heating, heat storage systems and others. There are many pros and cons, but the fact remains that most central heating systems in new houses and bungalows use conventional radiators, and that a popular heating system makes a house a better investment than one with a less popular system. However, the place of electricity in the central heating league table may improve soon with the development of heat pumps. These have many advantages for large homes, and have a chapter of their own starting on page 60.

When considering alternative heating systems it is important to keep in mind the relation between capital cost and running cost. In the early 70's the running costs of a system were probably under 20% of the capital cost. Now this is probably significantly over 50%. Modern control systems are relatively inexpensive and will significantly reduce this important ratio. Any new heating appliance deserves the best controls available provided that they are recommended by the manufacturers. Thermostatic radiator valves and zone heating thermostats are essential, and there are many other 'black boxes' which deserve serious consideration. As with all else, choose from personal recommendation rather than from advertisements if you possibly can.

The business of selling and installing central heating systems is very competitive, and it is comparatively easy to get systems designed and quoted by installers who hope to be given your contract. Make sure that their work is to approved standards, and that they can offer a back-up service for repairs and maintenance. Probably your best guarantee of this comes if they are approved as installers by the major fuel agencies or appliance manufacturers.

To get the best from modern central heating appliances you need the best possible ways of distributing and controlling the heat which they make available. Radiators, such as the Funrad Skirting radiators shown on the left, should be fitted with thermostatic control valves like the Pegler valve shown below right. They will both give of their best if the whole system is fitted with a sophisticated temperature controller such as the Drayton Temperature Controller shown below left.

Heat pumps

Everyone building in the eighties is concerned that their new home has an appropriate level of insulation, and has a central heating appliance that will combine economy with efficiency. In making decisions about the system to install you have a bewildering range of options, and one of the most intriguing and least understood, is the opportunity to heat your house with a heat pump.

Domestic heat pumps are appliances which generate heat for central heating and domestic hot water in the same role as an oil, gas or solid fuel boiler. They are an alternative to these older appliances. In the right situation they have many advantages and are potentially one of the most important developments in housing for many years.

How do they work? Heat pumps do not 'make' heat by burning a fuel like every other heating appliance. Instead they collect heat from one place, and deliver it where it is wanted, using electrical energy to drive the pump to collect the heat energy. A heat pump enables 1kW of electricity to be used to collect up to 3kW of heat while if the electricity had been used in an ordinary electric fire it would only have generated 1kW of heat. This is not new technology having been used in industrial and commercial applications for many years. What

A house built in 1981 which is heated with a heat pump. The unit is to the extreme left of the photograph above, and better seen in the picture below.

is new is its application to the housing scene.

There are many ways in which small heat pumps can be used in a new home, and unfortunately the way in which they are described is often very confusing. Just as the word 'vehicle' can describe anything from a forklift truck to a racing car, so the name 'heat pump' is used to describe a wide variety of machines. All of them are gadgets which move heat from one place to another. Some collect waste heat and re-cycle it, some collect heat from the air, others collect heat from the ground, or a river or the sea. Some deliver hot air, others hot water. Most are powered by electricity, but some are driven by gas or oil. All of these machines are heat pumps, and the general use of the same name to describe them all is very confusing. Let us end the confusion as far as this book is concerned, and look only at heat pumps which are of interest to anyone building a new home; those which take heat from the air, use it to provide hot water for a conventional radiator system, and are driven by electricity.

Heat pumps which are specially designed for this job are well developed and are widely available. They are efficient and reliable. They are also several times as expensive as any other boiler or appliance. Their advantage has to be that the running costs are low enough to offset the high capital cost, and that over the years they will provide a total package investment, capital cost plus running cost, which is cheaper than any alternative.

This would seem to be a relatively simple concept, but unfortunately it is not. Evaluating a heat pump, driven by electricity, against other appliances which use other fuels, involves considering how you think the prices of the different fuels will move in relation to each other. Even more important is considering how inflation is going to affect the equation. If you are building a large house and buy an expensive heat pump instead of a cheap oil boiler, and inflation rockets along at 15%, then

in four years the extra cost of the heat pump will have been more than covered by the savings in running costs. After that you will be enjoying very cheap central heating. If inflation runs at 7% then it is unlikely that your heat pump will pay for its extra cost by savings on energy bills in much less than ten years — assuming that energy costs keep in line with inflation. But in the seventies energy costs increased far ahead of inflation. All very complicated, but no more so than the other investment pros and cons of building a new home anyway.

To sum up, if you are building a new house or bungalow there may be a very strong financial case for a heat pump installation if you consider that inflation is likely to continue to be a feature of the economy, and that fuel costs will rise at least in pace with inflation, and probably faster.

Whether this is applicable to your own particular house depends on various other considerations. First of all, what is the fuel that you would use if you did not buy a heat pump? If it is oil, which is the most expensive way of buying heat, then the financial advantage will be at its most convincing. If gas, then the financial advantage is not nearly as attractive until gas prices rise in the way which both the government and the gas industry forecast. If you are considering using solid fuel then you have to bring the business of handling coal or anthracite into your decision. The Heat Pump Association and the various manufacturers publish calculations and tables showing the savings which heat pumps will give against all other fuels, and at present these are most significant where the other fuel is oil. Nearly all these published figures are concerned with the cost of putting heat pumps in existing buildings, where they replace existing boilers and VAT cannot be reclaimed. In new homes the saving made by not buying the alternative boiler can be set against the price of the heat pump, and VAT is not charged. Because of this you may find the advantages of

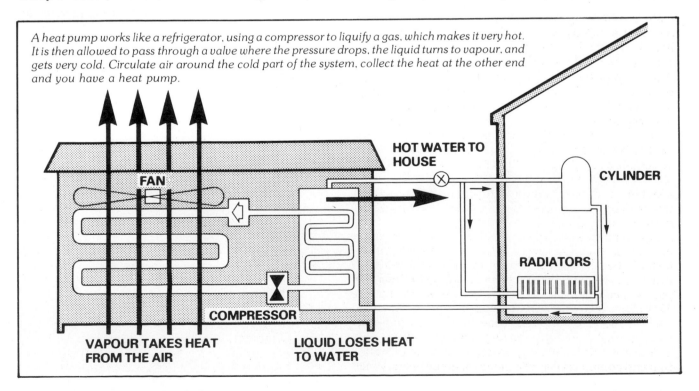

A heat pump works like a refrigerator, using a compressor to liquify a gas, which makes it very hot. It is then allowed to pass through a valve where the pressure drops, the liquid turns to vapour, and gets very cold. Circulate air around the cold part of the system, collect the heat at the other end and you have a heat pump.

FAN

HOT WATER TO HOUSE

CYLINDER

RADIATORS

COMPRESSOR

VAPOUR TAKES HEAT FROM THE AIR

LIQUID LOSES HEAT TO WATER

a heat pump in a new home are better than the advertisers claim — which is rather unusual.

A further consideration is that you will have to have somewhere to put your heat pump. When used in new homes they normally stand outside in a position where they can gulp down large quantities of air. They are not inherently beautiful, which is why advertisements often show them together with a distractingly attractive girl. The girl does not come with the heat pump. Since it will not look well by itself on your front lawn it is normally sited behind a garage, or by a back door where it is out of the way.

Secondly, the savings made by installing a heat pump depend on the machine being used to the full. Large heat pumps of about 14kW output are little more expensive than smaller models, so that the greatest advantage is obtained when a heat pump is installed in a larger home. The cost figures are not nearly so attractive for a small property.

Finally, the characteristics of the machine have to be understood to get the best from it. All heat pumps come with fully automatic controls, and these have to be set with care to give the best results. The control panel itself is no more complicated than the controls of an electric cooker, and the housewife who can manage a cooker will cope with a heat pump, although it may seem rather frightening at first acquaintance.

To sum up, the right heat pump installation in a larger home will be a very good investment, particularly if the alternative fuel is oil. It will be quiet and reliable, but you must have somewhere to site it that is out of the way and yet not enclosed.

If your new home is in this category, and you can afford to buy an expensive machine now to save on heating bills in the future, then you will want firm advice on the energy requirements of the building and the cost of heating it in different ways. You will probably have to go to the fuel agencies and heat pump manufacturers for this help, and you will have to make your own mind up about the probable reliability of the advice that you are given. As with so much else, ask the salesman where you can find one of his satisfied customers in your local area. With heat pumps this is not usually a problem, as they are novel enough for proud owners to delight in showing them off!

One important point to keep in mind when considering buying a heat pump is the importance of choosing a machine that is designed to work in our relatively humid climate. All heat pumps have to cope with moisture in the air which freezes as ice on their evaporator coils and they all have elaborate automatic de-icing arrangements. Machines that are designed for dryer American or Continental climates may not cope with this as effectively as machines which are specifically designed for the British market, and this is one aspect of your choice which has to be given careful consideration.

There is an excellent consumer's guide to heat pumps called *Heat Pumps and Houses* published by Prism Press. This is not a text book about the machines themselves, but is wholly concerned with their performance in homes of all sorts. It has over fifty photographs of installations, and quotes the actual running costs and the real savings. Details are given in the bibliography.

The Eastwood 14/11 heat pump which is the model usually installed in large detached houses.

Heat pumps can extract heat from a stream or river and use it to heat a home. These photographs show the indoor and outdoor parts of an Eastwood installation in the midlands.

Photographs of heat pumps used in this chapter were kindly provided by Britain's largest heat pump manufacturer, Eastwoods of Shirebrook. Full details of their machines and installation service can be obtained from them at Portland Road, Shirebrook, Mansfield, Notts NG20 ATY.

The legal side

PLANNING

Serious consideration cannot be given to building a new home without an understanding of the various consents and approvals necessary before you can even make a start. This subject is not nearly as simple or straightforward as you may think it should be, and applications to build a home must be made with care, and with an understanding of the options. It is equally important to understand how the system works, and find out how you can best arrange to get the various permissions that you want. This involves all sorts of special procedures, and sometimes these do not seem to have much relevance to the commonsense fact that the plot of land that you are buying is obviously the best place for the bungalow of your dreams.

There are two basic rules to be observed in dealing with the planners and others concerned with all of this. One is to know what it is that you want, and the other is to ask for what you want in the way most likely to succeed. Often this is a job for a professional, but the general public have every right to handle these formalities themselves, and often do so. Whether employing an agent, or submitting applications yourself, you must know the way in which these things work, and how to use the system to have the best chance of obtaining the consents that are required with as little fuss as possible.

Planning consents are impersonal things, and it is always the land which obtains planning consent, not the person who made the application for it. When land with planning consent is sold, the consent is available to the new owner. One does not have to own a piece of land to apply for planning consent on it, and it is quite usual for a prospective purchaser to make an application before actually buying the land to which it relates, although he is legally obliged to advise the actual owner that he is doing this.

As a general rule the personal circumstances of the applicant play no part in consideration of a planning application. The criteria is that it should be seen to be a good thing for society at large that the proposed development should take place. A planning consent for a new home on a particular site is granted because new homes are required, and this is a good place for one, and not because the applicant is a good chap who deserves to be allowed to do what he wants. On a farm, consent will be given for a new farm bungalow because it is essential to the proper management of the farm, and not because a rise in milk prices enables the farmer to afford it. This is the theory behind the Planning Acts; the practice is sometimes different, but you have a better chance of arranging to get your own way if you understand the concept.

There are various types of planning consent, and the differences between them are important. They are as follows:

Outline Consent. This is simply permission for a dwelling of some sort to be built, and is normally granted subject to a large number of conditions or 'reserved matters'. These require that before any work starts it is necessary to submit details of the proposed design, materials, access, etc, and all these matters have to be approved. An application for Outline Consent can be made before any expense is incurred in buying plans.

Approval of Reserved Matters. This is given in respect of an application dealing with the reserved matters in the Outline Consent which has already been granted.

Full Planning Permission. This is granted when an application is made which covers everything regulated by the planning authority in one application. There may be reserved matters in such a consent, but they will deal with minor issues such as the bricks to be used, or the drainage arrangements.

Conditional Consent. This is a convenient term for a planning consent which has been issued on special conditions. This normally is that the dwelling should be occupied by a person whose job requires that he should live on the site. In these circumstances the actual wording used is most important. Typically it may read: 'Occupation shall be limited to a person solely employed in agriculture or forestry in the local area, or a person last so employed, or the widow of such a person'.

Such a consent makes it very difficult for the dwelling to be sold separately from the farm or other enterprise to which it relates, and this is the purpose of the condition. Sometimes this is reinforced by a condition requiring that the applicant enters into a legal agreement with the local authority promising not to sell the house or bungalow separately from the enterprise. This is called a Section 52 Agreement. As a general rule a dwelling covered by a conditional consent will not qualify for an ordinary building society mortgage.

Planning Applications. A planning application is a legal document in its own right, and has to be acted on by the planning authority within a set period. Once a decision has been given on a planning application it is a matter of record in the local authority planning register which is available for inspection by the general public.

A Planning Refusal. A refusal of a planning application is a matter of record but does not normally preclude a further application being made to do the same thing in a different way. However, a refusal of an application for approval of reserved matters may mean that any re-submission must be as a new full planning application, so that if problems arise in discussions with a planning officer it is usual to withdraw such an application before a decision is made.

Conservation Areas. These are areas of particular scenic importance where all proposals are subject to special scrutiny, and where any new building is expected to blend in perfectly with its surroundings. Conservation areas are usually found in the centre of old towns, in particularly attractive rural villages, in National Parks, and at beauty spots.

Green Belt, White Land, Residential Zoning, etc. These are phrases which are often used in different ways and usually are not very specific. They relate to development plans for a town or village which have been adopted as a basis for dealing with planning applications. 'Green Belt' refers to land where no development is to be permitted, and 'White Land' is land not yet specifically zoned for residential development. This seems very simple, but only small areas of the country have development plans, and these are constantly being redrawn. In addition to this, they are regarded by different authorities in different ways, and may be considered as anything from a vague statement of principle to a firm policy. These terms are only really specific to a particular development plan, and the standing of that plan can vary.

Planning Appeals. One can enter an appeal against a refusal of a planning application, or against the unreasonable imposition of reserved matters, or refusal to approve proposals covered by reservations in the consent. Just over a quarter of all planning appeals succeed and in certain areas where conservation groups and others put a lot of pressure on planning committees, there is a tendency to refuse any application in a sensitive situation knowing that the worthwhile applications will succeed at appeal. Planning appeals are dealt with by the Department of the Environment, and virtually all appeals relating to single houses are dealt with by exchange of letter. It is not at all unusual for private individuals to handle their own appeals, and the Department of the Environment have a booklet giving help and advice in doing this. Anyone receiving a planning refusal is automatically sent full details of how to appeal against the decision.

The wording of any planning document has to be read very carefully. All the conditions mean exactly what they say, but there are some special things to look out for.

Any outline consent that reads: 'The area is of outstanding architectural importance, and a high standard of design and materials will be required' means that the local authority's requirements may be prohibitively expensive, and that this is certainly not a site on which anyone should consider building a low budget home without a lot of investigation into what will be permitted.

Any condition that requires that natural stone or natural slate shall be used, or which calls for the subsequent approval of materials in an area where stone, slates or small plain tiles may be required, may involve significant additional costs.

A planning consent for a building on a site where there are trees which are protected by a Tree Preservation Order will normally have a condition drawing attention to this. If it does not, the Planning Consent certainly does not cancel the Tree Preservation Order. You will have to seek separate approval to fell any trees that are in the way. If you have to do this it is always a good idea to offer to plant replacement trees elsewhere on the site.

Most planning refusals list half a dozen reasons why the application has failed. Some planning authorities set out as many reasons for their decision as possible. The only reason for this can be that it makes entering an appeal rather more difficult, as each reason for refusal has to be challenged separately. On the other hand, when a planning refusal contains only a single reason for refusal, particularly when this relates to access or to some other particular aspect of the proposal, it can be taken as an indication that a further application which meets the authority's requirements in this particular respect will be approved.

When one looks at the different sorts of consent it seems sensible to apply first for outline consent to

Outline consent to build on a site like this will be subject to very stringent and expensive conditions.

establish whether a house or bungalow can be built at all, and when this is granted to have detailed plans prepared and submit an application for approval of the reserved matters. However, this is a lengthy procedure, and frequently it is preferable to make a full planning application as a first approach to the authority. This saves time, and is often believed to demonstrate that an application is for a new home that someone really wants to build, and is not simply being made to establish an enhanced value for a piece of land. Another advantage of this approach is that it clears any uncertainty regarding the conditions in an outline consent. This can be very important as such conditions can often make a very significant difference in the total cost of a new home.

The general public have free access to planning officers, who invariably have set times at which they are available to discuss planning matters with members of the public. At most council offices they have an interview room set aside for this purpose where their treatment of visitors is invariably friendly and open compared with, for instance, the attitude at the rating office. However, in dealing with them, whether by letter or face to face, it is important to recognise two things. Firstly, no planning officer will discuss planning policy, but must restrict himself to advising how planning

policy will affect your proposals, without committing himself or the council in any way. Secondly, if you ask for advice you will get it — but you may wish you hadn't had it! To elaborate the first point, a planning officer will advise that an application 'could normally be expected to be approved' or that he 'would not anticipate being able to recommend approval'. He is not allowed to be more specific, and it is pointless, and rude, to try to tie him down.

What he will do is to explain policy in such a way that there are plenty of lines to read between. What he will not do is debate the policy itself, or give any sort of promise regarding an application. The only exception to this is when he is discussing reserved matters in a full consent, such as a requirement that a type of brick or design detail should be approved by him under powers delegated to him by the planning committee. In these matters he will be specific, and will often negotiate a compromise.

The second point concerns detailed advice given by a planning officer. This advice, although obviously the best advice as to how the planning authority view a situation, is a counsel of perfection, and it may not suit you to take it. For instance, suppose you are buying a particularly attractive site with outline consent. As a first stage in establishing a design you may decide to

---

TP 6P   NOTICE OF PLANNING PERMISSION   Planning
Reference No. 326/C/172883

TOWN AND COUNTRY PLANNING ACT

THE SHERWOOD DISTRICT COUNCIL having considered an Application

by or on behalf of Mr & Mrs J.B. Smithson

to erect a detached two storey dwelling with garage

on part O.S. 371   at Clay Lane, Carlton

as shown on the plans submitted with the application, which application and plans and any relevant correspondence are hereinafter referred to as "the application" hereby in pursuance of their powers under the above mentioned Act.

GRANT PERMISSION

for the development in accordance with the application, subject to compliance with the conditions imposed and or the reasons set out below.

CONDITIONS

1   The development hereby permitted must be begun either before the expiration of 5 years from the date of this outline permission, or the expiration of 2 years from the final approval of the reserved matters.

2   Application for approval of reserved matters must be made no later than the expiration of 3 years from the date of this outline planning permission.

3   Details of the siting, design and external materials for the dwelling and the means of access thereto shall be the subject of a separate application for the approval of reserved matters.

4   The colour type and finish of all external material shall be approved by the planning authority before development commences.

5   Any gates provided shall be set back at a distance of 4.5 metres from the edge of the carriageway of the adjoining highway.

6   The access shall be splayed back at an angle of 45°.

7   Provision shall be made for the parking of a minimum of 2 cars within the boundary of the site.

8   An adequate turning space should be provided on the site to enable vehicles to enter and leave the highway in a forward gear.

9   A landscaping scheme shall be submitted and approved before any work starts on site.

10   The existing trees and hedges shall be protected to the satisfaction of the planning authority while all the work is in progress.

11   The occupation of the dwelling shall be restricted to a person solely employed in agriculture, or in forestry, or a pensioner last so employed or the widow of such a person.

REASONS

To comply with section 41 of the Town and Country Planning Act 1971.

Date.. 3.2.83

Authorised Officer

This means a two storey house. If you prefer a bungalow you can discuss the matter with the Planning Officer, but he will certainly require you to make a new full application, and not simply an application for approval of reserved matters.

These dates are not negotiable. Note work must "be begun" — there is no restriction on when it is finished.

Samples will usually be required. Do not leave this to the last minute.

But you don't have to provide gates.

There will be trouble if you ignore this.

You usually need only to show large trees, indicating species, and the position of the drive and turning area. Everything else is usually shown as "flowerbeds and lawns".

This makes it a conditional consent, and there will be trouble with an ordinary mortgage. Seek advice if you are in doubt about this condition.

An Outline Planning Consent.

call at the planning office to ask for the free advice which is available there. If you do this you will be well received, and you will be impressed by the trouble which will be taken to explain how the site needs a house of sensitive and imaginative design to do justice to its key position. You may be shown drawings of the sort of thing that the planning officer has in mind, or a sketch may be drawn for you while you watch. All this is splendid, until you realise that the ideal house being described suits neither your life-style nor your pocket. You will then wonder what the reaction is going to be to your application for the quite different house that you want, and which is all you can afford. The simple answer is that your application will be dealt with on its merits and that the planning officer has an obligation to approve what is acceptable, and not what he thinks best. However, it is obviously preferable to discuss your own specific requirements which have been drawn up for you before the meeting.

Planning Applications are made by filling in forms which you obtain from your local planning office, and sending them in together with four or five copies of your plans — the number of plans required varies from council to council. The various details that have to be shown on the plans are explained in a leaflet which will accompany the application forms. Plans purchased for

Building Regulation Inspection Notices.

designs in this book come with elaborate notes on making planning applications.

Fees are payable in respect of planning applications, and although there are various exceptions, the general rule is that every time you sign a planning application form you will have to pay £44. You will pay the one fee if you are making a full planning application, but if you make an outline application followed by an application for the approval of reserved matters you will be paying a total of £88. Everyone grumbles about these fees, but they are negligible when considered in the context of the total cost of the project.

If you have got planning consent and want to make an alteration to the design it is not usually necessary to make a fresh application. The alteration should be shown on an amended drawing and two copies should be sent to the Planning Office with a letter asking that they are accepted as 'amendments to the approved drawing'. There is rarely any difficulty over this if the alteration does not significantly change the appearance of the building.

BUILDING REGULATION APPLICATIONS
Our building regulations grew out of early public health legislation. The original intention was to ensure that new buildings were healthy, with minimum standards of ventilation and damp proofing. Over the years this has gradually changed to concern that the building is structurally sound and built according to the best building practice from wholly durable materials. More recently still this has been extended to concern over safety features, such as the design of balustrades, and the latest regulations are now concerned with standards of insulation. There are no building regulations yet about fixing curtain rails, but at the present rate of progress we will have them before long!

It is usual to make a building regulation application at the same time that one submits a planning application, but it is not essential. If you are not in a hurry it may be a good idea to get planning consent first. Fees for building regulation applications are payable on a fixed scale and are normally £30 for a detached dwelling and £6 for a detached garage. When the approval certificate is received it is accompanied by a sheaf of post cards which have to be sent back to the local authority at various stages as the building progresses, and the building inspector will then visit the site to ensure that the work is up to standard. Not surprisingly there are fees payable for these inspections as well — usually twice as much again as the original application fee. There is no escape from any of this, and if these procedures are disregarded you can be legally required to take parts of the building to pieces so that hidden workmanship can be inspected, and in the last resort a sub-standard dwelling may have to be demolished. Things rarely come to this, but, as with planning legislation, building regulations must be taken very seriously.

The application is made by filling in a simple form and sending it to the local authority with two copies of the plans. Here it will be examined and invariably you will get a letter asking for further information, usually requiring various details to be shown on the drawing with a note about how they conform with the building regulations. If all this is dealt with within a statutory six week period then the approval will be issued. If not, a refusal notice will be sent as the council is legally obliged to make a decision within six weeks. Do not worry too much about a refusal notice of this sort because when you send the information required the file will be reopened without you paying any more fees.

A whole schedule of queries on a building regulation application is quite usual, and does not imply that whoever drew your plans is less than competent. Individual local authorities have a great deal of freedom in how they interpret the building regulations, and no two authorities ask for additional information on the same topics. Architects expect these queries, which can vary from a request for a soil stability investigation and full foundation design calculations through to a request to show the actual headroom half way up the stairs.

Sometimes building regulation queries can only be dealt with by going to considerable expense in having a structural engineer provide the information required. This usually happens when the application is to build a house or bungalow in a mining area, or over a geological fault, or where the design proposed is unusual. Your architect or whoever drew your plans will usually arrange this for you, but the fees will have to be paid by you, and it is a good idea to arrange to pay them direct, with the bill made out to you as the client, so that you have the direct benefit of the engineer's professional indemnity insurance.

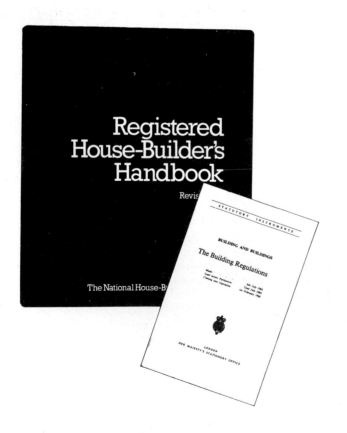

*Building Regulations — **what** you build*
*N.H.B.C. standards — **how** you build*

CONTRACTS, CONVEYANCES AND COVENANTS

This part of the book is about legal procedures, and so we include a brief look at the terms used when you make arrangements to buy a piece of land on which to build your new home. However, this is not a D.I.Y. guide for doing without a solicitor, and it is extremely unwise for most people to enter into any commitment to buy or sell land without legal help. A title to a house is sometimes conveyed without a solicitor, and there are savings to be made by doing this. Whether they are worthwhile is a matter of opinion. However, buying a piece of land on which to build a new home involves many more factors. A solicitor is essential. Some of the terms that he or she will use are as follows:

A Reservation Fee or **Reservation Deposit** may be paid to an estate agent or to the vendor simply to establish your interest in buying the land. Ensure that it is no more than this by writing on the back of your cheque 'returnable deposit — subject to contract'. This is as far as you should ever get without a solicitor.

Searches are investigations which are made by your solicitor into the title and all aspects of it. They take at least a month, during which time you will be looking very carefully at whether you can build the home you want within the terms of any existing planning consent, and within your budget.

A Contract is a firm undertaking to buy the land, and once you have signed it you cannot back out. It is usual to pay 10% of the purchase price when the contract is signed.

A Conveyance is the final transfer of the title to the land, and usually takes place a month after the contract is signed. This is when the balance of the money is paid over and the land becomes yours.

Covenants are specific obligations which you undertake when you sign the contract, and which you cannot escape without a great deal of difficulty, if at all. They are very important, and their long term implications must be considered with great care. Your solicitor will advise. Typical covenants might be: 'not to use the land conveyed other than for the erection of a *single* dwelling of one storey'. This is bad news if you want to build a two storey house and would like to build another in the garden if you could ever get planning permission in the future. 'To keep the east boundary wall in good repair at all times'. The east boundary wall may be O.K. now, but what would it cost to replace if it started to lean in twenty years time? 'To obtain the written approval of the vendor to the design of all buildings erected on the land'. A very common one. You must get 'Such consent not to be unreasonably withheld' added to it.

Discuss each and every covenant with your solicitor, and remember that you will have to pass on these obligations to anyone who buys from you in the future. This is important; you may not object to a covenant which prohibits keeping pets, but this may make it difficult for you to sell to a dog lover in the future.

Easements are formal permissions given by another landowner to let you do something on his land. Many people who build on their own land in the eighties are building on in-fill plots, and share access and services with others. The arrangements for them to do this are called easements, and they are important to both parties.

Beware any arrangement to share an access or service without a formal easement, even if another member of your family is involved. When you sell your house — and remember than on average every house is sold every seven years — the purchaser will certainly not want to buy it without formal easements, and at that time you may find that you cannot arrange things easily. To fall out with any neighbour is unfortunate, but to fall out with one who controls your drains can be disastrous. In the same way, do not grant any easement other than on a formal basis. If an informal use of an easement goes on for long enough a presumptive right is established, and this may extend to far more than you would have permitted in a formal arrangement.

Easements for shared drains and shared drives usually involve shared responsibility for maintenance and repairs. Look at the wording of such arrangements carefully, and consider how they are likely to work in the future. Who is to say when a drive needs to be repaired, or when a drain needs maintenance? Your solicitor will advise on this, and his fees for arranging the right wording for an easement are well worth the money.

Easements for overhead power lines are a great source of heartbreak to those who build on in-fill plots. If there are electricity lines running over the site for your new home, then a previous owner of your land has given the electricity board an easement to have them there. Now, if the easement was granted under one of the original nineteenth century electricity supply acts, there may be a condition in it that any owner of the land can serve a notice on the board to move the power lines at the board's expense if he wants to build a house for himself. If the easement was granted under modern legislation it will probably say that the board has to do the same, but at the landowner's expense. The difference can be thousands of pounds. However, beware taking this for granted. In the 1950's the electricity boards offered the other parties to their easements small sums of money to extinguish these rights, and a claim that the board has to move its power lines out of the way of your new home at its own expense may be met by evidence that your predecessor in title accepted £10 to extinguish this right in 1952!

There are similar situations when other main services are buried in a plot. There will be an easement somewhere that sets out the terms on which they are allowed to be there, and the exact wording of this can be very important.

RIGHTS OF WAY

Rights of way for others to cross your land are a common feature of rural in-fill building plots. Often the site was left undeveloped precisely because there was a right of way across it, which was then in use, but is not now used. The right of way as a legal right is invariably still there, and can cause problems. Again, this is a job for a solicitor.

If you have a public footpath across your building plot you can often get it diverted, but will have to tread very carefully in dealing with this. The procedures involved are lengthy, and any proposal of this sort has to be widely advertised and can easily become a conservationist's *cause celebre*. Remember that use of public footpaths or bridle paths are among the oldest of our civil rights, and politely ask all concerned for their support as a favour. Avoid calling the footpath 'disused' — there are those who dedicate their lives to re-establishing disused footpaths.

More usual rights of way concern access to neighbouring fields, or sometimes to properties which no longer exist. In these cases someone owns the right of way over your land in the way that you own the land itself. It is your land, but he can use it for access. This will have happened in one or two ways; either it will be written into his title to his own land (and should also be noted in your deeds), or else it is an acquired right which results from it having been used for a certain number of years. If it is not used it may be possible to buy it, so that only you have a right of way over your own land. If this is not possible then it is important to know exactly the extent of the right, and here your solicitor will advise.

Easements and rights of way can be very important indeed.

ROADS AND DRAINS

The drive and the drains from your new home are yours where they are inside your boundary, but what is the legal position outside your boundary? For most people the answer is that their drive leads across the council's footpath to a council road, and that their drains connect into the water authority's sewers, and their planning consent implies that the Council permits them to use the road and sewers. These roads and sewers are maintained by the authorities as a charge on the rates, and in exchange for this they will require either that their own workmen make the necessary sewer connections or footpath crossings at your expense, or else that your workmen do the job to their own exacting and expensive requirements.

Another possibility is that the road and sewers have been recently constructed by whoever sold you the land, and that the authorities will not take them over until all the new properties have been built. In these circumstances you will almost certainly have bought your land with the benefit of Road and Drainage Bonds which are guarantees that the local authority will eventually take over the road at no expense to you. These are often called Section 40 or Section 18 agreements.

The alternative is that you are involved in a special situation where your access is off a private road, or an unadopted road. In these circumstances it is likely that your drains are either your responsibility although they run under someone else's land, or else you share them with others. In some parts of the Home Counties these arrangements are not uncommon, and if this is your case it is essential that you understand clearly what your rights are when you think the services need repair or improvement, and what your obligations are to help pay for it. Your solicitor will advise on this.

Road charges are payments which are sometimes demanded by local authorities for making up or improving sub-standard roads which give access to a property. Again, this is more common in some parts of the country than others, and any liability to road charges will be discovered by your solicitor when you purchase the land. If you already have the land— perhaps a paddock at the bottom of your garden, or a plot which has been inherited— then it is a very good idea to check whether by building a house on it you are incurring a liability for road charges. The answer will probably be 'No' but it is nice to be sure.

Drains. A new dwelling requires two sorts of drains, and while this presents no problems when buying a serviced plot in a built up area, the options for a rural site without main drains can be confusing. The difference in costs between different arrangements can be considerable, and it is important not just to find out what is practicable, but also which is the cheapest of any alternatives. Whatever is approved will be satisfactory from a technical viewpoint, as the building regulations standards are very high.

Surface water drains take rainwater from the roof and from any drains in a drive, and nothing else. Except in urban areas they usually lead to soakaways, which are simply large holes which have been filled with stones and covered over. Soakaways have to be a minimum distance from the house, and wholly on your own land. Make sure they are not constructed in a place where you might want to build an extension at some time in the future. If you are a farmer you can avoid soakaways by simply leading surface water drains into land drains, or into a ditch. Incidentally surface water is called top water in some parts of the country.

All the other drains are foul drains, and take bath water, and water from the kitchen sink besides connecting to W.Cs. They are normally connected to council sewers (alias main drains) and the details of how this is to be done have to be shown very precisely on the plans which accompany your building regulation application. It is not essential that they should connect directly to the sewer, and it is often acceptable that they connect into a neighbour's drain instead. This can save a great deal of money and it is often well worthwhile paying a neighbour a couple of hundred pounds and meeting the legal costs of an easement to do this if it avoids an expensive drain connection in the road. Such an arrangement is called a shared system, although in East Anglia some local authorities insist on calling it a combined system. Everywhere else a combined system means an arrangement for surface water to be put into foul drains.

If you are building a new home where there is not a sewer available at a depth where your drains can run into it at an acceptable gradient, you are involved in a special situation, and require advice from someone who has a great deal of relevant recent experience. Recent experience is important as drainage technology is changing quickly. There are many options.

First of all, if there is a sewer within your reach but it is uphill from the new house you can install your own sewage pump. These have improved tremendously in recent years, and the whole installation, including sophisticated automatic controls, is hidden in a manhole below ground and costs under £1000. This seems a large sum, but if it enables a house to be built where it would otherwise be impossible to build it, it may be worthwhile. Usually it is only a small fraction of the value of the finished property.

Next we move to septic tanks and cess pools, which are not a very glamorous subject, but as the difference in cost is enormous it is worthwhile reading on. Septic tanks are digesters, being tanks with a series of baffles inhabited by bacteria that break down the solids in the raw sewage and render it unobjectionable. When they have done the job the effluent runs out of the exit pipe from the septic tank, and is disposed of in some suitable way. It is clean and odourless, but not surprisingly the authorities will take a very keen interest in what happens to it. Their requirements vary in different areas and the differences are sometimes inexplicable. If the site is isolated and the sub-surface drainage is good, a simple soakaway may be acceptable. More usually a system of land drains is required. Sometimes a sand filter chamber is required between the septic tank and the final discharge point. In some areas a special permit is required to discharge septic tank effluent anywhere near a watercourse, and the building regulation consent for the installation will be conditional on obtaining the permit.

Septic tanks have changed a great deal in recent

years, and are now invariably prefabricated in either fibreglass or concrete. The 600 gallon size for a single household costs under £500. The solids which accumulate in the bottom of a septic tank have to be pumped out every year or two, and it should be situated where the tanker can reach it. There are also statutory requirements that it should be at least 16 yards from a dwelling.

Where there is a high water table, or in some water supply catchment areas, it is not possible to obtain approval for a septic tank, and a cess pool is required. This is simply a very large buried tank which is pumped out by a sewage tanker at intervals — at least monthly — and not only is the initial installation costly, but the cost of emptying it can be significant. Sometimes the council provides this service on the rates, sometimes charges are levied which vary from high to exorbitant. The general rule is to try to avoid having a cesspool if at all possible, and to get the best advice on alternative pumped or sophisticated digester systems.

A septic tank (below) is cheap and effective and a cess pool (above right) is to be avoided if possible. Tanks by Condor.

SERVICES

The standard services to be considered when thinking about a new house are water, electricity, gas and telephones. Compared with much else with which you will be involved these are comparatively simple matters as the authorities concerned are in business selling their services, and will want you as a customer. However, there are things to watch.

A water supply is provided by the local water authority who will want a formal application for a supply, and a connection fee. They may also want a separate application for a tap for water for the builder to use while he is building, and may make a special building water charge. Many people building on an in-fill site arrange a temporary water supply from another dwelling, and thus avoid the building water charge. This can be well worth doing.

The water authority will be concerned that all plumbing work meets their own standards, and will want to inspect it before they provide the permanent connection. Your plumber will know their requirements, and is probably on Christian name terms with the Inspector. A connection is made at the boundary of your property, and you have to provide the pipe from the boundary to the house.

The electricity supply is arranged in much the same way, and it is worth noting that a temporary supply can be made to a building site if a locked box is provided for the meter. This enables electric mixers and other power tools to be used, and is often a good idea. When filling in the application form for the permanent supply it is important to give consideration to the possible advantages of opting for the Economy 7 Tariff, with cheap electricity after midnight. If you are considering a heat pump it is also worth asking if a three phase supply is available without extra charge.

One matter, which is very important, is to settle exactly where the meter box is to be fixed. These boxes are supplied by the electricity boards for building into the outside wall of a house so that the meters can be read without entering the premises. The Boards expect them to be fixed in a prominent position, preferably by the front door. Now these boxes are singularly unattractive in appearance, and it is unlikely that you will want the meter box to be a key feature on the front of the building. If this is so, you will have to say very clearly to all concerned at an early stage and settle where it is to be. The board may ask for a few pounds extra to cover the additional length of cable: pay it, it is worthwhile.

If you are building in the country you may find that the electricity board will quote for an overhead supply. If you want a buried cable they will quote for this as well, and you may be able to get the price down if you offer to dig the trench for them. This must be a trench on its own, and may not be shared with other services.

If there is a gas main within reach to give you a gas supply, the procedures are exactly the same as those for an electricity supply, even down to the meter box. If there is a gas supply available but you doubt if you will want to use it, it may be worth considering putting in the supply simply to enhance the value of your house when you sell it.

Telephones are becoming more and more part of our lives, and arrangements to put them in a new house should be planned as carefully as the other services. You will probably want the wires underground, and once again you may be able to negotiate on the cost of this if you offer to dig the trench. When the time comes to put the wiring in the trench, try asking the foreman to drop in a two pair cable as you expect to have a second phone before long. He will usually oblige and you can give your teenagers their own phone in the future. (Whether or not this is a good idea is a matter of opinion, but you will have the option.) A spare line may also be useful for cable t.v. or a burglar alarm link.

It is essential to insist that meter boxes are not positioned where they spoil the look of a house. The ones in the sketch should be round the corner at the back door.

Finance

If you buy a house from a developer or through an estate agent you will find that the person who you are dealing with will advise and help you with the various financial arrangements that have to be made. Usually they will be anxious to arrange a mortgage for you, and to sell you insurances. This help is not available if you are arranging to build on your own land, and you will have to handle all the financial planning yourself. This is not at all difficult providing that you have a clear view of your long term objectives.

Start by considering your position when the new home is completed, and you have moved in. Will you want a mortgage? If not, then you are very fortunate and your only problem is to work out whose name is to be on the title deeds in order to put your family in the best Capital Transfer Tax situation.

If you will be involved with a mortgage then there are various alternatives, from endowment insurance-linked mortgages at one end of the scale to Option Mortgages on the other. Your mortgage may be with either a bank or a building society. All of this may be something with which you are very familiar, or you may need specialist advice. If you need advice the best people to start with are your Bank Manager, or a reputable mortgage broker. The important thing is to consider these long term objectives quite separately from the actual business of financing the building work.

Paying for the land and the actual construction work is something which has to be carefully budgeted, and arranged with care, as all the people who will be working for you are working for money. They will expect to be paid on time, and you will find that their cooperation and help will evaporate very quickly if anything goes wrong with your arrangements to meet your bills. To maintain the enthusiasm of all concerned you must be a good payer, and must be seen to be a good buyer.

If you do not already have a site then the first thing that you have to pay for is the land, and the solicitor's fees and land registry charges involved in buying the land. The only exception is if you are buying a serviced plot from one of the local authorities who will give you a licence to build on the land, and only require you to pay for the plot itself when the house is finished. This sounds a good idea, but it can make it difficult for you to borrow the money for the building work as you will not have the deeds to the land to offer as security. In this case the authority selling the land will help with advice on how to get round this problem.

The next commitment is to pay your architect or designer, to pay planning and building regulation application fees, and perhaps to pay some special insurance premiums. None of these will be very large sums, but it is important to pay them promptly and to start the way you intend to go on.

At this stage you will be getting firm price quotations for the actual building work, and will be relieved to find these are in line with the guideline project costs which you have been using so far. If you are placing a contract with a builder then he will almost certainly want stage

payments — typically 20% when the ground floor slab is cast, 25% when the roof is tiled 25% when the house is plastered out, and the balance when you move in. Your contract with him probably involves deducting a 5% retention from each payment, which you will pay at the end of a three month period after the builder has returned to deal with any minor snags.

Building using sub-contractors involves many more payments to be made, and you will have to draw up your own cash flow projection, probably using a book like *Building Your Own Home* as a guide.

If you are building using one of the package service companies they will help you to establish your budget, will give you a firm quotation for their own work which will explain exactly when their bills have to be paid, and will advise on budgeting for other expenditure.

At the end of the whole job you will move into your new home, and will probably get the mortgage which we have already discussed. When you know where you are going to get this, and what sort of a mortgage it is going to be, you can find out if you can get progress payments as the building goes up, or whether the mortgage money can only be paid when the building is completed. If you can get progress payments then you will need only a modest bank balance or overdraft to pay the bills that come along before the first progress payment arrives, and another advantage of a mortgage with progress payments is that you will also get the tax benefits of the mortgage right from the start.

If you cannot arrange progress payments on the particular mortgage that you want then you must get a bridging loan to cover the cost of the work until you receive the mortgage money on the finished job. This is an arrangement with the bank to lend you all the money that you require to build, sometimes as a lump sum loan, but preferably as an overdraft. As a security the bank will want your personal guarantee and also the title deeds to the land and whatever you build on it. When you finish the bank will transfer the deeds to your building society, and the building society will transfer its cash direct to the bank. The banks and building societies are well used to working together in this way.

A disadvantage of this arrangement is that the bank will want rather more interest than a building society, and may insist on a fixed loan instead of an overdraft, which is more expensive still. They will sometimes demand a commitment fee on top of everything else. Tax relief can be claimed on the interest, but not normally until you make your annual tax return.

If your mortgage is with a bank then all of this is arranged by your bank manager. If you are getting a building society mortgage your bank manager will want to see a letter from your building society confirming that a mortgage will be available in due course before he authorises a bridging loan.

As an alternative to using the title to the land on which you are building as security for all of this, it is sometimes preferable to take out a second or increased mortgage on your existing home. It is all very complicated, but the banks and building societies are in business to lend money, and they will help and advise on the various ways in which everything can be arranged. When you find that you are about to sign the relevant papers to commit yourself to all of this, you will be less than human if you do not start wondering exactly what you have let yourself in for, and what will happen if you become ill, or fall under a bus. This is where you start thinking about insurances.

INSURANCES

Having made arrangements to build a new house, probably using borrowed money, you will be very conscious that you have entered into some pretty formidable obligations and that you must try to cover any risks with appropriate insurance. This is relatively easy, and although you may find yourself involved with a number of different policies, the premiums involved are quite small.

First of all, once you have bought the land you are liable to third party claims arising from anything to do with the land. The obvious hazard is that a tree may fall and injure someone. Third party claims of this sort may be covered by your existing householder's insurances, but once you start any building operations the risks are very real and you must make sure that they are covered.

If you have a formal contract with a builder then the wording of the contract itself should put the responsibility on him to insure against all risks, including the risk of the uncompleted building catching fire. However, if you are handling any part of the work yourself, either working yourself or using sub-contractors, you should certainly take out your own insurance cover, as well as insisting that your builder has the insurances required under his contract. You will need contractors 'All Risk' insurance, employers' liability insurance if you are employing any one at all, and standard third party insurance. The latter is essential; you must realise that if you have any responsibility for a building site a trespassing child who falls off your scaffold may have a valid claim for damages against you.

There are standard builders' policies available to cover all of this, and details are available from leading insurance companies. The package firms will help with this if you are using their services.

If you think that the success of the whole project depends on you, and that your own supervision is necessary for everything to be the huge success that it will be, then you must take out special insurance cover to enable someone to take over if you are killed or taken ill. This is even more important if you are building using sub-contractors, or relying on some of your own labour. Short term life insurance for one year only is very cheap, and a special policy for a sum adequate to enable your executors to employ the best builder in town to get the job finished is a very sensible investment. Short term health insurance may be equally appropriate. Everyone's personal situation is different in this, but whatever it is, suitable arrangements must be made.

VAT

The VAT situation for new homes is all good news. If you are building a completely new home, and are not altering, renovating or otherwise involved with an existing building, you will get back virtually all the VAT which you pay whether or not you are VAT registered. The VAT position for extensions, alterations, or repairs is different and complex, but for a completely new building it is quite simple.

If you are already VAT registered with a business of some sort, and the new house is financed as a part of the business, as on a farm or at a garden centre, then you simply reclaim the VAT through your normal returns.

If a builder has a contract for the whole job he will 'zero rate' the VAT and you will not have to pay the VAT on anything that he buys for you. If you want to buy any fittings yourself — light fittings for example — give him the receipt and ask him to put it through his books as if he had bought it himself. All the normal fittings and fixtures can be zero rated except for a few unusual items. These are mainly items of kitchen equipment as opposed to kitchen units — cookers, washing machines, etc. Some fitted furniture is also outside the scope of the regulations, as are for some reason, extractor fans.

If you are building using sub-contractors then you reclaim the VAT using what are called 'Notice 719 procedures'. This is a bit involved; full details and the relevant Customs and Excise notice are given in *Building Your Own Home*. The essential is to keep all your bills, as you will need them to support your claim for a VAT refund when the house is finished.

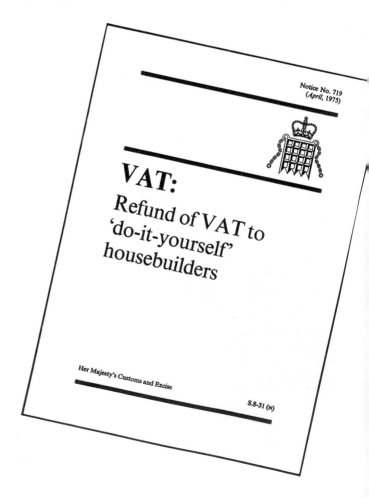

Notice No. 719 (*April, 1975*)

VAT: Refund of VAT to 'do-it-yourself' housebuilders

Her Majesty's Customs and Excise

S.8-31 (N)

How are you going to build?

The fundamental differences between the various ways of building a new home are the different levels of your involvement with the building process, from simply handing the whole job over to someone who is going to make it all happen for you, through to providing all the drive and management to get everything done yourself. These are the choices.

USING AN ARCHITECT
The Rolls Royce way of having a new home built is to use an architect in private practice who specialises in individual houses. He will handle everything for you, and though you can tell him that you want him to arrange to use one of our designs, you will probably find that he will prefer to draw up his own design. He will find you a builder, prepare the contract for you to sign, supervise the work, and approve the bills before sending them on to you to pay. He will be concerned to see you get full value for money, but he does operate at the top end of the market. His fees will be around 6% of the cost of the building, plus expenses. If this is for you, then it is essential to make sure you explain exactly what your budget is, and to make it clear that the job must be completed within this figure.

USING A DESIGN CONSULTANT
A look at a typical local authority planning register will show just how many planning applications are made by design consultants. They are not subject to the control of the R.I.B.A. or the Architects Registration Council, and may not be fully covered by professional indemnity insurances. Their fees are invariably highly negotiable, and they will usually submit our plans for approval, find you builders, and supervise work if required. They will give you as much or as little help as you require. Make sure there is a clear understanding of your budget, and of the fees which they require.

USING A DESIGN FROM THIS BOOK
A full set of drawings for a design from this book will cost less than ½% of the cost of the building, and standard designs can be altered to meet your own requirements. The drawings come with very detailed advice on submitting your own planning and building regulation applications, or you can get a local surveyor or estate agent to do this for you, or P.S.S. Ltd who sell the drawings may arrange this. You also get three copies of a specification and copious notes on seeking quotations from builders, on insurances, VAT reclaim procedures and much else. See page 282.

LOCAL BUILDING COMPANIES
By this we mean well established local builders who work in the area where you want to build. They are probably concerned with commercial and development work as well as with one-off houses, and may not welcome your enquiry unless the contract is fairly large and the specification high. A phone call asking if they are interested in quoting for a one-off home in your price bracket may save time and trouble. They are invariably N.H.B.C. registered. Check whether they will build for you themselves with their own employees, or whether they propose to sub-contract the job. This sort of firm should be able to help and advise on every aspect of the project, but do make sure that you make your own decisions about the terms of the contract with them.

A LOCAL BUILDER
This is the chap who puts up most one-off houses on the client's own sites. He is usually a building tradesman who often works alongside his employees. He works from home where his wife takes the phone calls. N.H.B.C. registered. Do not be put off by his apparent meagre resources; he can do a first class job and with the N.H.B.C. arrangements and the right contract you are safe with him. His building work is usually better than his organising ability, and you may get involved in arranging for services and other matters.

THE NON N.H.B.C. BUILDER
If a non-registered builder wants to take a contract for the whole job you must ask yourself why he is not registered. Take advice and be cautious. Without an N.H.B.C. certificate you will have problems getting a mortgage, and will have to get architect's progress certificates — more about these later.

N.H.B.C. CERTIFICATES
The National Housebuilders Registration Council is an organisation formed by the building industry and virtually all responsible house builders are members, having satisfied the council about their competence and having given substantial guarantees. All their house building work is checked at intervals by the N.H.B.C. Inspectors, and they pay a large insurance premium on each house they build. In exchange for this their clients get the following benefits:
1. The N.H.B.C. Inspectors will ensure that all work is carried out to N.H.B.C. standards which are very high.
2. You get a ten year warranty against structural failure, and without this a bank or building society will want architect's progress certificates if you need a mortgage.
3. Your position is protected if the builder goes bankrupt or otherwise fails.

When you place a contract with an N.H.B.C. builder he will send you a form which is a legal undertaking to build to N.H.B.C. standards under N.H.B.C. supervision.

BUILDING CONTRACTS

If you employ an architect he will write a contract with a builder for you. Make sure it is a fixed price contract, with no escalation clauses to allow for inflation, and that any extras to be charged have to be approved by you as well as by the architect before the expenditure is incurred.

If you are using an established building firm they may present you with one of the various standard forms of contract used in the building industry. You will quickly see that 90% of the clauses protect the builder and not the client.

A quotation from a small local builder may well be handwritten on one side of a piece of lined paper. This may seem to you to be casual in the extreme, but if the price is right and the builder is right it can be the basis of an excellent contract. What you do is to send him a letter accepting his offer and *referring to an attached specification and drawing*. See the sample opposite.

In any arrangement to build a new home the essential is never to pay in advance for any work. Progress payment should always be for rather less than the actual value of the work done. Work that is extra to contract should also be costed and authorised in writing before it is put in hand. If these rules are followed, you will always be in the driving seat and will effectively control the contract. If you ever pay for anything in advance, or imply sanction for extra work for which you have not been quoted a firm price, you have lost control of the situation. 99% of disputes on contracts come from clients losing control of situations in this way.

QUOTATIONS AND PRIME COST SUMS

When you are seeking a price from a builder he will not want to quote for the particular kitchen that you require, and so will allow a prime cost sum for this. This is called a p.c. sum. If a p.c. sum is £900 he has allowed in his price for a kitchen with this value. If the kitchen that you want costs £500 more than this, then the contract price will be increased by £500; if less then there is saving on the contract price. Typical features covered by p.c.sums are kitchens, bathrooms, central heating, fitted furniture, fireplaces, feature staircases, wall tiling and floor tiling. It is a very useful arrangement, but make sure that you know the basis on which the extras or savings on p.c. sums will be charged — list price, trade price, special offer or what.

Another aspect of quotations is the obvious need to allow for unforeseen extra work in the foundations. This is dealt with by the builder quoting for the foundations as shown on the drawing. Any extra work in the foundation which is required by the Building Inspector or the N.H.B.C Inspector is charged at standard trade rates; these are published monthly and are well known. Special features such as display shelving, parquet flooring, built-in hi-fi wiring or garden floodlights are best kept out of quotations and contracts altogether, and settled separately as extras to the contract. This has many advantages, one of which is that a request for elaborate sounding features in the basic quotation often gives the builder the idea that cost is not particularly important to you! Get your contract price fixed on a basic specification, with realistic p.c. sums, and obtain special quotations for extras later.

TYPICAL SHORT FORM OF SPECIFICATION

A full architect's or quantity surveyor's specification is a long and complex document, couched in technical jargon, and defining materials, methods of construction and standards. Relatively few new homes on clients' own land are built with full specifications, and many are built without the essential definitions of key elements in the builder's contract. This short form of specification covers these definitions, but avoids technicalities by referring to well known published standards, particularly the NHBC Handbook.

This specification is an example only, and is intended as a guide to drawing up a specification for a specific contract for a specific house.

1. This specification relates to a contract established by . . . (detail form of contract, if any, or exchange of quotation and acceptance which establishes the contract) . . . and is a schedule to that contract. The contract is between the client . . . (name and address) . . . and the builder . . . (name and address) . . . and is a simple contract between the client and the builder. Neither the designer, any supplier of materials or any sub-contractor are party to this contract.

2. This specification refers to a house to be built to the drawings attached, which have been initialled and dated by both parties, and all notes on these drawings are part of the specification.

3. The builder shall obtain an NHBC certificate for the property, and shall provide the client with the documentation relating to this in accordance with standard NHBC practice before work commences. All materials and work shall be to the requirements of the NHBC Builders Handbook, and shall follow the further recommendations laid down in the NHBC site manuals and practice notes.

4. Time will be the essence of the contract and the builder is to start the works on . . . (date) . . . or as soon as practicable thereafter, and shall finish the whole of the works in the time stated in the tender.

5. Two sets of working drawings will be furnished to the builder for site use, and any further prints reasonably required shall be supplied on request.

6. The term prime cost when applied to materials or goods to be fixed by the builder shall mean the list price of such goods as published in the supplier's catalogue, and any trade discounts obtained by the builder shall be an advantage enjoyed by the builder. Prime cost sums shall include suppliers' charges for delivery. All expenses in connection with the fixing of such goods shall be allowed for by the builder in the contract sum.

7. All work and materials shall be to British standards and Codes of Practice and shall comply with Building Regulations. Proprietary materials and components shall be used or fixed in accordance with the manufacturers' recommendations.

8. The builder shall be responsible for the issue of all statutory notices and shall comply with the requirements of the Local Authority and statutory bodies. The client warrants to the builder that all necessary planning consents and appropriate building regulation approvals have been obtained, and shall be responsible to the builder for any delay or cancellation of the contract consequent on there not being such consents or approvals.

9. The builder shall be deemed to have visited the site and to have satisfied himself regarding site conditions.

10. The builder shall be responsible for all insurances against all risks on site, including public liability and fire risk, to date of hand over. The builder shall make security arrangements for the proper storage of materials on the site as appropriate to the local circumstances. The builder is to avoid damage to public and private property adjacent to the site, and to make good or pay for reinstatement of any damage caused. The builder shall extend to the client the guarantees available to him on proprietory materials and fittings, and shall provide the client with documentation required to take advantage of such guarantees.

11. The builder is to cover up and protect the works from the weather, and to take all action for the protection of the works against frost in accordance with the requirements of the NHBC.

12. Top soil shall be stripped from the site before commencing excavation of the foundations in accordance with the requirements of the NHBC, and shall be . . . (spread or left heaped) . . . Any trees removed shall have the whole of their roots excavated, and the back fill shall be with material appropriate to the works to be executed over the excavation.

13. The builder is to set out and level the works and will be responsible for the accuracy of the same.

14. Foundations shall be as per the drawings with footings under partition walls taken down to solid ground. Depth of the foundations shall be as per drawings, with any additional depths required by the Local Authority paid for at measured work rates.

15. Concrete for the foundations and solid floors shall be truck mixed concrete as specified. Foundation brickwork shall be in bricks or blocks to the requirements of the Local Authority. Fill shall be clean material to the requirements of the NHBC.

16. Ducting shall be provided for service pipes and cables through the foundations, and chases shall be formed in concrete for pipework inside the building in accordance with good building practice.

17. The ground floor if to be of solid construction shall have a sand cement screed, finished to receive . . . (tiles as defined or carpeting) . . . or if suspended floor construction shall be as per drawing with floor boarding to be . . . (define whether tongue and grooved boarding or interlocking flooring panels) . . .

18. Mat wells shall be provided at the front and back doors to be . . . (define type and size) . . .

19. The shell of the building is to be built with the materials specified on the drawings. The external walling material shall be . . . (make and type) . . . and shall be laid and finished in a manner to be agreed. The windows shall be . . . (make and range) . . . and shall be finished . . . (define finish). The external doors shall be . . . (make and types) . . . and shall be finished . . . (define finish). Other external joinery, including any cladding, fascias and barge boards shall be finished . . . (define finish). Internal door frames shall be . . . (material and finish). Window boards shall be . . . (material and finish) . . . Staircases shall be . . . (material and style, particularly style of balustrade and rails).

20. The roof shall be constructed strictly in accordance with the drawings, and any trussed rafters specified shall be of a type for which building regulation approval has been obtained.

21. The roof and any vertical external tiling shall be tiled with . . . (define tiles by manufacturer, type and colour) . . . and the tiling work shall be carried out by a tiling contractor approved by the tile manufacturer so as to obtain the most favourable guarantee available from the tile manufacturer. The subcontract shall be between the builder and the sub-contractor.

22. First floor boarding shall be . . . (define whether tongue and grooved boarding or interlocking flooring board) . . .

23. Access to the roof shall be provided to NHBC requirements, and a loft ladder shall be fitted within the contract sum.

24. All walls shall be plastered in . . . (define lightweight or traditional plaster) . . . to the plaster manufacturer's full specification, and all materials used shall be from the same manufacturer. Coveing and other plaster features shall be extras to the contract, to be specifically defined in a quotation and ordered with a written order.

25. Ceilings shall be boarded to suit the ceiling finish specified, which shall be . . . (define) . . .

26. The under surface of the stairs shall be . . . (define arrangements for below the stairs if this is a visible feature) . . .

27. Architraves and skirtings shall be . . . (define material, size and moulding shape after discussion of samples) . . .

28. Internal doors to be . . . (define doors specifically, by manufacturer and model) . . .

29. Any sliding patio doors shall be . . . (manufacturer and type) . . .

30. All windows shall be double glazed with sealed double glazing units to be . . . (manufacturer and type) . . . All glazed doors shall be single glazed. Obscure glass shall be used for glazing to . . . (define rooms) . . .

31. Garage doors shall be . . . (manufacturer and type) . . .

32. The door furniture to be as the schedule attached (The schedule should detail which internal doors are to have latches, which are to have locks, security locks to external doors, letter plates as required, plus any other fittings. Windows are supplied complete with furniture, but if security bolts or special fittings are required these should be specified.).

33. The central heating system shall be installed against a prime cost sum of £ . . . and the proposals for this system shall be as detailed separately. The system shall be designed to meet the heating requirements of the NHBC, and all work shall be to the appliance manufacturer's requirements. If the heating system requires the installation of an oil tank, the position and height of this shall be agreed, and the structure to support and/or conceal the tank shall be . . . (define) . . .

34. The chimney and chimney breast shall be built as per drawing, and the fireplace opening provided shall be for a . . . (name appliance) . . . This appliance and the fire surround shall be provided against a prime cost sum of £ . . . All work to the fireplace opening and chimney shall be to the appliance manufacturer's requirements.

35. Sanitary ware and bathroom fittings shall be provided against a prime cost sum of £ . . . (discuss).

36. The cold water tank shall have capacity of . . . (discuss) . . . and shall be situated in the roof in a position agreed, to give ease of access, on a stand to NHBC requirements. It shall be fitted with a lid, and frost protected as required under the Building Regulations. The hot water cylinder shall have a capacity of . . . (discuss) . . . in a position to give ease of access while providing for the maximum space for shelving alongside. The hot water cylinder shall be fitted with an immersion heater, to be . . . (discuss, including whether this is a dual model to provide both full and top-up heating). The cylinder shall be lagged to NHBC requirements.

37. The kitchen fittings shall be provided against a prime cost sum of £ . . . and this shall include all sinks down on drawings. Hot and cold water and drainage connections to a washing machine/dish washer situated . . . (define) . . . shall be provided.

38. Wardrobes, cupboard fronts and other fitted furniture shall be provided against a prime cost sum of £ . . .

39. The electrical installation shall allow for lighting points, power points and switching arrangements to be to the NHBC minimum requirements, and the builder shall quote the additional sum required for each extra ceiling light, extra wall light, and each extra socket outlet. Light switches and socket outlets shall be . . . (manufacturer and range) . . . Simple pendents shall be provided at all lighting points, or alternatively the client's fittings will be fixed if provided to programme. The fuse box shall be . . . (define fuse board and circuit breaker system) . . . Provision shall be made for television sockets and telephone points in . . . (define rooms and position in rooms) . . . Electricity meters shall be in a meter box fitted . . . (define position. The Electricity Board may try to define where this should be) . . . Provision shall be made for bells at the front and back door, and a simple bell shall be provided, or alternatively the client's chimes or other fittings to be installed if provided to programme.

40. All interior plaster surfaces shall be finished with . . . (define emulsion paint and colour) . . . which shall be applied in accordance with the manufacturer's recommendations for new work to give a consistent colour.

41. Wall tiling shall be quoted as a prime cost sum of £ . . . per sq yd. for a stated minimum area.

42. All Softwood joinery shall be knotted, primed and treated with two undercoats and one gloss finishing coat of interior paint to be . . . (define paint and colour) . . .

43. All timber surfaces which are not to be painted shall be protected by using Sadolin or similar protective stain to the manufacturer's requirements, and shall not be varnished (or other requirements as considered appropriate).

44. Foul drainage shall be as detailed on the site plan, and all work shall be to the requirements of the Local Authority.

45. Rainwater goods shall be . . . (manufacturer and range) . . . and shall discharge into open gullies or via sealed drain connectors . . . (as defined) . . . Surface water drains shall discharge into soakaways or elsewhere as detailed on drawings.

46. External steps, and the porch or step at the front door, shall be finished with . . . (quarry tiles or finish required) . . . A path shall be provided around the whole of the perimeter of the building, to a width of 2 ft., to be . . . (specify concrete surface or paving slabs) . . . and shall be laid to the full requirements of the NHBC for external works.

47. Other external works, including any work on the drive, or any fencing, shall be considered as extras to the contract, and shall be quoted for in writing, and the order for them placed in writing.

48. Any detached garage shown on the drawings is outside the contract, and any work to construct such a garage shall be an extra to the contract, to be quoted in writing and any order placed in writing.

49. Any other work required or fittings to be installed in connection with the contract shall be quoted in writing and any order placed in writing.

50. Any defect, excessive shrinkages or other faults which appear within 3 months of handover due to materials or workmanship not in accordance with the contract, or frost occurring before practical completion, shall be made good by the builder, and payment of the retention detailed in the payment arrangements at paragraph 51 shall only be made on completion of this making good.

51. Payment to be made on a progress rate of:
    20% of contract price at d.p.c.
    25% of contract price at roof tiled
    25% of contract price at plastered out
    30% at handover
The above all subject to a 2½% retention as provided in paragraph 50. All payments to be made within 7 days of notice that payment is due.

52. The client may but not unreasonably or vexatiously by notice by registered post or recorded delivery to the builder forthwith determine the employment of the builder if the builder shall make default in any one or more of the following respects:

i) If the builder without reasonable cause fails to proceed diligently with the Works or wholly suspends the carrying out of the Works before completion.

ii) If the builder becomes bankrupt or makes any composition or arrangement with his creditors or has a winding up order made or a resolution for voluntary winding up passed or a Receiver or Manager of his business is appointed or possession is taken by or on behalf of any creditor of any property the subject of a Charge. Provided always that the right of determination shall be without prejudice to any other rights or remedies that the client may possess.

53. The builder may but not unreasonably or vexatiously by notice by registered post or recorded delivery to the client forthwith determine the employment of the builder if the client shall make default in any one or more of the following respects that is to say:

i) if the client fails to make any interim payment due within 14 days of such payment being due.

ii) if the client or any person for whom he is responsible interferes or obstructs the carrying out of the Works.

iii) if the client becomes bankrupt or makes a composition or arrangement with his creditors.
Provided always that the right of determination shall be without prejudice to any other rights or remedies which the builder may possess.

54. In the event of a dispute between the parties arising out of the contract, the parties shall agree jointly to engage an architect independent of either of them to arbitrate between them, and shall be bound by the architect's findings as to the matter in dispute and to his apportionment of his fees as an arbitrator.

BUILDING USING SUB-CONTRACTORS OR YOUR OWN LABOUR

Any idea of building without having a contract with a builder who co-ordinates and controls the whole job takes you straight into the world of self-build. This is a practical proposition for those with organising ability and lots of confidence. At least 25% of one-off homes are built this way. Read *Building Your Own Home* — details are in the bibliography.

ARCHITECT'S PROGRESS CERTIFICATES

If you are building using sub-contractors you will not be able to get an N.H.B.C. certificate, and will usually have to arrange to get architect's progress certificates if you want bank or mortgage finance. This is fully discussed in *Building Your Own Home*; it can be a problem, and arrangements must be made at an early stage in the whole business. The various package service companies will help their own clients with this. Sometimes it is possible to offer chartered surveyor's certificates instead.

This owner-built house in Nottinghamshire was the original of our Woodchurch design on page 106.

For years the author has been writing and stating in broadcasts "at least 2000 people" build their own homes every year. In 1982 we got the accurate figures from the reply to a question in the House of Commons on the number of VAT notice 719 claims — seven thousand individual self builders, like the couple who built the bungalow on the facing page. A thousand more built as members of Self-build Housing Associations, like the association members left. Eight thousand people build their own homes every year, providing all the management and usually some of the labour involved.

Tim Skelton of the Milton Keynes Land Office, Alan Lake of Barclays Bank who finances self build projects, and Tony Wilson, Secretary of the Self Build Managers Association, all of whom help people's dreams of a new home come true at Milton Keynes.

Timber frame building

If you are thinking of building a new home you are almost certainly reading all the magazine features on new houses that you can find, are sending for brochures, and you are collecting all the information that you can about your options. From this you will know of the choice between traditional construction and the newer timber frame systems, and you are probably a little uncertain about it all, particularly as both ways of building are promoted as being the *only* way of building. Let us look at this situation.

First of all, timber frame homes are neither better nor worse than traditionally built homes. They look exactly the same and are just as good an investment. The costs are generally comparable. The difference is in the way in which they are constructed.

Timber frame houses and bungalows have a wooden frame which supports the roof. This usually has a skin of brickwork or other masonry outside. There is lots of insulation and damp proofing material around the frame itself, and the walls inside are formed by an inner skin of plasterboard or 'dry lining'.

Traditional housing usually has walls with two skins of masonry, with insulating blockwork as the inner skin. The walls between rooms are usually built in solid blockwork, at any rate on the ground floor, and all interior surfaces are finished with traditional wet plastering that takes some time to dry out.

There are various half-way compromises between these two systems of construction: traditionally built houses can be dry lined, and first floor walls between bedrooms are often timber framed. However, the essential difference between traditional and timber frame construction is that a timber frame supports the roof of the building, and gives the whole dwelling its structural stability. In traditional construction this structural stability comes from the masonry.

All new housing in the UK has to comply with some of the strictest building regulations in the world, and all new homes, traditional or timber framed, are built to exceptionally high standards. Timber frame housing is particularly closely controlled, and because the components are factory made there is an assurance of a measure of 'built-in' quality. The timber frame home will last as long as a traditionally built home, will be no better and no worse a fire risk, and will be just as easy to insure, and just as easily mortgaged. Their advantages and disadvantages compared with traditional construction are very minor matters in the whole context of building yourself a new home. On the other hand, a decision to build one way or the other is a very fundamental one, and you have to make your mind up early in the whole scheme of things. To help you in this, here are the points you should keep in mind.

1. Timber frame housing is very effectively advertised by the frame manufacturers, and their trade associations do an excellent public relations job. As a result you can go to the Ideal Homes Exhibition and collect an armful of timber frame brochures. You will not find many stands promoting traditional construction. This is a pity. It gives a one sided view because there are no comparable organisations concerned with the older way of building.

2. Timber frame construction was used for between 10% and 20% of new homes during the whole of the seventies, and is now heading for a 30% market share. However, much of this is on large developments where a whole site can be geared up for this form of construction. The proportion of timber frame used for one-off housing varies enormously in different parts of the country. In Scotland it has almost taken over the market, in some parts of England it is no more popular than it was 10 years ago. Beware generalisations, and look out for other new homes being built locally to get an idea of the way the trend is going in your own county.

3. Timber frame houses can be built more quickly than traditional buildings. The speed of construction comes from the walls being reared and the roof put on in two or three working days compared with two or three weeks for bricks and mortar. More importantly, the plasterboard internal surfaces do not have to dry out like traditional plastering, and this can save another month. However, the foundations, drains, drive, services and fitting out all take just as long whichever way you build. Ignoring the publicity stunts (the writer once built a traditional house in 7 days!), if time is important you can hope to move into a timber frame house 2 months after a start is made on site, and into a traditionally built home in 4 months. This will be after an average of between 3 and 4 months considering design, getting planning and building regulation consents, and waiting for the builder to start. If speed is essential, timber frame will save you 2 months, and perhaps more in bad weather.

4. Timber frame houses have a high level of thermal insulation. All the frame manufacturers put more insulation into the structure than the building regulations require, and more than is provided in most traditionally built homes. Of course, whatever insulation you wish can be specified in any new home, however it is constructed, but timber frame companies offer exceptional insulation as standard. Rather more importantly timber frame walls do not soak up heat themselves the way that blockwork walls do, so the house will warm up quickly when the heat is turned on. It will also cool down quickly when you turn the heat off, but then you won't be in to notice! This low thermal capacity and quick thermal response of a timber frame house is a very real advantage if your home is going to be unoccupied for part of the day, or when both husband and wife are at work.

5. Costs are more or less comparable. The only meaningful comparisons are the final costs per square foot for the finished job, and timber frame houses are firmly in the middle of traditional costs. Certainly if you are wanting to build for yourself using sub-contractors you will probably find it cheaper to build traditionally, and at the very top end of the market you can pay more for a traditional home than average timber frame costs, but in most cases the prices that you will be quoted will be in the same general bracket.

6. Finally, service. Most timber frame companies will handle everything for you from planning application onwards, and because they are so concerned to advertise they are customer conscious, and will look after you. They usually have show houses for you to inspect before you settle anything at all, and the nationally known companies have got where they are by giving a good service. Usually they have an area manager who will act as your liaison man in everything as the job progresses, and perhaps the real appeal of timber frame to those building on their own land is that it is all made so easy.

This traditional style house is by Prestoplan, and has a timber frame.

Top: The insulation in a timber frame bungalow.
Centre: Prestoplan's Harelaw bungalow.
Left: The Prestoplan Dunvegan House (top) and its lounge (below).

Virtually all single and two storey homes can be built in timber frame, but there are obvious advantages in using designs that were specifically drawn for this type of consideration. In particular, a building regulation application to build using a frame requires the submission of special drawings with the structural design calculations, and usually can only be handled by the trade manufacturer.

Twenty of the designs in this book are by Prestoplan, Britain's leading timber frame manufacturer, and are to be found between page 171 and page 190. Plans for these designs are available from Plan Sales Services like the plans for all the other designs in the book, and these are for making planning applications only. Prestoplan have the full frame drawings and structural calculations for building regulation applications for all these designs, and purchasers of drawings are put in touch with the company who will quote for their full

service. If one of these designs is built using a Prestoplan frame, the company will refund the sum paid to Plan Sales Services for the basic plan. Fuller details of these arrangements will be found on page 282.

Material for this feature was provided by Prestoplan Limited, timber frame housing specialists, who can be contacted at Stanley Street, Preston PR1 4AT. Their telephone number is Preston (0772) 51628. They have area staff who can advise on their service throughout the country.

The package companies

There are many ways of arranging to build a new home, and one very straightforward approach is to use one of the companies that offer a specialised service to those who have their own land. There are a number of them to choose from, and they can be very useful indeed to those who feel they want help in co-ordinating the whole job.

Many of the designs in this book are from Design & Materials Limited, who specialise in traditional construction. Whether you buy plans from this book, or other plans from the D & M range, or whether you want a design drawn specially for you, D & M will be happy to quote you for making a site survey, advising you in detail on costs and many other matters, handling your planning and building regulation applications, obtaining quotations from builders for you, and supplying all the structural shell materials for your home. They have experienced field staff who cover the whole of Britain except the Scottish Highlands and N. Ireland, and have an associated company in Eire.

A proportion of the plans are by Prestoplan Ltd, and were specially drawn for timber-frame construction. As with the D & M plans, buying these drawings does not involve you in any obligation to use a Prestoplan timber-frame, but obviously Prestoplan will be delighted to quote you. Again, they will handle everything for you, from discussing the potential of your site through to arranging the actual building work. Prestoplan will also quote for help with any of the other designs in the book which are suitable for this type of construction. It must be emphasised that if you are building with a timber-frame you will have to use the services of a specialist supplier to provide you with the design calculations that will be needed for your building regulation application. It is not practicable for the average home builder to handle this himself, and advice on this subject in many American publications is not relevant to British conditions.

Besides D & M and Prestoplan there are many other companies in this field, and most of them will help you to build using a set of plans purchased using the order form at the back of this book. They should all be able to give you firm quotations for everything they offer to do for you, and the best way of evaluating the service offered is to ask to see their completed homes and jobs under construction for ordinary clients —*not* show houses. If you are buying their experience, make sure how wide it is and ask how many houses they handle a year. This is particularly important when talking to agents for continental firms.

The D. and M. Carlton design.

84

A question often asked is whether it is more economical to buy materials through a package company. The answer is that in direct terms there is probably no saving, and that given the bill of quantities, the time to spare, and the right contacts you can probably just beat the price that they quote. However, it is the convenience and efficiency of their total service that is the real attraction, together with the advice that they can give about local builders, sub-contractors, insurances and many other matters. People tend to get involved with a package company at project planning stage, and are more concerned at the ability of the company to help them realise their total objective within their budget than with the possibility of buying their double glazing units marginally cheaper elsewhere.

All the package companies aim at the middle and top end of the market, and their specifications are always very high, with above average standards of insulation. Materials supplied are invariably first class, especially the joinery, which they usually manufacture themselves. Walling materials and tiles which they supply come directly from the manufacturer's works against long term contracts, and this enables them to guarantee

deliveries — something which is very important when work starts on site.

Package companies will not usually enter into a contract to build for you themselves, instead they obtain competing quotations for you from local builders and help you to place a contract direct with the contractor whose tender you wish to accept. This procedure avoids legal complications, and the client has the direct benefit of the builders N.H.B.C. Certificate with its ten year warranty.

Those who are building on their own using sub-contractors find a package service even more useful, as it takes one whole area of organisation and uncertainty out of their hands. This enables them to concentrate on the job that only they can do, which is to see that the work on site is carried out properly, on programme, and at the right price. They also find that professionally prepared estimates of costs from the package companies are useful in putting up their proposals to building societies and banks who are providing loan finance, besides getting help from package companies in arranging for the architect's progress certificates which will be required as a condition of obtaining loan finance.

All the materials for a new home. The photograph was posed for The Sunday Times *by D & M Ltd., and shows their clients with the architect, the engineer, the materials manager, and everyone else involved in providing the D & M service. In the background are the materials supplied — a giant Lego set.*

Above: The Prestoplan Ilkley design bungalow.
Below: A D & M house designed to the client's own requirements.

Home Plans
for the 80's

Design Pages

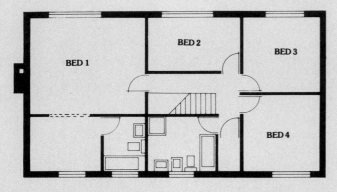

102 BUNGALOW DESIGNS

104 HOUSE DESIGNS

13 GARAGE DESIGNS

All of these designs are for new homes that can be built at realistic unit costs. All of them have been built, and a large proportion have been built many times.

When choosing a design it is essential to consider the constraints of the site and the requirements of the planning authorities as detailed in earlier chapters. All the designs can be built using any materials acceptable under the Building Regulations, and there is considerable scope for making alterations to windows and roof styles. Other alterations are often practicable but may increase unit construction costs.

Details of how to obtain the detailed plans for these designs are given on page 282 to 284.

INDEX

This index is in alphabetical order. The last three digits of the design numbers are the page numbers in this book, so the whole book acts as a numerical index. The areas given are the areas enclosed by the internal faces of the external walls. The notes under 'Aspect' are a general indication of whether the principal rooms look out to the front (F), rear (R), both front and rear (F&R), all round (A), or only to the side (S). The front is usually taken as the side with the front door.

NAME	DESIGN	HOUSE OR BUNGALOW	AREA SQ.FT.	BEDS	ASPECT
Abingdon	82160	B	994	3	F
Albany	83151	B	1447	3	R
Alderwood	83214	H	1440	3	F
Allington	83169	B	1582	4	R
Almondbank	83104	B	1550	4	F
Amberley	83133	B	1920	4	F
Anston	83242	H	1668	4	F
Appleton	83222	H	1404	4	R
Ascot	83159	B	1060	3	F&R
Ashgrove	82125	B	1640	4	A
Avonmere	83265	H	3200	6	F&R
Aylesbury	83226	H	1506	4	F&R
Bakewell	83264	H	2465	4	R
Balmoral	83180	H	1936	4	F
Banbury	83160	B	994	2	F
Bardsey	83190	H	2106	3	R
Bathampton	83269	H	2204	4	F&R
Battlebridge	83156	B	1296	3	F&R
Beaumont	83184	H	1026	3	F
Beechwood	83147	B	1330	3	R
Berkeley	83134	B	700	2	R
Beverley	83236	H	1614	4	F&R
Biddenden	83124	B	1512	3	A
Blyth	83240	H	1695	4	F&R
Bridgewater	83116	B	1592	4	A
Broadwell	82096	B	1566	5	S
Brockenhurst	83225	H	1357	4	F&R
Bromyard	82206	H	1160	4	R
Buckingham	82194	H	1004	3	F
Buckland	81261	H	1796	4	R
Buxton	83271	H	2378	4	A
Camberley	83148	B	840	2	F&S
Cardigan	83144	B	840	2	F&R
Carlton	83098	B	1715	4	F
Carolina	82150	B	1438	5	F&R
Carsholme	83274				
Charnock	83175	B	1177	3	R
Chatsworth	83266	H	2052	4	A
Cheltenham	83218	H	1415	4	F
Chesterton	82132	B	1360	4	F
Chevington	83205	H	936	3	F
Chiltern	83155	B	1060	3	R
Chippenham	82252	H	1905	5	R
Clevedon	83168	B	1582	4	F
Colwyn	83127	B	1880	3	A
Coneyhurst	82143	B	950	4	A
Connecticut	83152	B	1767	4	A
Conway	83142	B	840	2	R
Corsham	82227	H	1560	5	R
Cotswold	83199	H	2084	4	F&R

NAME	DESIGN	HOUSE OR BUNGALOW	AREA SQ.FT.	BEDS	ASPECT
Cranbrook	83118	B	1120	2	A
Creswell	83108	B	1020	2	R
Cromer	82137	B	830	3	F
Crosshaven	83157	B	2030	4	F
Danehill	83105	B	1360	2	F
Dartmouth	83257	H	1836	4	F&R
Deansgate	83153	B	1661	3	A
Denham	83110	B	1304	3	R
Dereham	83237	H	1700	3	F&R
Donegal	82156	B	1296	4	F&R
Douglas	83172	B	1771	4	F
Dunholme	83261	H	1796	4	R
Dunvegan	83181	H	1980	4	F&R
Eastgate	83243	H	1750	4	F&R
Eastwood	83231	H	1442	4	F
Elmhurst	83125	B	1640	3	A
Evesham	83145	B	840	3	F&R
Exeter	83112	B	1650	4	R
Fairford	83196	H	1054	4	F&R
Farnborough	83120	B	1600	3	F
Ferndale	83213	H	1675	4	F&R
Folkstone	83135	B	882	4	R
Fordcombe	83247	H	1998	4	F&R
Forest Gate	83143	B	720	2	A
Fossebridge	83223	H	1570	4	A
Foxton	83170	B	1720	3	A
Foxwood	83259	H	1614	4	F&R
Gainsborough	83111	B	1060	3	R
Glen Dun	83171	B	1555	3	F&R
Glen Farg	83177	B	1026	3	F
Glen More	83179	H	1242	3	F&R
Glen Shee	83176	B	1026	3	F&R
Glen Urquhart	83178	B	1296	4	F
Glyndebourne	83107	B	1800	2	A
Grafham	83193	H	1011	3	F
Granchester	83233	H	1825	4	F&R
Grantley	83187	H	1400	4	F
Grasmere	83141	B	860	3	F
Greenwood	83258	H	2075	5	F&R
Halstead	83207	H	1000	3	F&R
Hambleton	83182	H	1675	5	R
Hardwick	82266	H	2052	4	A
Harewood	83186	H	1620	4	F&R
Harrow	82110	B	1450	4	R
Haslemere	83158	B	2948	4	R
Hartfield	83197	H	1097	4	F&R
Haverhill	83094	B	1150	4	F

INDEX

Designs featuring a Sunken Lounge

Holiday Homes

Designs often built as Farmhouses

Designs with a Study or Office for those who work at home

INDEX

Designs suitable for a Sloping Site or with a Split Level Layout

Designs suitable for a Narrow Site

Designs with Granny Flats or Other Self-Contained Accommodation

Designs of interest to the Disabled

Small Family Houses of less than 1200 sq.ft.

Small Family Bungalows of less than 1000 sq.ft.

Small Retirement Bungalows

HAVERHILL

The Haverhill bungalow suits a site where a natural slope permits the garage floor to be significantly lower than the level of the living accommodation, giving an interesting and very cost effective roof arrangement. Although it is illustrated with flat tiles, this emphasis on the roof is very well suited to parts of the country where traditional pantiles are appropriate.

Design Number 83094

Floor Area	1150 sq.ft.	107 sq.m.
Dimensions overall	64'8'' x 26'6''	19.7 x 8.1
Lounge/Dining (overall)	21'6'' x 18'0''	6.55 x 5.48
Kitchen	11'6'' x 7'8½''	3.50 x 2.35
Garage	19'0'' x 10'2½''	5.79 x 3.11
Master Bed	13'6'' x 11'0''	4.11 x 3.35
Bed 2	12'0'' x 11'0''	3.65 x 3.35
Bed 3	10'0'' x 10'6''	3.05 x 3.20

How do you arrange a patio window in a living room that is the full width of a gable? Just the single opening rarely looks right from outside, but it is invariably what is needed when considered from inside. One answer is to have a narrow slit window on each side of the main opening as in this successful design.

Another feature is the sunken lounge, with two steps down to the new level. This gives a remarkable feeling of space to the whole bungalow, and is the one feature of the house that guests always remember. An incidental result of this arrangement is that a whole flight of steps is required up to the front door, which gives the emphasis to the entrance that is so necessary when it is in the angle between the two wings of the building.

This is a big bungalow, with four bedrooms and study that can become a fifth bedroom if required, but it is a very cost effective design. The only problem area is the chimney, which comes through the roof far too near the valley for simple construction — but where else can the fireplace go? Never mind — our drawings include a special detail to show how the chimney, the roof and the valley all relate to each other!

Design Number 83095

Floor Area		
(exc. garage)	1700 sq.ft.	158 sq.m.
Dimensions Overall	68'10'' x 34'1½''	20.97 x 10.40
Lounge	15'3½'' x 20'4''	4.66 x 6.20
Dining	9'6'' x 11'11½''	2.90 x 3.64
Kitchen	15'2½'' x 10'0''	4.64 x 3.05
Study	9'6'' x 7'10½''	2.89 x 2.40
Utility	10'0'' x 7'10½''	3.05 x 2.40
Cloaks	6'0'' x 7'10½''	1.80 x 2.40
Master Bed	15'1'' x 11'7½''	4.60 x 3.54
Bed 2	10'7½'' x 11'7½''	3.24 x 3.54
Bed 3	12'6'' x 7'10½''	3.82 x 2.40
Bed 4	12'6'' x 7'4½''	3.82 x 2.25

This bungalow can be built in two stages if required, without bedrooms 3 and 4, and extended later if desired. The smaller version is called the Collingham and the reference is 82095.

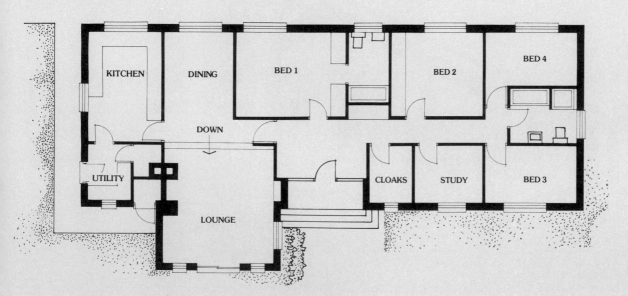

THORNHILL

The Thornhill bungalow suits either a site of generous size, where the lounge window can be in the side wall as illustrated, or a narrow plot where the lounge window changes place with the fireplace. There are other options as well, and one is to turn the en-suite bathroom to the guest room into a cloakroom with a door from the hall. Altogether it is a very versatile and popular design.

A five bedroom version of this bungalow is the Broadwell, reference 82096.

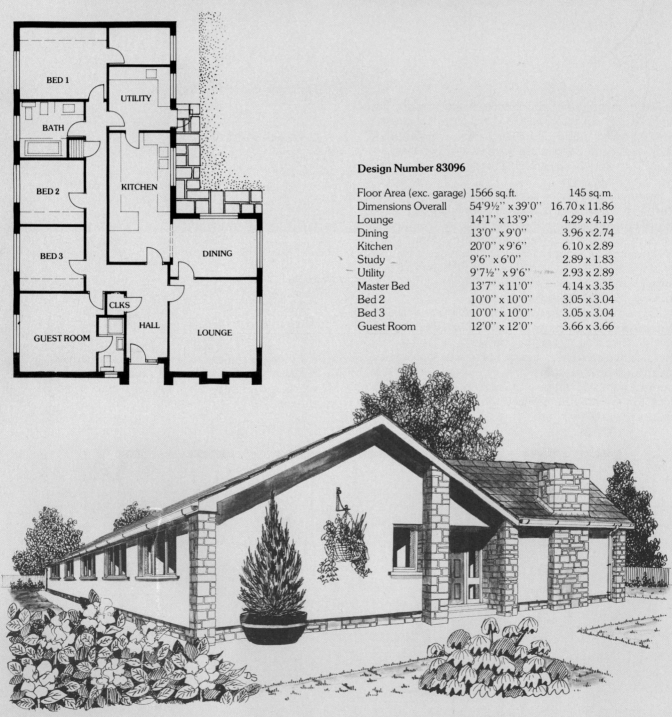

Design Number 83096

Floor Area (exc. garage)	1566 sq. ft.	145 sq. m.
Dimensions Overall	54'9½'' x 39'0''	16.70 x 11.86
Lounge	14'1'' x 13'9''	4.29 x 4.19
Dining	13'0'' x 9'0''	3.96 x 2.74
Kitchen	20'0'' x 9'6''	6.10 x 2.89
Study	9'6'' x 6'0''	2.89 x 1.83
Utility	9'7½'' x 9'6''	2.93 x 2.89
Master Bed	13'7'' x 11'0''	4.14 x 3.35
Bed 2	10'0'' x 10'0''	3.05 x 3.04
Bed 3	10'0'' x 10'0''	3.05 x 3.04
Guest Room	12'0'' x 12'0''	3.66 x 3.66

SHREWSBURY

Like many of our designs, the Shrewsbury bungalow was first drawn to meet a clients requirements, proved popular with others, and then became a standard. It is shown with an open-plan lounge/dining/kitchen arrangement, with these 3 rooms linked by wide arched openings that relate to each other in a particularly effective way. Open-plan living is a personal choice, and if desired these arches can be replaced by either single or double doors.

Building Regulations require that the window to bedroom 3 shall be 12 foot from any boundary, so the bungalow as drawn requires a minimum 53 feet width of plot. However, it has been built with the master bedroom increased in size and with bedroom 3 as an en suite bathroom. This arrangement will fit on a plot only 44 feet wide. It has also been modified for another client with a cloak room in the hall turned round to make a shower room to bedroom 2. The permutations are endless!

A two bedroom/two bathroom luxury version of this bungalow is the Parkhead, reference 82097.

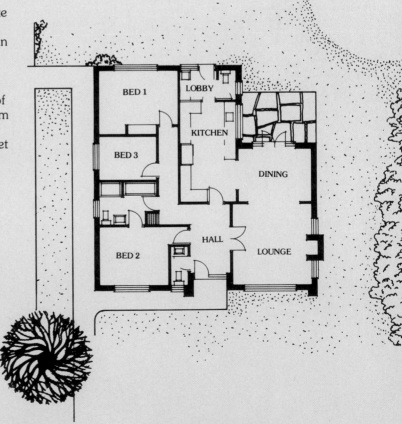

Design Number 83097

Area	1194 sq.ft.	211 sq.m.
Overall	38'4'' x 38'4''	11.69 x 11.69
Lounge	14'1'' x 13'10''	4.29 x 4.21
Dining	12'11'' x 9'0''	3.95 x 2.74
Kitchen	16'11'' x 9'6''	5.15 x 2.89
Bed 1	13'7'' x 11'5''	4.15 x 3.47
Bed 2	12'1'' x 10'0''	3.67 x 3.05
Bed 3	10'0'' x 7'0''	3.05 x 2.13

CARLTON

This large and imposing bungalow has been built on more than 100 sites in one form or another, and at one time was the design used by D & M Limited as its trademark. Designed by Jean Dunkley, R.I.B.A., in 1973, it seems to be nearly everyone's idea of a dream home for a dream site. In the real world it requires a site with at least a 100ft. frontage, preferably with some trees about to give a broken skyline behind the simple roof.

The Carlton is a very economical structure, with no load bearing internal walls and a simple trussed rafter roof. It is illustrated with landscape style windows, with top opening lights, which suit it better than casement windows although it can be built with either. In both sketches it is shown in a garden which slopes away from the front door. When building on a site like this it is most important to establish the floor level at just the right height for the building to look at its best. So often clients who are most concerned about the exact position of the corner pegs for a new home seem content to leave the actual floor level to others. It is much too important for that.

The recess off the back porch of this bungalow is for the central heating boiler with short pipe runs to the large airing cupboard, but sometimes the boiler is put in the back of the porch itself, giving more cupboard space in the utility room.

Design Number 83098

Area	1715 sq.ft.	160 sq.m.
Overall	74'6'' x 25'1''	22.71 x 7.64
Lounge	23'5'' x 20'7''	7.14 x 6.27
Dining Kitchen	22'7'' x 9'4''	6.90 x 2.85
Bed 1	21'2'' x 11'10''	6.46 x 3.61
Bed 2	10'5'' x 10'0''	3.19 x 3.05
Bed 3	13'5'' x 10'0''	4.10 x 3.05
Bed 4	9'4'' x 7'0''	2.85 x 2.15

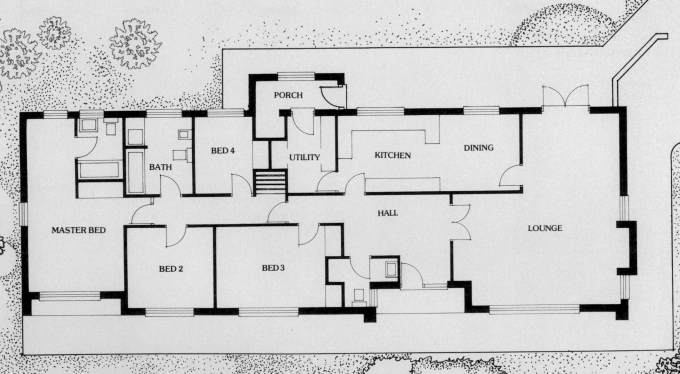

HUCKNALL

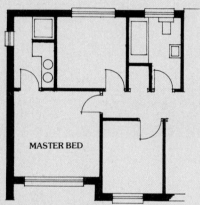

MASTER BED

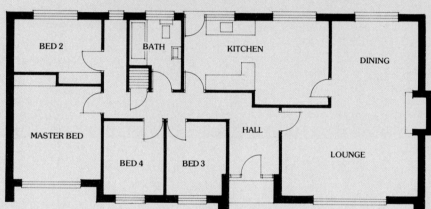

BED 2   BATH   KITCHEN   DINING

MASTER BED   HALL   LOUNGE

BED 4   BED 3

Design Number 83100

Floor Area	1270 sq.ft.	118 sq.m.
Overall dimensions	56'1" x 26'4½"	17.0 x 8.0
Lounge (overall)	23'5" x 18'6"	7.14 x 5.64
Kitchen/Dining (overall)	19'7" x 11'4"	5.96 x 3.45
Master Bed	12'2" x 11'11"	3.70 x 3.63
Bed 2	10'0" x 8'0"	3.05 x 2.43
Bed 3	10'0" x 8'0"	3.05 x 2.43
Bed 4	11'11" x 6'10"	3.63 x 2.08

This is a variant of our popular "Carlton" bungalow, with the overall length reduced from 74ft to 56ft. There are two arrangements shown, one with an en suite bathroom to the master bedroom, and one with a single family bathroom. In the latter layout we show a window in a recess at the head of the passage, but this can easily be omitted and the window recess used for a separate W.C. or a walk-in airing cupboard.

WASHINGTON

This interesting bungalow is unusual in having a hall that gives access to both the front and the back doors, and can be built with a screen door across the front of the porch to give a lobby at the front door if you are concerned about draughts!

There is a lot of cupboard space, and in many ways this is a very compact design, with a lot of accommodation in a small area. The garages need not be built if they are inappropriate

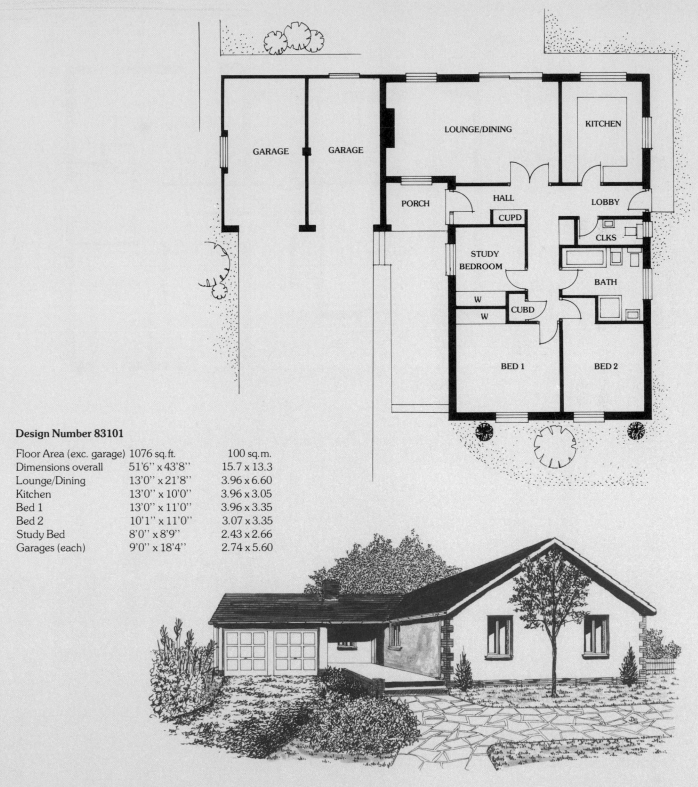

Design Number 83101

Floor Area (exc. garage)	1076 sq. ft.	100 sq.m.
Dimensions overall	51'6'' x 43'8''	15.7 x 13.3
Lounge/Dining	13'0'' x 21'8''	3.96 x 6.60
Kitchen	13'0'' x 10'0''	3.96 x 3.05
Bed 1	13'0'' x 11'0''	3.96 x 3.35
Bed 2	10'1'' x 11'0''	3.07 x 3.35
Study Bed	8'0'' x 8'9''	2.43 x 2.66
Garages (each)	9'0'' x 18'4''	2.74 x 5.60

PEMBERTON

A three level house: the garage at ground level, up half a flight of stairs to the hall, lounge and kitchen, and then up another half flight to the bedrooms. This arrangement always seems to suit the use of contrasting materials for the walls to bedroom part of the house, shown here panelled in shiplap timber boarding. A rendered finish with a "bell" bottom edge over the stonework to the garage gives the same effect.

This design is often set back into a bank, and it is possible to save on excavations costs by omitting the store at the back of the garage if the levels permit this.

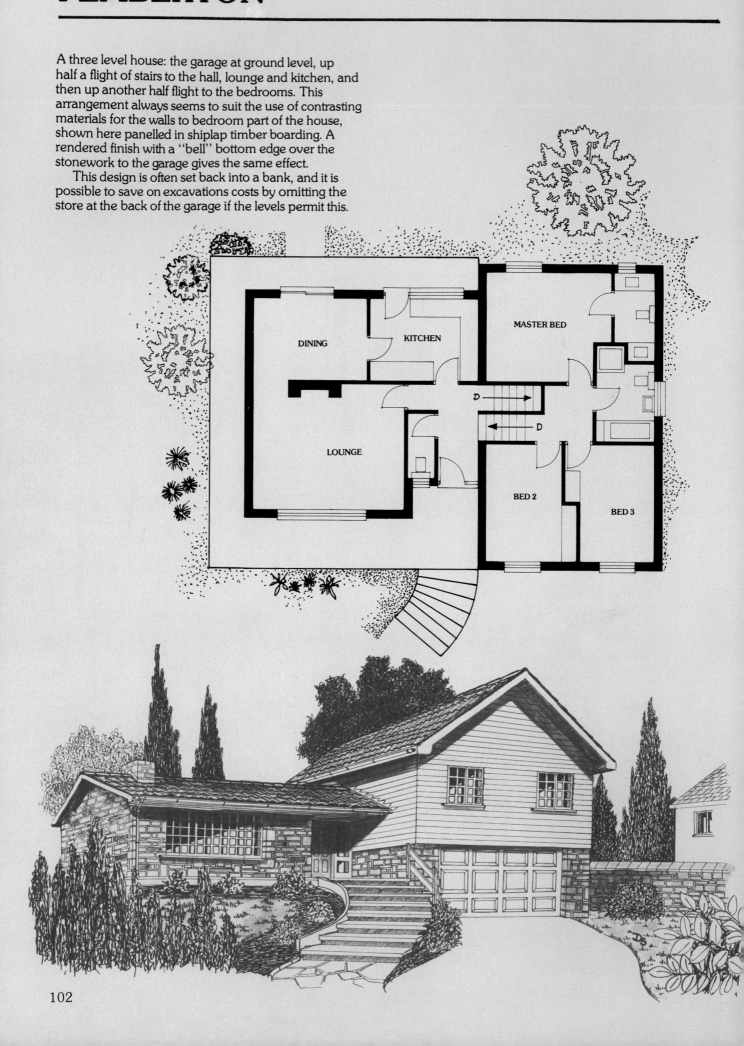

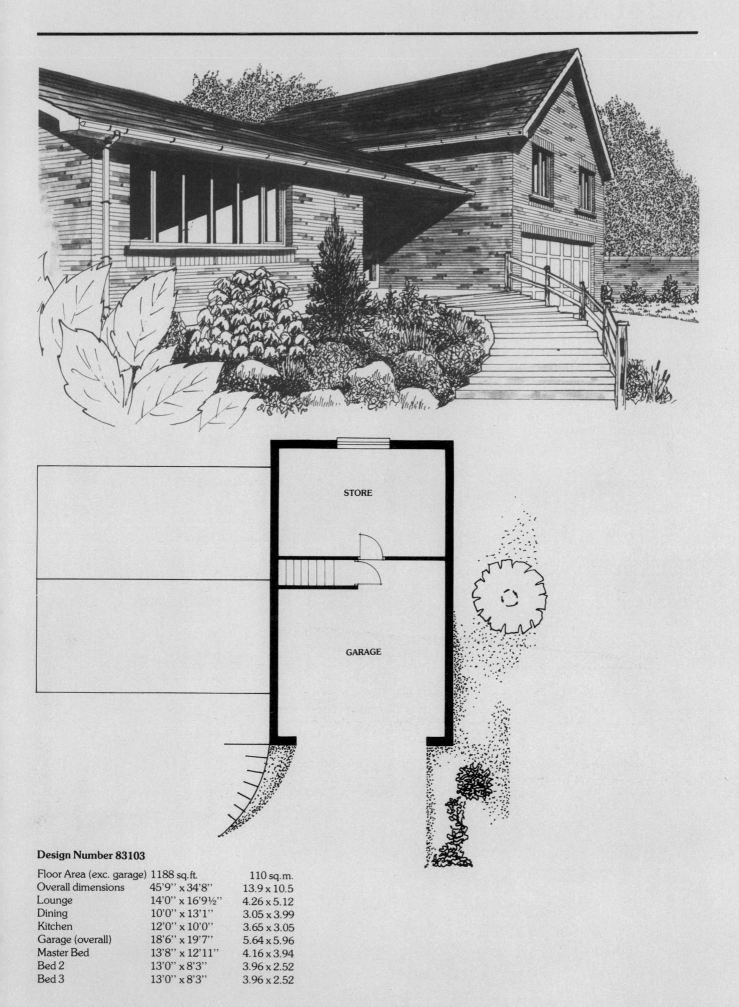

Design Number 83103

Floor Area (exc. garage)	1188 sq.ft.	110 sq.m.
Overall dimensions	45'9" x 34'8"	13.9 x 10.5
Lounge	14'0" x 16'9½"	4.26 x 5.12
Dining	10'0" x 13'1"	3.05 x 3.99
Kitchen	12'0" x 10'0"	3.65 x 3.05
Garage (overall)	18'6" x 19'7"	5.64 x 5.96
Master Bed	13'8" x 12'11"	4.16 x 3.94
Bed 2	13'0" x 8'3"	3.96 x 2.52
Bed 3	13'0" x 8'3"	3.96 x 2.52

ALMONDBANK

This large bungalow has the low level lounge which is such an effective way of dealing with a sloping site. The carpeted steps leading up from the lounge have been drawn in a way that makes them a key feature, and the open plan dining area all adds to the effect. This sort of layout is well suited to the gable wall inside the lounge being built in hand-made brick, with a very carefully chosen modern fireplace.

Design Number 83104

Floor Area (exc. garage)	1550 sq. ft.	144 sq.m.
Dimensions overall	48'10'' x 44'11''	14.8 x 13.6
Lounge	20'0'' x 16'7''	6.09 x 5.05
Dining	14'0'' x 9'6''	4.26 x 2.89
Kitchen	17'7'' x 9'6''	5.37 x 2.89
Utility	7'6'' x 6'10''	2.29 x 2.07
Breakfast Area	14'10'' x 9'6''	4.51 x 2.89
Master Bed	13'7½'' x 9'5''	4.15 x 2.87
Bed 2	12'1'' x 10'0''	3.67 x 3.05
Bed 3	10'0'' x 7'0''	3.05 x 2.13
Bed 4	10'0'' x 7'0''	3.05 x 2.13

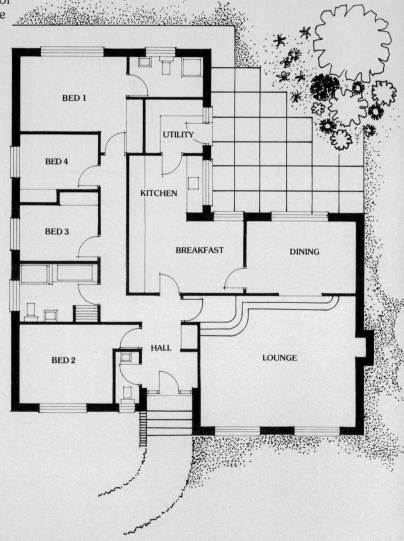

DANEHILL

This is another design with the lounge at a lower level than the rest of the bungalow, with steps down from both the hall and back up again from the lounge into the dining room. This is a very effective way of showing off your dining room suite!

There are two large bedrooms and two bathrooms: the arrangement of these will be altered to suit individual clients requirements. Normally at least one bathroom will be en suite with a bedroom.

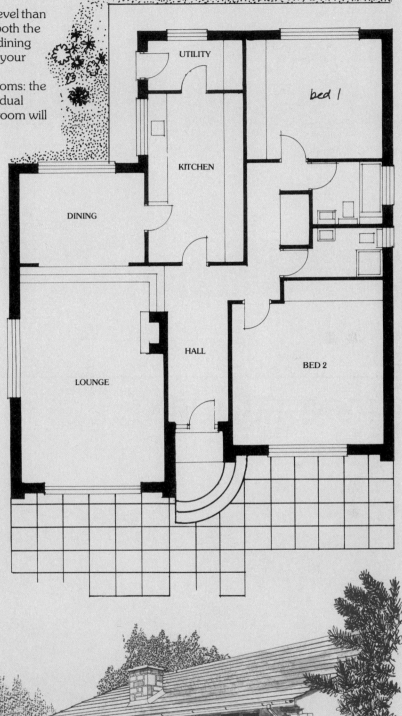

Design Number 83105

Floor Area		
(exc. garage)	1360 sq.ft.	126 sq.m.
Dimensions overall	46'1½'' x 38'10''	14.0 x 11.3
Lounge	21'8'' x 15'0''	6.60 x 4.57
Dining	13'3'' x 9'0''	4.03 x 2.74
Kitchen	16'11'' x 9'6''	5.15 x 2.89
Utility	9'6'' x 5'0''	2.89 x 1.54
Master Bed	12'1½'' x 11'7½''	3.69 x 3.55
Bed 2	15'4'' x 14'4½''	4.67 x 4.38

WOODCHURCH

GLYNDEBOURNE

This attractive bungalow has a conservatory next to the kitchen, which is an ideal arrangement for a family with young children, and a big garden. It suits a site where the view is to the front, and is another design that is popular with those housewives who think the kitchen window is the most important window in the house.

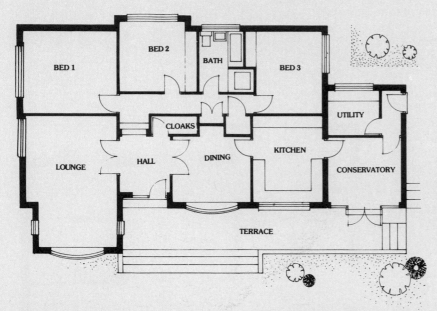

Design Number 83106

Floor Area	1452 sq.ft.	135 sq.m.
Overall dimensions	58'1'' x 34'8''	17.7 x 10.5
Lounge (overall)	14'0'' x 20'0''	4.26 x 6.10
Dining	11'9'' x 10'0''	3.58 x 3.05
Kitchen	10'6'' x 13'0''	3.20 x 3.96
Utility	11'3'' x 7'0''	3.43 x 2.13
Conservatory	11'3'' x 10'0''	3.43 x 3.05
Bed 1	12'6'' x 14'0''	3.81 x 4.26
Bed 2	11'9'' x 10'6''	3.58 x 3.20
Bed 3	12'6'' x 10'0''	3.81 x 3.05

Originally built for a distinguished musician, the Glyndebourne design provides the maximum of gracious living in a sensible overall size for a two bedroomed home. It is a derivative of our very popular "Carlton" bungalow, and has the same front elevation but with a small projecting gable to the rear.

It is shown here with a rendered finish on a stone plinth, with stone window sills. The junction of the rendered wall and the plinth is always very important, and the specification for the plasterer should require a bell shaped aluminium render stop to give a clean edge that is at least an inch clear of the stone work. The stone sills are a regional feature; until recent times they would have been installed in the full thickness of the wall; however, modern legislation discourages such "cold bridges" in today's thermally efficient cavity walls. We are aware of this and our drawings embody suitable methods of solving the problem.

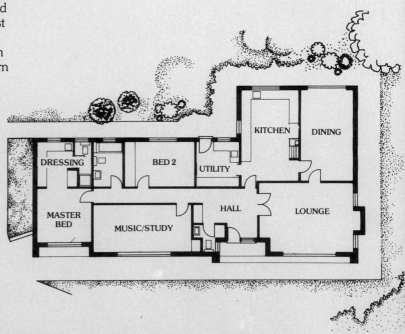

Design Number 83107

Floor Area	1800 sq.ft.	167 sq.m.
Overall	67'11'' x 36'0''	20.69 x 10.97
Lounge	19'8'' x 14'10''	5.99 x 4.52
Dining	11'0'' x 19'4''	3.35 x 5.89
Kitchen	12'1'' x 19'4''	3.69 x 5.89
Music/Study/		
Guest Room	20'6'' x 10'0''	6.25 x 3.05
Utility	9'2'' x 9'6''	2.80 x 2.89
Master Bed	11'6'' x 11'5''	3.49 x 3.47
Bed 2	14'8'' x 9'6''	4.46 x 2.89

CRESSWELL

Clients who are building a home for their retirement often ask for a design of modest overall size, easily run, but with big rooms that suit furniture bought for a larger home. This is a design that meets all the requirements where the site has its principal views to the rear. An alternative version with views to the front is the Welbeck opposite.

Although the Cresswell will fit on a 45ft plot, both the lounge and the master bedroom are over 20ft. long. The unusually deep wall between the hall and the bedroom accommodates display shelves with concealed lighting, and many other features of this sort can be built into this attractive, but cost effective design.

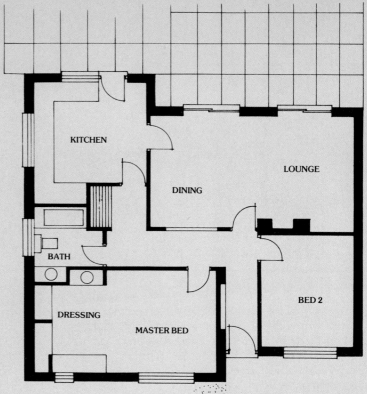

Design Number 83108

Floor Area (exc. garage)	1020 sq.ft.	95 sq.m.
Dimensions overall	36'10½'' x 34'2''	11.2 x 10.4
Lounge/Dining	13'0'' x 23'0''	3.96 x 7.00
Kitchen (overall)	12'6'' x 13'6''	3.81 x 4.11
Master Bed	20'4'' x 11'6''	6.20 x 3.50
Bed 2	12'6'' x 10'4''	3.81 x 3.15

WELBECK

This is the "views to the front" version of our popular Cresswell design which is illustrated opposite.

When it was designed by Tim Woods the specification was for a retirement bungalow about 1,000 sq. ft. with two bedrooms, one of which was to be at least 20ft. long. The size of the rooms, and the well balanced proportions give this bungalow the feel of a far larger property, and it is in many ways the ideal retirement bungalow.

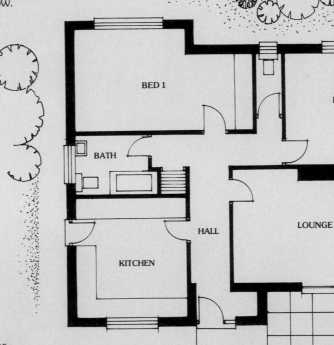

Design Number 83109

Floor Area	1020 sq. ft.	95 sq.m.
Dimensions overall	30'10½'' x 34'2''	11.2 x 10.4
Lounge	18'1'' x 12'6''	5.50 x 3.81
Kitchen	12'6'' x 13'6''	3.81 x 4.11
Bed 1 (overall)	20'0'' x 11'6''	6.10 x 3.50
Bed 2	13'0'' x 10'4''	3.96 x 3.15

DENHAM

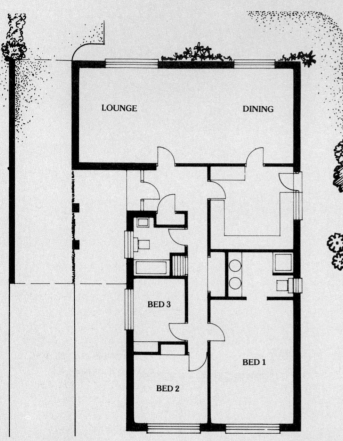

This bungalow design with its twin staggered car ports comes from France, and is essentially for a site with the view to the rear. The windows on the rear elevation can be positioned to suit the view, the design of the back garden, or simply the decor of the room. This must be arranged with care, as the windows will determine the whole of the character of the lounge, which is very large for a home of this size.

From the road the appearance is dominated by the arrangement of the car ports. If appropriate the right hand one can be paved as a covered approach to the front door, leaving the car or cars on the left. Whatever the arrangement, the supporting pillar should be massive, with deep timbers at the eaves and masonry flower boxes or other features below to balance things up.

A very distinctive home with a lot of character within a very simple basic structure.

Design Number 83110

Area (exc. garage)	1304 sq. ft.	121 sq.m.
Dimensions overall	42'5'' x 53'10''	12.9 x 16.4
Lounge/Dining	31'4'' x 14'0''	9.55 x 4.26
Kitchen	12'0'' x 12'0''	3.65 x 3.65
Master Bed	12'0'' x 18'0''	3.65 x 5.50
Bed 2	11'0'' x 10'0''	3.35 x 3.05
Bed 3	9'0'' x 7'8''	2.74 x 2.35

A slightly larger 4 bedroom version of the Denham is the Harrow bungalow reference 82110

GAINSBOROUGH

The Gainsborough bungalow is another design for sites where the view and outlook are to the rear, and the entrances have to be to the front. It is shown here with the big kitchen/family room arrangement which suits those who work in the country, and has a chimney breast which is central to the internal walls of both the lounge and the kitchen. This can take flues from both the fire in the lounge and from an Aga type cooker up the same stack — it is surprising how many of our farming clients list ''room for an Aga'' at the top of their list of design requirements.

The three large bedrooms have built-in cupboards and there are two more and a large airing cupboard in the hall. If the shower is not required in the bathroom it can be replaced by the airing cupboard, giving an extra cupboard in the hall.

Design Number 83111

Area	1060 sq.ft.	99 sq. m.
Overall	47'11'' x 25'1''	14.61 x 7.64
Lounge	19'9'' x 12'1''	6.01 x 3.69
Dining Kitchen	19'9'' x 11'0''	6.01 x 3.35
Bed 1	13'10'' x 10'7''	4.23 x 3.24
Bed 2	10'7'' x 10'1''	3.24 x 3.07
Bed 3	10'1'' x 10'0''	3.07 x 3.05

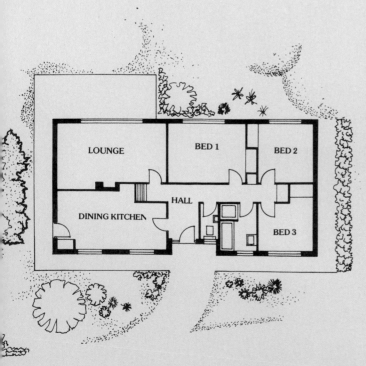

EXETER

HAWKHURST

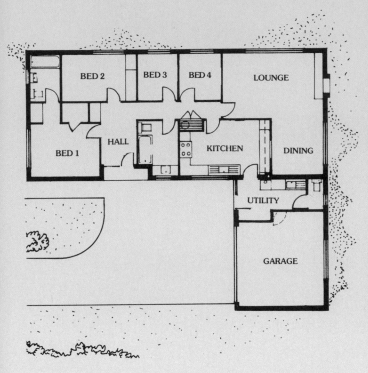

The Exeter design is an old favourite, particularly in rural areas. It is a bungalow that needs plenty of space around it. The main block of the design does not often change, but the variations to the garage wing have been endless. One of the most common is to reduce the size of the utility room to little more than a porch and to build a farm office behind it. Another interesting possibility is to arrange for the garage foundations to be built to suit its conversion into a granny flat at a later date.

The huge walk-in wardrobe with hanging rails on either side is an unusual feature, and one that has proved very popular. We now often incorporate it in new designs.

Design Number 83112

Area (inc. garage)	1650 sq. ft.	153 sq. m.
Overall	57'6" x 40'3"	17.54 x 15.29
Lounge	19'2" x 12'7"	5.84 x 3.84
Dining	10'10" x 9'10"	3.30 x 3.00
Kitchen	17'3" x 10'6"	5.25 x 3.20
Bed 1	14'1" x 13'1"	4.30 x 3.99
Bed 2	14'5" x 9'0"	4.40 x 2.74
Bed 3	9'0" x 7'9"	2.74 x 2.35
Bed 4	9'0" x 7'9"	2.74 x 2.35

A five bedroom version of this design is the Honiton, reference 82112 with a gable extension to the rear.

This design has some unusual and attractive features. The large living area has a big island fireplace which splits it into two halves — an informal living room, and a more formal lounge. The fireplace itself is the first thing that is seen when one enters through the front door. This is real "open plan" living — attractive to some, and less so to others. The decision as to whether this is for you may depend on whether all the family like the same television programme. At any rate, the layout can be built with solid dividing walls if required.

Two bathrooms and exceptionally large wardrobes give luxury bedroom accommodation, and if required the main bathroom can be reduced in size to permit a cloakroom at the front door.

As drawn the garage roof arrangement depends on differential floor levels; if the site requires that the garage floor is at the same level as the bungalow floor, then a gable roof will be required over the garage door.

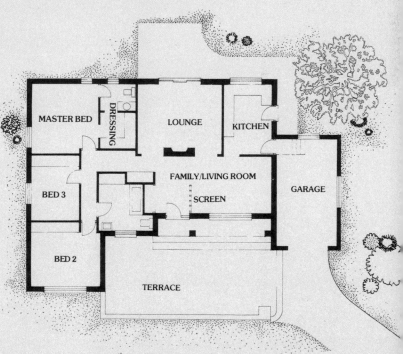

Design Number 83113

Floor Area (exc. garage)	1230 sq. ft.	114 sq. m.
Dimensions Overall	59'0" x 39'6"	18.00 x 12.04
Lounge	15'9" x 13'0"	4.80 x 3.96
Family/Living Room	10'6" x 15'0"	3.20 x 4.57
Kitchen	9'0" x 13'0"	2.74 x 3.96
Garage	11'3" x 20'0"	3.43 x 6.10
Master Bed	12'6" x 13'0"	3.81 x 3.96
Bed 2	13'0" x 12'0"	3.96 x 3.65
Bed 3	12'0" x 9'0"	3.65 x 2.74

MIDHURST

TAUNTON

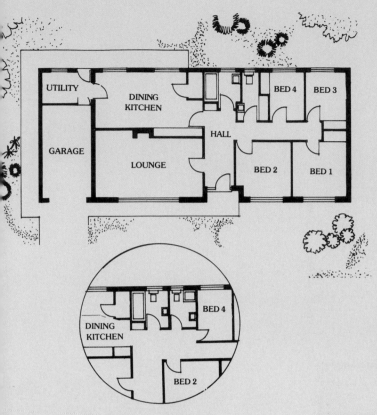

The Midhurst design is the 4 bedroomed version of our Ascot design, and is one of our series of rural designs with very large "living in" kitchens.

The garage and utility room shown can be omitted from the design altogether if required, and a small porch built at the back door for muddy boots and somewhere for the dogs to sleep!

The WC has its own wash basin, or room for a vanity unit, and is a very popular feature in a home with 4 bedrooms for a young family. Taking this concept further, the Midhurst has been built a number of times with a WC extended to become a shower room, although this cuts down the size of the 4th bedroom and involves moving the bedroom door. The inset drawing shows how this is arranged.

Design Number 83114

Area	1060 sq. ft.	99 sq. m.
Overall	47'11" x 25'1"	14.61 x 7.64
Lounge	19'9" x 12'6"	6.01 x 3.81
Dining Kitchen	19'9" x 10'7"	6.01 x 3.23
Bed 1	10'4" x 10'1"	3.14 x 3.07
Bed 2	10'4" x 10'1"	3.14 x 3.07
Bed 3	9'2" x 7'5"	2.80 x 2.27
Bed 4	9'2" x 6'7"	2.80 x 2.00

When you look at L shaped bungalow plans note carefully if a wall that supports the main roof continues straight through at the point where it joins the subsidiary roof. If it does, as with the Taunton, the roof design is simple, easy to build and cost-effective. Of course, there are many ways of building when this cannot be a design feature, but all of them involve special structural components which not only have to be designed, purchased and built in, but which also have to be approved by the local authority after the submission of structural engineers design calculations.

But enough of this — if you buy the plans from us we provide the design calculations anyway. The Taunton bungalow is a popular design with the single drawback that visitors to the front door have to walk down a passage to get to the lounge. Whether or not you think this a disadvantage is a personal choice. The windows in the lounge, and in the two end bedrooms, can be moved around to suit the view, and the back door can be moved from the back of the utility room to the front of it if this is desired.

Design Number 83115

Area including single garage	1616 sq. ft.	149 sq. m.
Overall	57'6" x 45'9"	17.54 x 13.94
Lounge	23'4" x 13'7"	7.11 x 4.15
Dining	11'10" x 8'11"	3.60 x 2.72
Kitchen	13'5" x 10'5"	4.10 x 3.18
Bed 1	13'0" x 12'10"	3.96 x 3.92
Bed 2	13'0" x 10'2"	3.96 x 3.08
Bed 3	10'6" x 8'11"	3.21 x 2.72
Utility	15'11" x 7'11"	4.89 x 2.42
Garage	15'11" x 11'7"	4.89 x 3.51

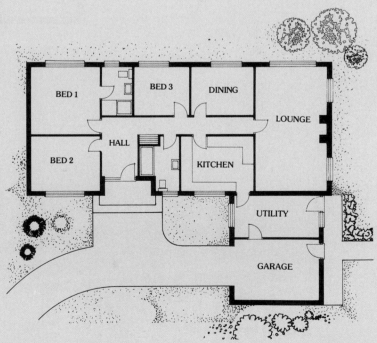

BRIDGWATER

This is a variant of the popular Taunton bungalow, with the double garage replaced by a Granny Flat. The overall dimensions are identical, and it is practicable to build the Bridgwater design with minimum additional foundations and lintels so that it can be turned into a Taunton if ever required. In the same way a Taunton can be built with everything ready for it to be turned into this design. Some clients have found this very convenient.

The windows in the Granny Flat can be moved about to suit the view.

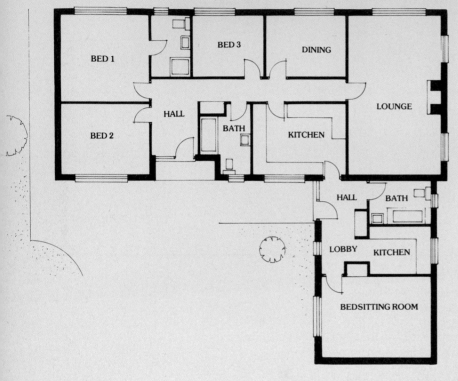

Design Number 83116

Total Floor Area	1592 sq. ft.	148 sq. m.
Overall dimensions	52'2'' x 52'4''	15.8 x 15.9
Main dwelling:		
Lounge	23'5'' x 13'7''	7.14 x 4.15
Dining	11'10'' x 9'0''	3.60 x 2.74
Kitchen	10'6'' x 13'5''	3.19 x 4.10
Bed 1	13'0'' x 13'0''	3.95 x 3.96
Bed 2	13'0'' x 10'1½''	3.96 x 3.08
Bed 3	9'0'' x 10'6''	2.74 x 3.21
Bedsitting	12'0'' x 16'0''	3.65 x 4.87

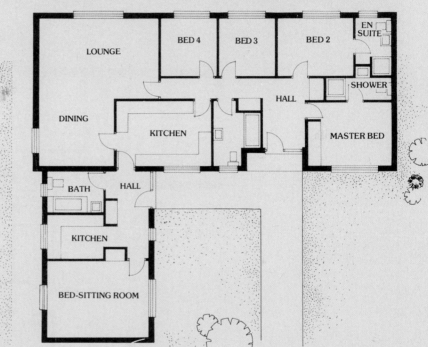

This is a version of the popular Exeter design bungalow with an integral Granny Flat. The flat has its own front door, an arrangement that is always very popular with Grannies who like to feel that they have retained their independence.

This design is suitable for a site with all round views, and the windows can be changed round to suit the clients' requirements.

Design Number 83117

Floor Area (inclusive)	1765 sq. ft.	164 sq. m.
Dimensions overall	57'9'' x 52'4''	17.6 x 15.9
Lounge/Dining (overall)	23'5'' x 19'2½''	7.14 x 5.85
Kitchen	10'5½'' x 15'1''	3.18 x 4.60
Bed 1	13'1'' x 10'2''	3.99 x 3.08
Bed 2	11'10'' x 9'0½''	3.61 x 2.75
Bed 3	9'0'' x 9'0½''	2.74 x 2.75
Bed 4	9'0'' x 9'0½''	2.74 x 2.75
Annexe:		
Bed-Sitting Room	15'11'' x 12'0''	4.89 x 3.65
Kitchen	7'0'' x 9'0''	2.13 x 2.74

CRANBROOK

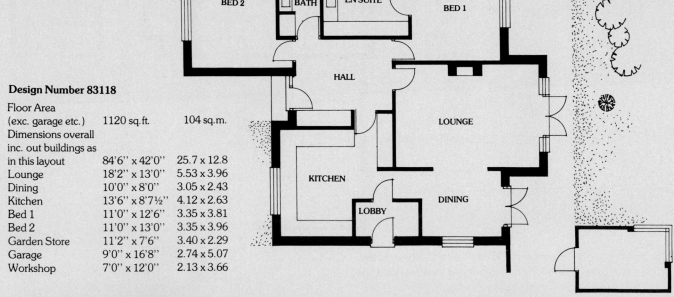

Design Number 83118

Floor Area
(exc. garage etc.)	1120 sq.ft.	104 sq.m.
Dimensions overall		
inc. out buildings as		
in this layout	84'6'' x 42'0''	25.7 x 12.8
Lounge	18'2'' x 13'0''	5.53 x 3.96
Dining	10'0'' x 8'0''	3.05 x 2.43
Kitchen	13'6'' x 8'7½''	4.12 x 2.63
Bed 1	11'0'' x 12'6''	3.35 x 3.81
Bed 2	11'0'' x 13'0''	3.35 x 3.96
Garden Store	11'2'' x 7'6''	3.40 x 2.29
Garage	9'0'' x 16'8''	2.74 x 5.07
Workshop	7'0'' x 12'0''	2.13 x 3.66

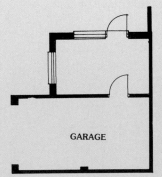

The Cranbrook was originally designed for a woodland site in Lincolnshire and was built in stone under a pantile roof instead of the flat tiles shewn in our sketch. Unpainted softwood joinery was specified and this was stained to a dark oak colour. The result was one of the most attractive bungalows ever built to our drawings.

Note that the biggest bathroom is en suite with the main bedroom: this is a growing trend, with more and more of those who pay the mortgages deciding that they deserve the best washing facilities!

The little building by the dining room window is an amateur radio station, and was built at the same time as the bungalow to match it in materials and style. If you have a hobby, then make provision for it in your plans and do not let it be an afterthought.

PENHURST

The Penhurst bungalow was drawn by John Gwilliam RIBA for a large and valuable site on the W. coast, where only a 58' strip could be used for the building. The open plan layout was designed in conjunction with the clients, who wanted a clear view from the kitchen across the dining area and through the glazed screen into the lounge. It all worked very well indeed, and became a striking and much admired home.

The car port has wrought ironwork in the arched openings. This is a very effective way of giving character to a screen wall, and looks particularly well when associated with generous areas of paving.

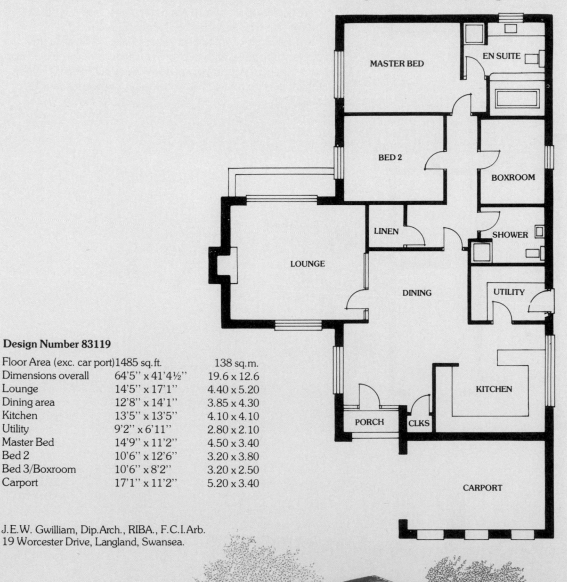

Design Number 83119

Floor Area (exc. car port)	1485 sq.ft.	138 sq.m.
Dimensions overall	64'5'' x 41'4½''	19.6 x 12.6
Lounge	14'5'' x 17'1''	4.40 x 5.20
Dining area	12'8'' x 14'1''	3.85 x 4.30
Kitchen	13'5'' x 13'5''	4.10 x 4.10
Utility	9'2'' x 6'11''	2.80 x 2.10
Master Bed	14'9'' x 11'2''	4.50 x 3.40
Bed 2	10'6'' x 12'6''	3.20 x 3.80
Bed 3/Boxroom	10'6'' x 8'2''	3.20 x 2.50
Carport	17'1'' x 11'2''	5.20 x 3.40

J.E.W. Gwilliam, Dip.Arch., RIBA., F.C.I.Arb.
19 Worcester Drive, Langland, Swansea.

FARNBOROUGH

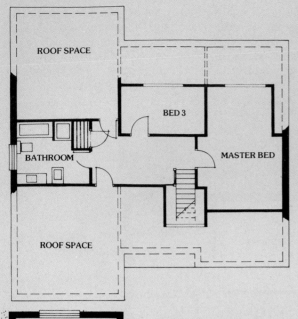

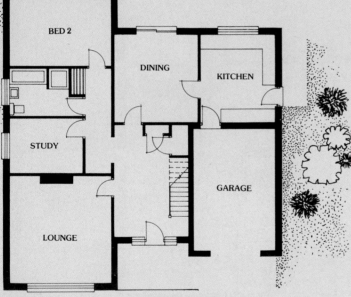

A common design requirement is for a home with one bedroom and its bathroom downstairs, and the other bedrooms and another bathroom above. The Farnborough demonstrates one way of providing this accommodation with two big roof space areas that will not be counted for rating purposes when the house is built, but which can be turned into additional bedrooms if ever required.

Design Number 83120

Floor Area (exc. garage)	1600 sq. ft.	148 sq.m.
Dimensions overall	41'3'' x 43'7''	12.5 x 13.2
Lounge	14'9'' x 15'11''	4.50 x 4.85
Dining	13'0'' x 13'0''	3.96 x 3.96
Kitchen	13'0'' x 11'0''	3.96 x 3.35
Study	8'0'' x 10'6''	2.43 x 3.20
Garage	12'0'' x 18'0''	3.65 x 5.48
Master Bed	12'7'' x 18'4''	3.83 x 5.60
Bed 2	14'9'' x 9'10''	4.50 x 3.00
Bed 3	13'0'' x 7'0''	3.96 x 2.13

SHERWOOD

The Sherwood bungalow is a very popular D & M design, and particularly appeals to housewives who want the kitchen windows to look out over the drive to give a good view of everything that is going on. This is well illustrated in the sketch, but what the artist was not able to show is the projecting gable on the rear elevation, with wide patio doors. The lounge is big enough to have two sets of double doors leading into it, and these are very important features. The pattern of door should be chosen with great care, as it will give a lot of character to the room.

This design can also be drawn with a sunken lounge, and the lounge gable can be extended if required. For one client we provided plans for the lounge increased in depth by 10ft, with room for a grand piano on the right of the door from the hall, and two steps down from this level to a conservatory area with doors out to a very special garden.

A four bedroom version of this design is called the Thoresby, reference 82121

Design Number 83121

Area	1485 sq.ft.	138 sq.m.
Overall	61'3'' x 31'8''	18.66 x 9.66
Lounge	20'6'' x 16'1''	6.25 x 4.91
Dining	12'0'' x 11'5½''	3.65 x 3.49
Kitchen	13'6'' x 11'8''	4.11 x 3.55
Bed 1	15'2'' x 13'1''	4.61 x 3.66
Bed 2	14'7'' x 10'0''	4.45 x 3.05
Bed 3	12'0'' x 10'0''	3.65 x 3.05

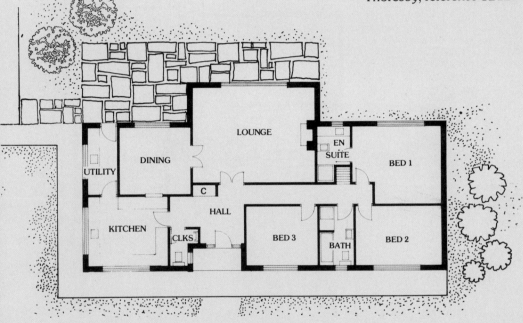

MISTERTON

The Misterton design bungalow provides a large living area and an interesting and complex shaped structure that can be accommodated on a relatively narrow site. The frontage depends on the width of the garage required: with a single garage it can be built on a 40 foot side plot, and it only requires 54 feet for a double garage as shown.

The internal hall giving access to the bedrooms lacks a window and requires that at least 2 of the doors leading from it have glazed lights above. This is not an unusual arrangement. The wall between the utility room and the kitchen is not structural, and can be ommitted if required.

Flat roofs are not as fashionable now as they were ten years ago, but in areas where they are an established feature of local architecture this design is deservedly popular.

Design Number 83122

Area (exc. garage)	1070 sq.ft.	102 sq.m.
Overall	46'7'' x 55'9''	14.20 x 17.00
Lounge	14'6'' x 15'9''	4.42 x 4.80
Dining	14'6'' x 9'10''	4.42 x 2.99
Kitchen	10'2'' x 8'10''	3.09 x 2.69
Bed 1	10'2'' x 10'6''	3.09 x 3.20
Bed 2	10'11'' x 10'6''	3.32 x 3.20
Bed 3	9'10'' x 8'6''	2.99 x 2.59
Garage	18'5'' x 15'6''	5.61 x 4.72

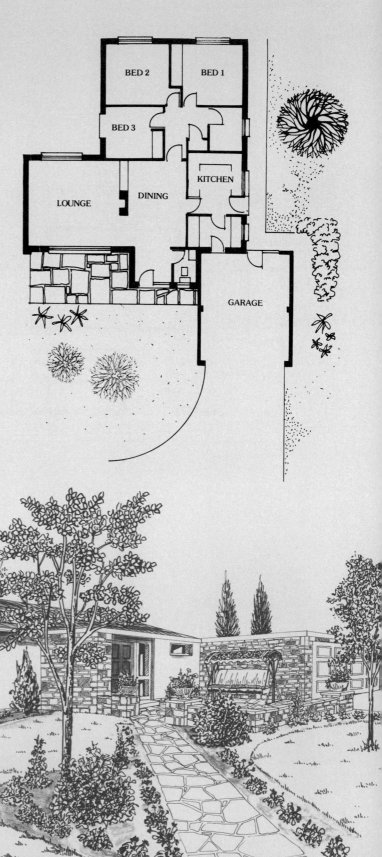

MOORCROFT

The Moorcroft bungalow was originally drawn for a north country site, where it was built in stone with the stone tabling to the gables that is illustrated. In a softer landscape in the south it would probably be built in brick or have a rendered finish and so look far less austere.

The room sizes are very generous, and this is definitely a luxury home. The layout can be re-arranged to provide a two bedroom — two bathroom home if required. A very attractive bungalow for a retired couple looking for larger-than-average rooms.

Design Number 83123

Floor Area	1240 sq. ft.	115 sq.m.
Dimensions overall	48'5'' x 38'6½''	14.7 x 11.7
Lounge/Dining (overall)	26'4½'' x 20'7''	8.04 x 6.27
Kitchen	10'0'' x 11'5''	3.05 x 3.48
Utility	6'6'' x 10'0''	1.98 x 3.05
Master Bed	15'1'' x 12'0''	4.60 x 3.65
Bed 2	10'0'' x 11'1''	3.05 x 3.38
Bed 3	8'0'' x 8'0''	2.43 x 2.43

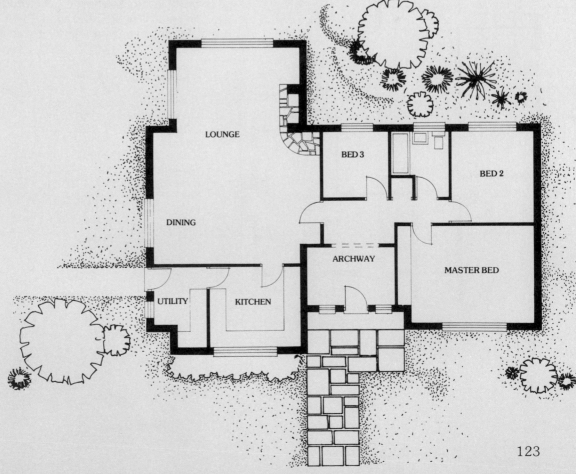

BIDDENDEN

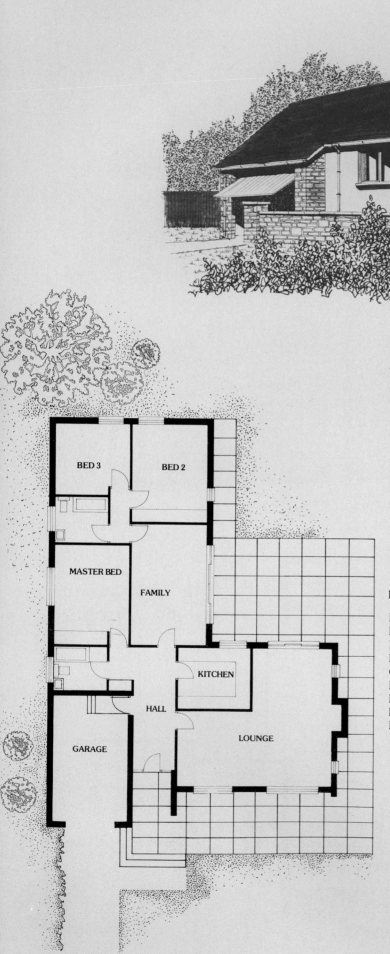

This large bungalow uses a family room as a passage to give access to the second and third bedrooms, and as these are usually childrens bedrooms this is a logical and sensible arrangement. (Incidentally it is as common in American designs as it is unusual here.)

The dining table can either be in the family room or in the lounge as required: if the latter then a door can be opened from the lounge into the kitchen.

The Biddenden is illustrated here with a barbeque built against the outside of the chimney breast, using a special fire built into the chimney when the house was built. If you like out-of-doors entertaining this is an excellent way of ensuring that the smoke keeps out of your guests eyes!

Design Number 83124

Floor Area (exc. garage)	1512 sq.ft.	140 sq.m.
Dimensions Overall	62'2'' x 44'7''	18.95 x 13.59
Lounge (overall)	23'7'' x 21'0''	7.20 x 6.40
Kitchen	11'0'' x 9'0''	3.35 x 2.74
Garage	11'6'' x 19'0''	3.50 x 5.80
Family Room	11'6'' x 18'2''	3.50 x 5.55
Master Bed	15'0'' x 11'6''	4.57 x 3.50
Bed 2	14'9'' x 11'6''	4.50 x 3.50
Bed 3	11'6'' x 11'0''	3.50 x 3.35

ELMHURST

This interesting design demonstrates a way of getting a large luxury bungalow on a site with a width of only 45ft, while enjoying most of the advantages of a home on a far larger frontage. The lounge and dining room have patio doors which open to an enclosed Courtyard and the bedroom wing has views to the rear. If your problem is how to build a large single storey home on a narrow plot then the Elmhurst or modification of the Elmhurst may provide the answer.

A four bedroom version of this bungalow is the Ashgrove, reference 82125

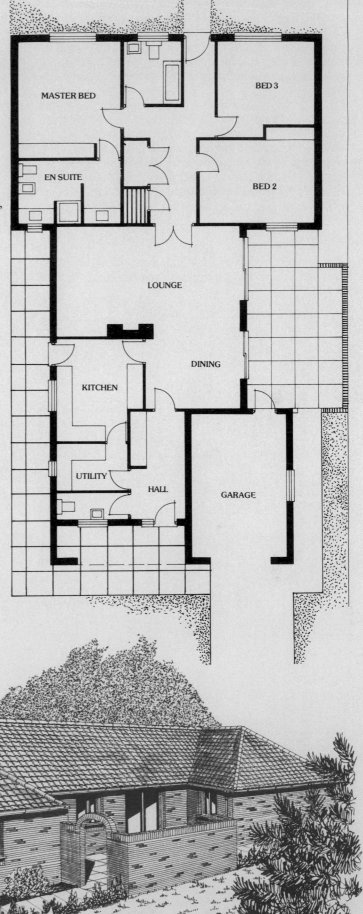

Design Number 83125

Floor Area (exc. garage)	1640 sq.ft.	152 sq.m.
Dimensions overall	39'6'' x 67'4''	12.0 x 20.5
Lounge/Dining (overall)	23'5'' x 23'0''	7.14 x 7.01
Kitchen	13'0'' x 11'1''	3.96 x 3.38
Utility	7'3'' x 6'0''	2.20 x 1.83
Garage	18'0'' x 12'0''	5.48 x 3.65
Master Bed	13'1½'' x 13'0''	4.00 x 3.96
Bed 2	14'5'' x 10'6''	4.40 x 3.20
Bed 3	12'7'' x 12'2½''	3.84 x 3.72

LICHFIELD

The Lichfield design bungalow has a very large living area combined with three double bedrooms, a utility room that can have the external door omitted so that it can be used as a small fourth bedroom or study, and two bathrooms. The lounge/dining/kitchen layout can be varied to suit the clients requirements and the opportunities offered by the site.

In the plan we show the lounge floor dropped to give feature steps up to double doors that lead into the hall, with extra ceiling height. The roof carries on at the same level, so the cost of this is minimal while the effect can be most impressive and gives enormous character to the home. The only snag with this arrangement is that changes of levels in bungalows are not always popular with prospective purchasers when the property is sold. The choice is yours.

The Tamworth design is a 4 bedroom version of this bungalow. The design reference number is 82126

Design Number 83126

Area (exc. garage)	1431 sq.ft.	136 sq.m.
Overall	62'0'' x 29'6''	18.89 x 8.99
Lounge	23'4'' x 13'2''	7.11 x 4.02
Dining	12'5'' x 10'6''	3.80 x 3.20
Kitchen	12'5'' x 12'6''	3.80 x 3.81
Bed 1	13'5'' x 11'8''	4.10 x 3.56
Bed 2	16'5'' x 9'10''	5.00 x 3.00
Bed 3	10'6'' x 9'10''	3.21 x 3.00
Utility	9'2'' x 8'1''	2.78 x 2.46

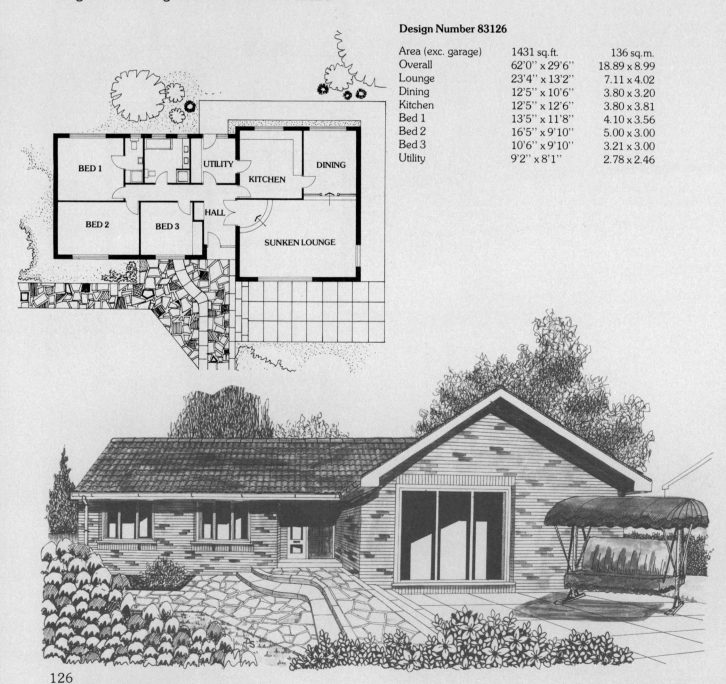

The Colwyn bungalow was originally designed for a splendid coastal site at Colwyn in North Wales. With a study isolated from the rest of the accommodation, it has proved particularly popular with those who work from their own homes, as well as for clergymen and others who wish to talk to callers away from family hubbub.

The two gables give it an interesting appearance from all angles, and the "window seat" window in the lounge adds a lot of character. The dining room usually has a patio window, but this can be changed if required.

Note the walk-in airing cupboard with the cylinder on one side of the door and linen racks to the ceiling on the other.

Design Number 83127

Area (inc. garage)	1880 sq. ft.	176 sq. m.
Overall	62'0'' x 46'6''	18.89 x 14.16
Lounge	23'5'' x 12'4''	7.14 x 3.76
Dining	12'3'' x 11'6''	3.74 x 3.50
Kitchen	14'9'' x 11'10''	4.50 x 3.60
Bed 1	13'0'' x 12'3''	3.97 x 3.72
Bed 2	16'2'' x 10'10''	4.92 x 3.31
Bed 3	10'10'' x 10'6''	3.31 x 3.20

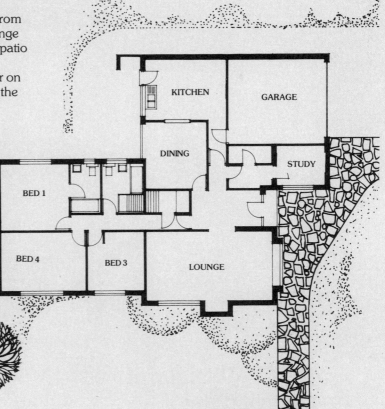

WINDERMERE & ULLSWATER

The Windermere and Ullswater designs meet a specific requirement in the most practicable way, and are good examples of a design concept that evolved to meet building regulation requirements for narrow sites.

Both designs provide 3 bedroom accommodation with all the bedrooms grouped at one end of the home, and to achieve this one bedroom window has to be in a side wall. A bedroom is classified by the authorities as a "habitable room", unlike a bathroom or kitchen, and the principal window of a habitable room must be at least 12 feet from a boundary.

On the other side of these designs there are nearly 40 square feet of window and door openings, and another building regulation requirement is that they should be at least 3 feet from any boundary.

The third critical dimension is that the most cost effective span for a simple rectangular structure with a trussed rafter roof is about 25 feet.

Add these three dimensions together and we arrive at a minimum 40 foot plot width for the standard solution to the problem. If three bedrooms are required on a plot which is less than 40 feet wide, then either two bedrooms have to be at one end and one at the other, or else a structure with a more complex shape is involved.

Ullswater

Design Number 83128

Area	850 sq.ft.	79 sq.m.
Overall	38'4" x 25'1"	11.69 x 7.64
Living Room	16'8" x 13'1"	5.08 x 3.99
Kitchen	10'6" x 10'0"	3.19 x 3.05
Bed 1	12'1" x 10'6"	3.68 x 3.20
Bed 2	11'0" x 10'6"	3.36 x 3.20
Bed 3	8'10" x 6'11"	2.70 x 2.10

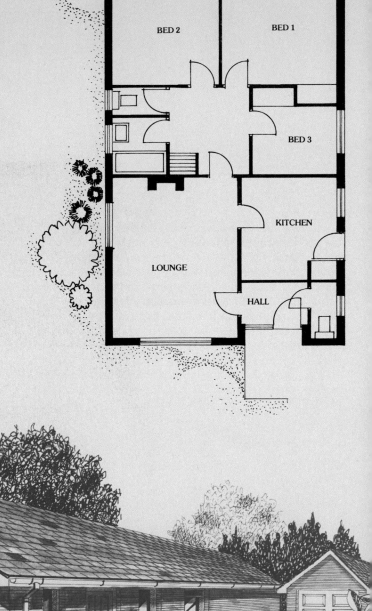

Windermere

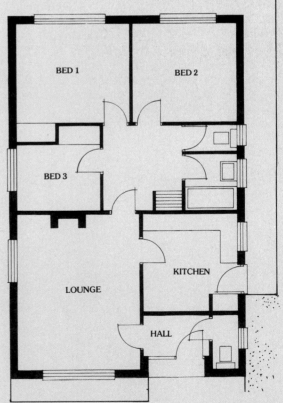

The Ullswater has the kitchen door on the same side as the bedroom window, and the 12 foot distance to the boundary is wide enough for the drive and a garage adjacent to the back door. The Windermere is obliged to have the garage and drive on the opposite side to the back door. The two bungalows are otherwise the same.

Both designs have an optional cloakroom at the front door, which, if it is not required is just the right size for a cloaks cupboard and somewhere to leave a pram — a requirement that is often overlooked in a compact house, but which is a very important matter.

The 12 foot width for a garage enables it to be built right up to the boundary, with a 3 foot gap between the garage and the main building. This space is often advantageously filled with a wrought iron gate or similar feature.

Design Number 83129

Area	850 sq.ft.	79 sq. m.
Overall	38'4'' x 25'1''	11.69 x 7.64
Living Room	16'8'' x 13'1''	5.08 x 3.99
Kitchen	10'6'' x 10'0''	3.19 x 3.05
Bed 1	12'1'' x 10'6''	3.68 x 3.20
Bed 2	11'0'' x 10'6''	3.36 x 3.20
Bed 3	8'10'' x 6'11''	2.70 x 2.10

PARKLANDS

The Parklands bungalow is another design which suits a site with all round views. The angled fireplace is the principal feature in the large living room, and is often built of stone or handmade bricks and these may be used for the adjacent walls. This layout is particularly popular with those who like plenty of space around them, especially if they do a lot of entertaining. However, if this is not your scene the Parklands can be built with a dividing wall between the dining and the lounge areas. In this case the double doors are replaced with two ordinary doors into the hall, one from each room.

If the garage is not required it is usual to build a small porch at the back door, and this can have either a flat or a pitched roof depending on the area, and the probable requirements of the Planning Officer. The decision whether to build an integral garage or a detached one is not easy: the convenience of an integral garage has to be set against a detached garage being cheaper to build. Another factor is that a separate garage can be built at a later date, and those who are building on their own using sub-contractors often like to arrange to delay starting their garage until they know that the main building is going to be within their budget costs.

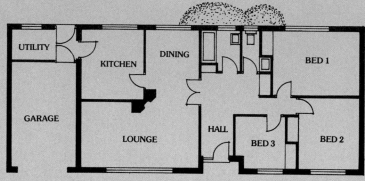

Design Number 83130

Area	1060 sq.ft.	99 sq.m.
Overall	47'11'' x 25'1''	14.61 x 7.64
Lounge	19'9'' x 11'0''	6.01 x 3.36
Dining	12'4'' x 8'11''	3.78 x 2.72
Kitchen	12'0'' x 10'6''	3.68 x 3.19
Bed 1	14'4'' x 10'11''	4.37 x 3.33
Bed 2	12'1'' x 10'1''	3.71 x 3.07
Bed 3	8'10'' x 8'1''	2.71 x 2.47

This bungalow is sometimes built with the garage turned into a small flat to give separate accommodation for an elderly relative. The design for this is called the Newhall, and has the reference number 82130

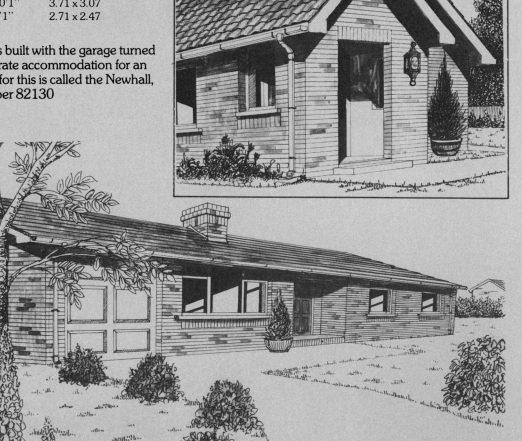

130

MARLOW

The Marlow is a 4 bedroomed version of the Parklands design opposite, and is very popular with those who like a really large living area in a bungalow of only 1060 square feet. There are two alternative bathroom arrangements, as we find that this house is often built by those with a large family who prefer one bathroom for the parents and a shower room for everyone else.

As with the Parklands, the garage need not be built, in which case it is usual to provide a porch of some sort or another at the back door.

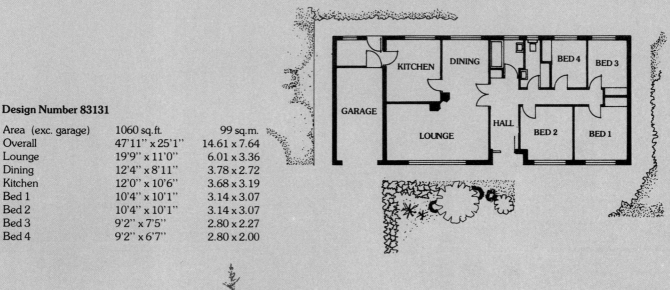

Design Number 83131

Area (exc. garage)	1060 sq.ft.	99 sq.m.
Overall	47'11" x 25'1"	14.61 x 7.64
Lounge	19'9" x 11'0"	6.01 x 3.36
Dining	12'4" x 8'11"	3.78 x 2.72
Kitchen	12'0" x 10'6"	3.68 x 3.19
Bed 1	10'4" x 10'1"	3.14 x 3.07
Bed 2	10'4" x 10'1"	3.14 x 3.07
Bed 3	9'2" x 7'5"	2.80 x 2.27
Bed 4	9'2" x 6'7"	2.80 x 2.00

PETWORTH

This is a D & M design, and D & M will never forget the client for whom this design was drawn as they took a vintage Bentley in part exchange for their service!

The low level lounge is entered down a feature staircase that leads from the dining room, which is completely open plan with the lounge except for the changes of levels and an attractive room divider.

The fireplace wall is in handmade brick. The whole effect is quite stunning and it is difficult to realize that the whole bungalow is only 1360 sq. ft. Note the small shower room off the main bedroom with a sliding door to save space.

There is a four bedroom version of this bungalow called the Chesterton. The reference number is 82132.

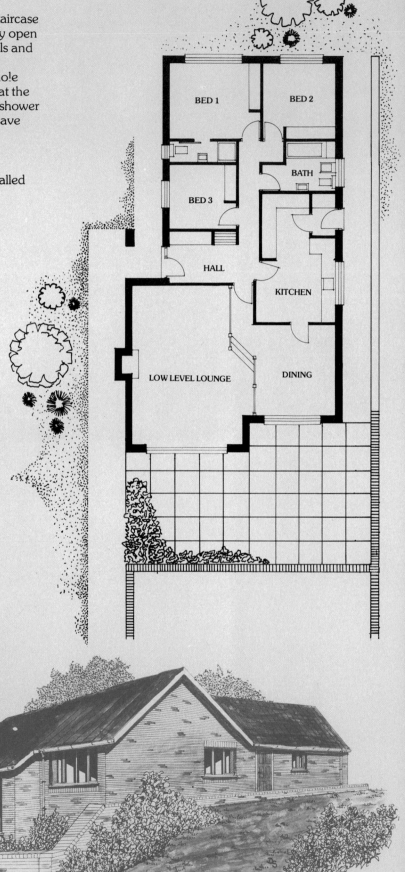

Design Number 83132

Floor Area	1360 sq. ft.	126 sq. m.
Dimensions overall	51'0'' x 30'0''	15.5 x 9.1
Lounge	22'2'' x 16'7½''	6.75 x 5.07
Dining	12'6'' x 11'3''	3.81 x 3.42
Kitchen (overall)	17'8½'' x 11'3''	5.40 x 3.42
Master Bed	12'8'' x 10'9''	3.86 x 3.27
Bed 2	10'9'' x 10'3''	3.27 x 3.12
Bed 3	9'3'' x 9'0''	2.82 x 2.74

132

AMBERLEY

This is another design with a dropped lounge to take advantage of a sloping site, although it can be built on the level if required. The carpeted steps by the side of the fireplace lead up to the dining area. Your dining suite at this high level with windows behind it will look very striking, and add tremendous character. If required the bedroom wing can be at a higher level than the hall, as there is plenty of room in the passage between bedrooms 2 and 4 for the steps that would be required.

Design Number 83133

Floor Area	1920 sq.ft.	178 sq.m.
Dimensions overall	65'10½'' x 44'5''	20.0 x 13.5
Lounge	19'9'' x 20'0''	6.00 x 6.10
Dining	11'10'' x 10'10½''	3.60 x 3.30
Kitchen	16'5½'' x 10'10½''	5.01 x 3.30
Study	12'6'' x 8'7½''	3.82 x 2.63
Utility	10'10½'' x 7'6''	3.30 x 2.28
Master Bed	14'1'' x 11'7½''	4.30 x 3.54
Bed 2	15'1'' x 11'6''	4.59 x 3.50
Bed 3	17'1'' x 11'7½''	5.20 x 3.54
Bed 4	15'1'' x 9'6''	4.61 x 2.90

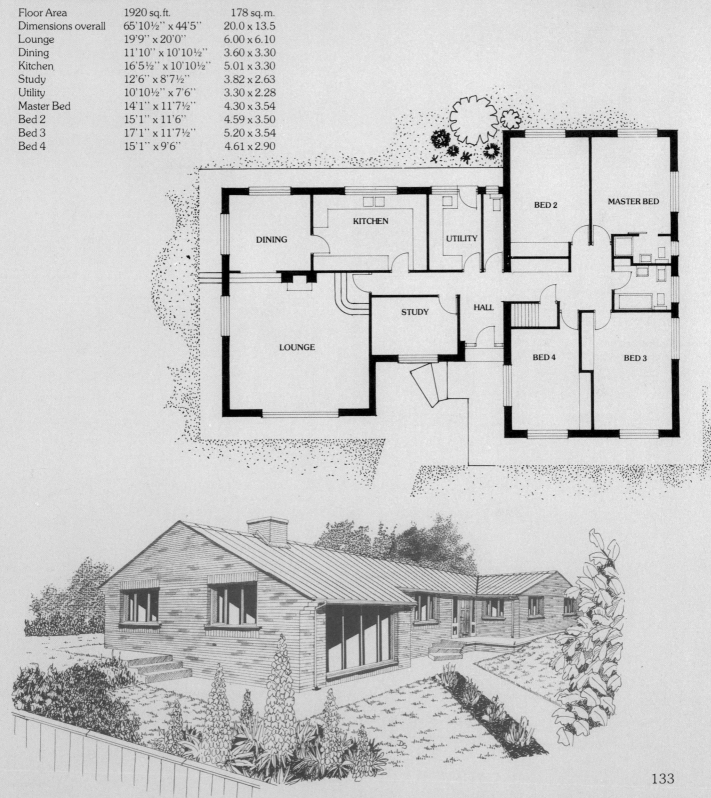

BERKELEY

The Berkeley bungalow is only 700 square feet, and is usually built as a weekend cottage, although it has all the features of a home to be permanently occupied and makes an economical retirement home.

It is this versatility which makes it a good investment as a second home, as the re-sale potential is much better. Small chalets and wooden holiday homes are often depreciating assets, while a miniature full size home in permanent material will appreciate with the housing market.

The illustration shows the rear elevation with a 12ft. patio window. Patio windows of this size in a small lounge have to be double glazed if the house is to be used all the year round, and triple glazing can be appropriate in these circumstances. Of course, the patio window can be replaced with an ordinary window if required, or a smaller french window into the end wall. Provided that the end of the window is 2ft. 3 inches from the corner of the building this is easily done, but a true corner window requires special consideration as it may have to be a structural part of the building. We are well used to dealing with this.

Design Number 83134

Area	700 sq. ft.	65 sq. m.
Overall	31'8" x 25'1"	9.66 x 7.64
Living Room	16'8" x 12'1"	5.09 x 3.69
Kitchen	11'0" x 8'2"	3.35 x 2.50
Bed 1	13'0" x 10'2"	3.97 x 3.09
Bed 2	11'0" x 9'10"	3.35 x 3.01

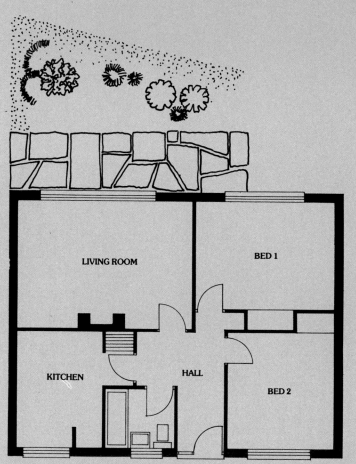

LIVING ROOM

BED 1

KITCHEN

HALL

BED 2

FOLKESTONE

This holiday bungalow has the living accommodation in the centre of the building, with two bedrooms at each end. This arrangement is very convenient for two families going on holiday together, and the open plan layout certainly suits holiday living.

A vacation home like this in permanent materials is a much better investment than a timber chalet, particularly as far as maintenance is concerned.

Design Number 83135

Floor Area	882 sq.ft.	82 sq.m.
Dimensions overall	39'6½'' x 25'3''	12.0 x 7.7
Lounge/Dining (overall)	18'8'' x 13'6''	5.70 x 4.11
Kitchen	7'0'' x 6'0''	2.13 x 1.83
Bed 1	11'6'' x 10'4''	3.51 x 3.15
Bed 2	12'10'' x 9'7''	3.91 x 2.92
Bed 3	9'7'' x 7'3½''	2.92 x 2.22
Bed 4	8'0'' x 13'6''	2.43 x 4.11

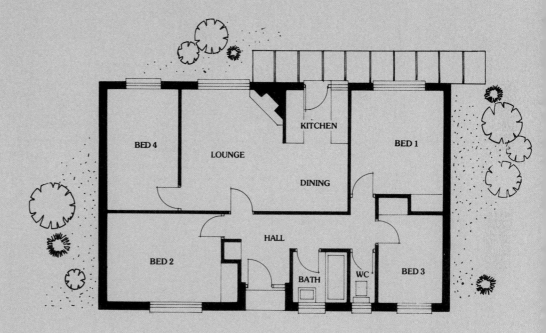

KESWICK

YARMOUTH

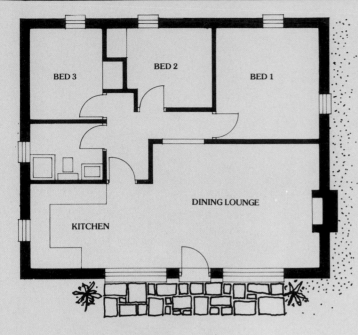

This holiday bungalow of only 650 sq. ft. was designed for holiday living in an area where a simple traditional design is a basic planning requirement. The accommodation is arranged on the basis that a family on holiday in these surroundings will want one double bedroom and two separate sets of bunk beds for children. The kitchen is open plan with the living room, and the windows are as big as one can realistically hope to get the approval of the planners.

A holiday home built in permanent materials like this is a much better investment than the wooden chalet that is often the alternative. The simple design, with the roof wholly supported on the external walls, lends itself to being built as a part time project, perhaps using local sub-contractors for the shell and finishing off the building oneself.

Remember the chimney and fireplace have to be massive to get the right effect with this design.

Design Number 83136

Area	648 sq. ft.	60 sq. m.
Dimensions overall	29'10'' x 25'0''	9.0 x 7.6
Lounge	16'0'' x 12'0''	4.87 x 3.65
Dining/Kitchen	12'0'' x 8'0''	3.65 x 2.43
Bed 1	10'0'' x 10'10''	3.05 x 3.30
Bed 2	8'2'' x 7'10''	2.50 x 2.38
Bed 3	7'0'' x 8'10''	2.13 x 2.70

A holiday bungalow has to be quite different from an ordinary home, and should be designed to suit holiday living — the realities of holiday living, not the image. One reality is that you will not spend all of the holiday sunbathing or fishing, and that the holiday home must have a character and a feel to it that will reflect and enhance a holiday mood.

The huge fireplace which is the key feature of this design gives interest and an outdoor living feel, as well as separating the living area from the galley and dining area. There are two double bedrooms and lots of storage. Storage is important in holiday homes, particularly these days when they are often shared by two or more families, and a large ceiling hatch so that one set of holiday clothes can be up in the roof space in suitcases when someone else is using the bungalow is an important design feature.

With two sliding glass doors on the key elevation, this design is suited to a situation where vacation homes are an established part of the landscape.

The Cromer bungalow, reference 82137 is a 3 bedroom version of the Yarmouth.

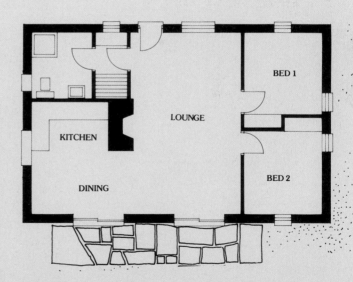

Design Number 83137

Area	713 sq. ft.	66 sq. m.
Dimensions overall	36'2'' x 22'1''	11.0 x 6.7
Lounge	13'0'' x 21'0''	3.96 x 6.40
Dining/Kitchen (overall)	12'0'' x 13'0''	3.65 x 3.96
Bed 1	9'0'' x 9'6''	2.74 x 2.90
Bed 2	9'0'' x 9'6''	2.74 x 2.90

NEWQUAY

TRURO

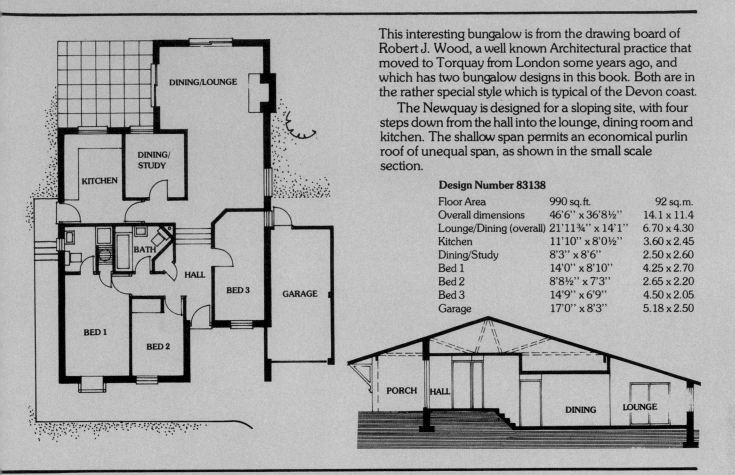

This interesting bungalow is from the drawing board of Robert J. Wood, a well known Architectural practice that moved to Torquay from London some years ago, and which has two bungalow designs in this book. Both are in the rather special style which is typical of the Devon coast.

The Newquay is designed for a sloping site, with four steps down from the hall into the lounge, dining room and kitchen. The shallow span permits an economical purlin roof of unequal span, as shown in the small scale section.

Design Number 83138

Floor Area	990 sq. ft.	92 sq. m.
Overall dimensions	46'6" x 36'8½"	14.1 x 11.4
Lounge/Dining (overall)	21'11¾" x 14'1"	6.70 x 4.30
Kitchen	11'10" x 8'0½"	3.60 x 2.45
Dining/Study	8'3" x 8'6"	2.50 x 2.60
Bed 1	14'0" x 8'10"	4.25 x 2.70
Bed 2	8'8½" x 7'3"	2.65 x 2.20
Bed 3	14'9" x 6'9"	4.50 x 2.05
Garage	17'0" x 8'3"	5.18 x 2.50

The second bungalow by Robert J. Wood is designed for a narrow site where the view from the principal rooms is to be to the rear.

The massive stone supports for the porch roof, and the sideways facing entrance, help the Truro to look larger than it really is. If necessary the garage can be dispensed with altogether, and the gable roof falling below the main roof will ensure that the bungalow is as distinctive as it is practical.

Design Number 83139

Floor Area	742 sq. ft.	69 sq. m.
Overall dimensions	30'6" x 42'8"	9.3 x 13.0
Lounge/Dining (overall)	20'4" x 17'10½"	6.20 x 5.45
Kitchen	8'6" x 8'2½"	2.60 x 2.50
Garage	8'0½" x 17'7"	2.45 x 5.35
Bed 1	8'10" x 11'2"	2.70 x 3.40
Bed 2	7'10" x 11'2"	2.40 x 3.40

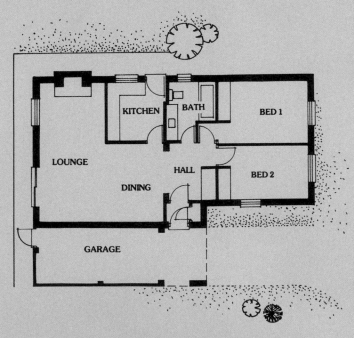

Robert J. Wood, Chartered Architect
70 — 71 Fleet St, Torquay, Devon.

LANGDALE

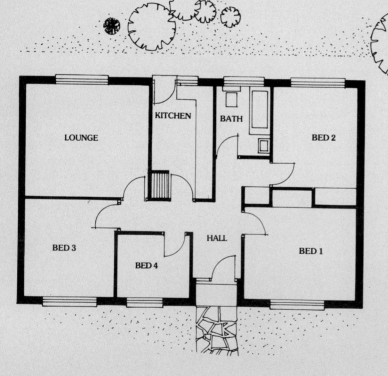

Design Number 83140

Floor Area	840 sq. ft.	79 sq.m.
Overall dimensions	25'3'' x 38'6½''	7.7 x 11.7
Lounge	13'3½'' x 13'6½''	4.05 x 4.12
Kitchen	7'0'' x 13'3½''	2.13 x 4.05
Bed 1	12'4'' x 10'1''	3.76 x 3.08
Bed 2	9'2'' x 11'0''	2.80 x 3.36
Bed 3	9'11'' x 10'1''	3.02 x 3.08
Bed 4	8'0'' x 6'10''	2.43 x 2.08

The Langdale bungalow provides four bedrooms in only 840 sq. feet, and to give this accommodation the lounge has to be fairly small. It is shown here in a rural setting with the windows to the front and rear, but if it has to be fitted on a narrower plot they can be moved into the gable walls.

This design is also useful as a holiday home or fishing cottage, providing the maximum of sleeping accommodation for those who expect to spend the whole day out of doors.

GRASMERE

This straight-forward bungalow for a 40ft. wide site has proved very successful over many years. The building is 25ft. wide, the garage can easily fit in a 12ft wide garden area, and there is a 3ft passage on the other side. This is the most practicable arrangement for a simple and cost effective rectangular structure on a plot of this size, and if it is possible to site the garage forward, as shown, the total effect is very attractive.

Design Number 83141

Floor Area (exc. garage)	860 sq.ft.	80 sq.m.
Dimensions overall	39'0'' x 25'3''	11.9 x 7.7
Lounge/Dining (overall)	17'3½'' x 17'0''	5.27 x 5.19
Kitchen (overall)	12'1'' x 10'2''	3.69 x 3.10
Master Bed	11'1½'' x 10'4''	3.39 x 3.15
Bed 2	10'4'' x 10'0''	3.15 x 3.05
Bed 3	9'0'' x 8'4½''	2.74 x 2.55

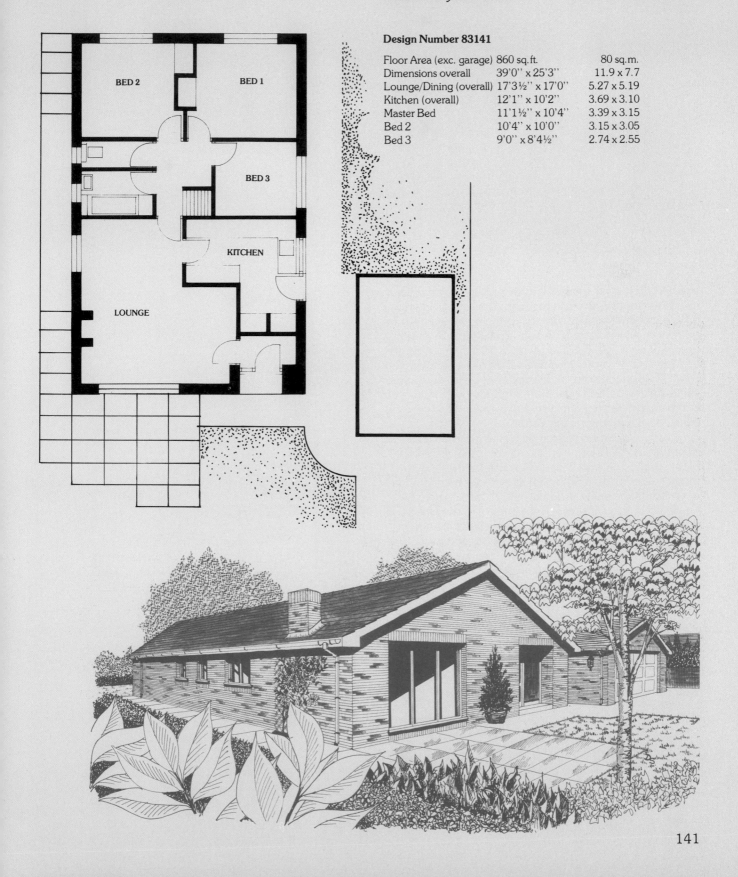

CONWAY

In architects jargon this is a "north frontage" design for a house where the view is to the rear. The large living room and main bedroom face the view, bringing the kitchen and bathroom windows into the front elevation. The area is only 840 sq.ft., yet the living room is 24ft long, giving a wide choice of ways of dividing off the dining end of the room. The windows in the lounge can be moved about to suit a client's particular requirements, although if unit cost is to be kept to a minimum no windows should be closer to a corner of the building than 2ft. 3".

The roof is entirely supported by the external walls, and although the walls between the rooms are built in solid block work to give good sound insulation, they can be moved around to change room sizes. A common change is to combine the bathroom and W.C. to give a larger hall.

The bungalow is shown here with a chimney for a coal fire, although this need not be constructed if it is not required. The heating requirement of this compact home when built with modern standards of insulation is so low that all the radiators required for full central heating can be run from the back boiler of a coal or gas fire in the living room

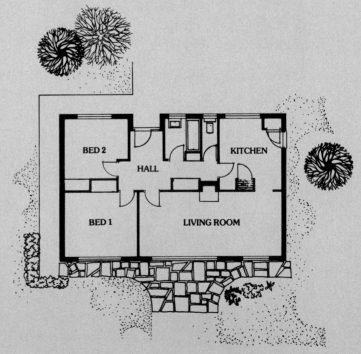

Design Number 83142

Area	840 sq.ft.	79 sq.m.
Overall	38'4" x 25'1"	11.69 x 7.64
Living Room	24'2" x 11'0"	7.36 x 3.36
Kitchen	12'0" x 10'6"	3.68 x 3.19
Bed 1	12'2" x 11'0"	3.72 x 3.36
Bed 2	10'11" x 10'1"	3.32 x 3.08

FOREST GATE

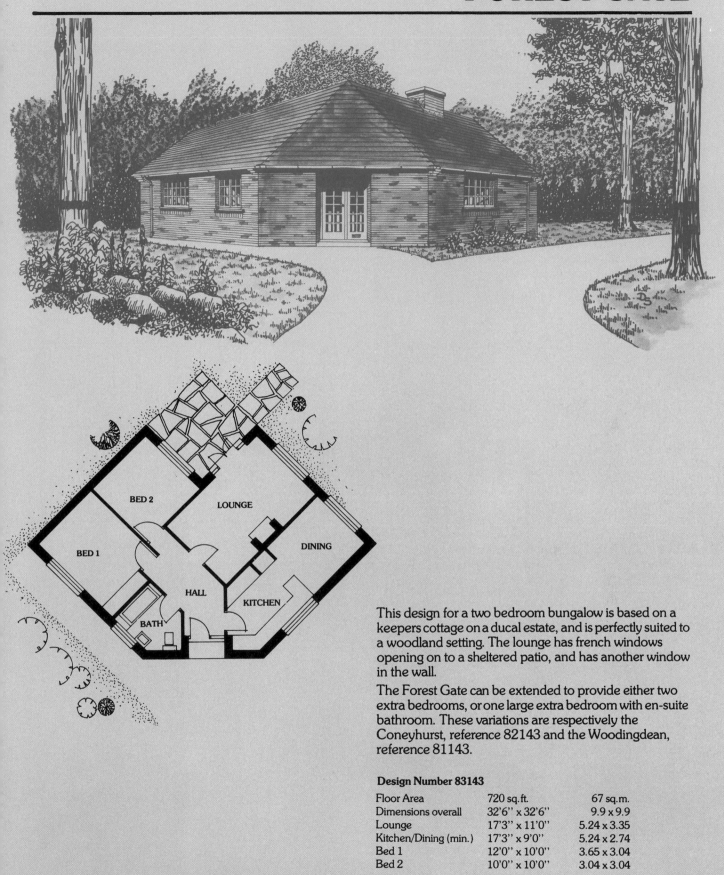

This design for a two bedroom bungalow is based on a keepers cottage on a ducal estate, and is perfectly suited to a woodland setting. The lounge has french windows opening on to a sheltered patio, and has another window in the wall.

The Forest Gate can be extended to provide either two extra bedrooms, or one large extra bedroom with en-suite bathroom. These variations are respectively the Coneyhurst, reference 82143 and the Woodingdean, reference 81143.

Design Number 83143

Floor Area	720 sq.ft.	67 sq.m.
Dimensions overall	32'6'' x 32'6''	9.9 x 9.9
Lounge	17'3'' x 11'0''	5.24 x 3.35
Kitchen/Dining (min.)	17'3'' x 9'0''	5.24 x 2.74
Bed 1	12'0'' x 10'0''	3.65 x 3.04
Bed 2	10'0'' x 10'0''	3.04 x 3.04

CARDIGAN

The Cardigan is an ideal retirement bungalow with a large living room which appeals to those who have been used to a larger house. The angled fireplace gives interest to the room, which has windows looking both front and rear. It is illustrated with a garage at the bedroom end of the house, which sometimes is unavoidable to suit an existing access. It is more usual to build it with a garage that gives access to the kitchen door, and this is shown in the inset plan. This arrangement, with the utility room at the back door, helps to keep draughts out of the kitchen.

The Cardigan is illustrated without a chimney, but we find that our clients who do not want an open fire invariably build a false chimney breast with an electric fire to give a focal point to the room.

In thinking how this bungalow would suit a site, remember that windows can be moved into the gable end wall to take advantage of a special view.

Design Number 83144

Area	840 sq.ft.	79 sq.m.
Overall	38'4'' x 25'1''	11.69 x 7.64
Lounge	19'0'' x 11'0''	5.79 x 3.36
Dining	12'5'' x 8'2''	3.78 x 2.50
Kitchen	12'1'' x 10'6''	3.68 x 2.19
Bed 1	11'7'' x 10'6''	3.54 x 3.21
Bed 2	10'7'' x 9'0''	3.23 x 2.75

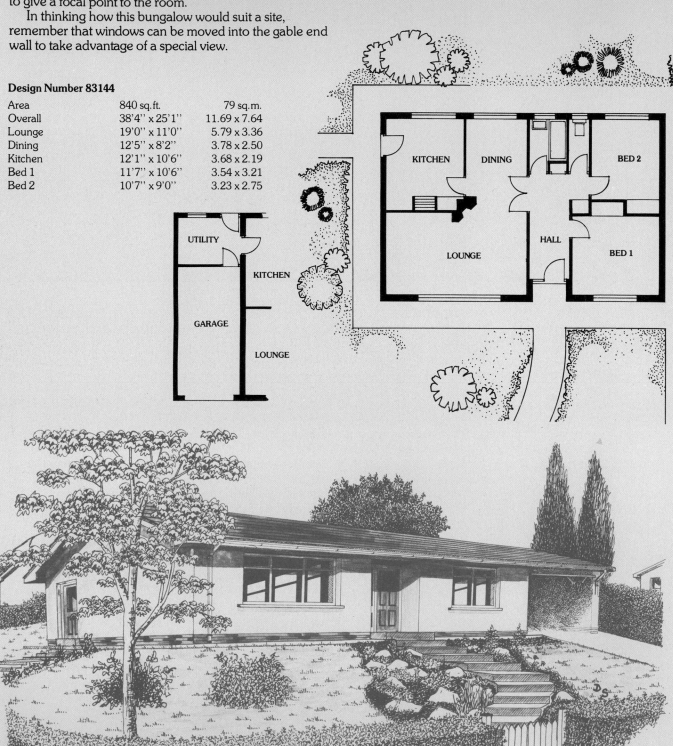

EVESHAM

This is a D & M design, and has been built more often than any of the other D & M bungalows. The garage and utility room are often left off, sometimes with the intention of building them later, and when this is done the bungalow is still pleasantly proportioned and seems much larger than its modest 840 sq. ft. The living room is a full twenty feet long, and if the fireplace is not required then the space which it occupies can be used to provide another cupboard in the hall. The kitchen is small: a decision has to be made whether to have a door from the kitchen to the living room, or whether to gain more space for kitchen units by having only a serving hatch.

We show this bungalow with a separate WC, but if required this can be moved into the bathroom, which will then have room for a shower, bidet, or airing cupboard. Once again, it is up to the householders to make their own decisions. There is room for another WC in the place of the utility room as shown on the inset drawing.

When built to todays high insulation standards this bungalow can have full central heating with the radiators run from the back boiler of either a coal fire or a gas fire in the lounge.

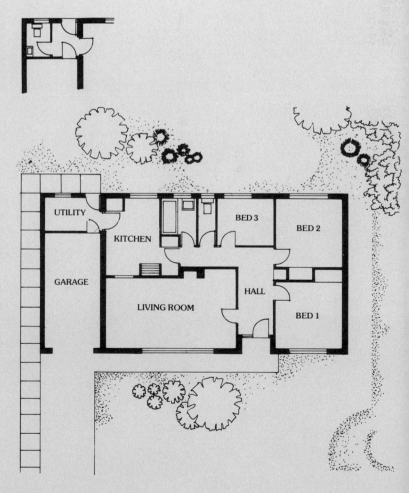

Design Number 83145

Area	840 sq. ft.	79 sq. m.
Overall	38'4'' x 25'1''	11.69 x 7.64
Living Room	20'6'' x 11'0''	6.24 x 3.36
Kitchen	12'0'' x 8'4''	3.68 x 2.55
Bed 1	10'6'' x 10'2''	3.21 x 3.08
Bed 2	10'7'' x 10'2''	3.23 x 3.08
Bed 3	8'9'' x 7'2''	2.68 x 2.18

WINSLOW

This is another example of a small bungalow without a back door — a matter of personal choice that is a heresy to some, and commonsense to others. It suits a narrow plot, and without a second entrance one saves the cost of a path, gains room in the kitchen, and avoids having the milkman walking around the house in his heavy boots early in the morning!

The front porch feature is a relatively inexpensive way of giving character and prestige to what is basically a very economical rectangular structure. In the same way the angled fireplace and chimney breast can be built as a feature to house an electric fire without the expense of a chimney. This is how the bungalow is illustrated, although the chimney for an open fire can be built if required.

Design Number 83146

Area (exc. garage)	896 sq.ft.	83 sq.m.
Dimensions overall	33'11" x 41'6½"	10.3 x 12.6
Lounge	12'0" x 17'0"	3.65 x 5.20
Dining	10'6" x 10'0"	3.20 x 3.05
Kitchen	8'6" x 10'0"	2.59 x 3.05
Carport	9'0" x 17'9"	2.74 x 5.40
Master Bedroom	12'0" x 12'0"	3.65 x 3.65
Bed 2	10'0" x 12'0"	3.05 x 3.65
Bed 3	10'0" x 8'6"	3.05 x 2.59

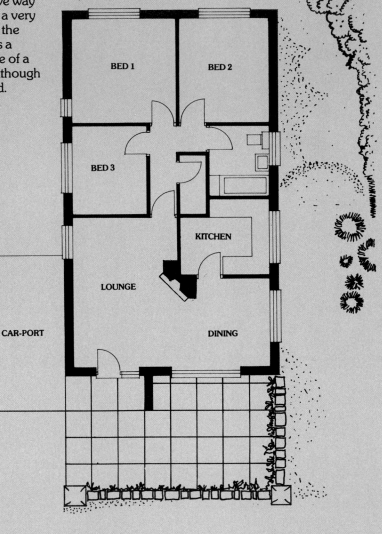

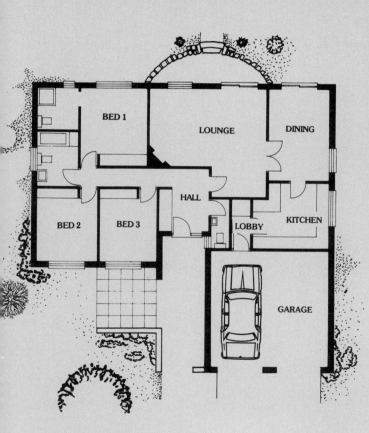

A narrow plot can make it necessary to build a garage projecting forward from a house or bungalow. If this is necessary it has to become an integral part of the whole design concept, and not "stuck on" as an after thought. This very attractive design achieves its effect by the clever balance between the different elements in the front elevation, and the unusually wide soffits to the roof. It is a striking and impressive building, and yet fits on a frontage of less than 60 feet.

Access from the garage into the kitchen is shown via a lobby with a useful store, or room for a deep freeze. As an alternative this lobby can be combined with the cloakroom, giving useful storage space. To comply with Building Regulations the door from the garage has to have a special fire-resistance rating and to be set in a frame with 25mm rebates. This is easily arranged.

If the width of the plot at the building line is very tight it is possible to reduce the width of this design slightly by substituting a double garage door for the two single garage doors shown. However, we feel that this unbalances the appearance slightly.

Design Number 83147

Floor Area (exc. garage)	1330 sq. ft.	123 sq. m.
Dimensions overall	49'10" x 47'7"	15.1 x 14.5
Lounge (overall)	19'0" x 17'9"	5.79 x 5.41
Dining	10'0" x 15'0"	3.05 x 4.57
Kitchen (overall)	12'6" x 10'9"	3.81 x 3.28
Garage	19'4" x 19'0"	5.90 x 5.79
Master Bed	11'0" x 12'9"	3.35 x 3.90
Bed 2	10'0" x 12'0"	3.05 x 3.65
Bed 3	10'0" x 12'0"	3.05 x 3.65

CAMBERLEY

This 840 sq.ft. 2 bedroom bungalow will sit on narrow sites, as all the windows which the Building Regulation requires to be at least 12ft from a boundary are in the gable end walls. However, it can also be used on a more spacious site like the one illustrated, and is useful in situations where as few windows as possible are wanted on the front elevation.

The Camberley has a very simple layout, and always feels larger than it really is. As with all small rectangular bungalows, the lower the roof pitch, the larger the building will seem.

If a storm porch is required there is room for a glazed screen and door inside the front door which is shown on the plan, and this is a popular feature with those who build the Camberley as a bungalow for their retirement.

Design Number 83148

Area	840 sq.ft.	79 sq.m.
Overall	38'4'' x 25'1''	11.69 x 7.64
Lounge	19'0'' x 11'0''	5.79 x 3.36
Dining	12'5'' x 8'2''	3.78 x 2.50
Kitchen	12'1'' x 10'6''	3.68 x 3.19
Bed 1	11'7'' x 10'6''	3.54 x 3.21
Bed 2	10'7'' x 9'0''	3.23 x 2.75

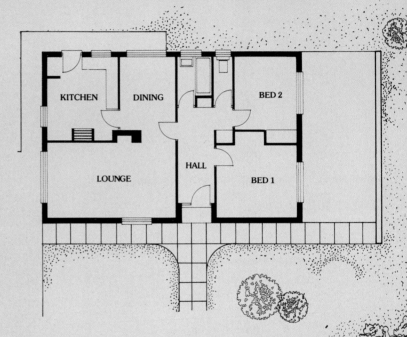

148

MENDIP

This design is for use on sites with very narrow frontages, and enables a three bedroom layout to be accommodated on a plot thirty five feet wide if a drive to a garage at the rear is required down the side of the bungalow, or only thirty one feet wide if access to a garage can be provided in some other way.

The Mendip design is fully reversible, and can be built with the lounge facing either the road or the back garden.

There is space for built-in wardrobes in all the bedrooms. If desired the bathroom and washbasin can be combined, giving room for a bidet or shower as well as the fittings shown, or else enabling the airing cupboard to be moved into the bathroom.

Design Number 83149

Area	840 sq.ft.	79 sq.m.
Overall	38'4" x 25'1"	11.69 x 7.64
Living Room	17'5" x 13'6"	5.30 x 4.11
Kitchen	13'6" x 8'4"	4.11 x 2.54
Bed 1	11'6" x 10'4"	3.51 x 3.15
Bed 2	11'10" x 9'7"	3.61 x 2.92
Bed 3	9'7" x 7'4"	2.92 x 2.22

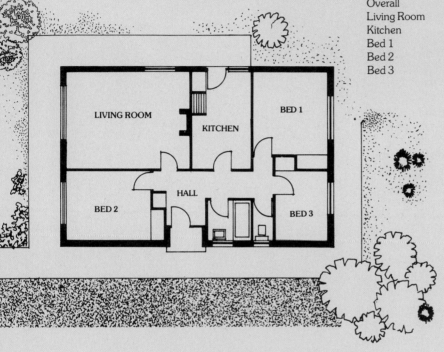

MARYLAND

The Maryland design bungalow features a large open plan dining hall with a full depth Georgian bay window. This is a most effective way of giving a prestige feel to a house of modest overall size, and it is an idea which is gaining in popularity. By pushing the garage forward the front elevation has a courtyard look, and flower boxes or other features can enhance this and make it a most striking home.

The three bedroom layout includes a master suite that is shown with both a dressing room and a shower room, but of course the opportunities for arranging your own layout here are limitless.

The massive chimney breast is designed to be a feature in both the lounge and the hall, to be built in either brick or stone as required. It can easily contain a gas fired central heating unit, with the controls hidden behind a specially designed door. This saves space in the kitchen and reduces pipe runs — and cost.

A five bedroom version of this bungalow with a gable extension to the rear is the Carolina design, reference 82150.

Design Number 83150

Area (exc. garage)	1188 sq.ft.	110 sq.m.
Dimensions overall	65'8" x 34'3"	20.0 x 10.4
Lounge (overall)	13'0" x 16'9"	3.96 x 5.10
Dining	11'0" x 11'4"	3.35 x 3.45
Kitchen	11'0" x 10'0"	3.35 x 3.05
Garage	21'0" x 20'0"	6.40 x 6.10
Master Bed	11'0" x 14'9"	3.35 x 4.50
Bed 2	11'0" x 11'0"	3.35 x 3.35
Bed 3	10'0" x 11'0"	3.05 x 3.35

Home Planners, Inc
23761 Reseach Drive
Farmington Hills, Michigan 48024, USA.

ALBANY

This large bungalow to an American design has many features which have been absent from our own domestic architecture for many years, but which are now coming back into fashion. The deep windows to the bedrooms are unusual, but give enormous character to the whole building. They can, of course, be replaced with windows of a standard sill height if required.

The deeply recessed porch with double doors gives a most prestigeous entrance. Our sketch shows classical pillars to the front of the porch. These are a key feature and must be absolutely right; in some situations it will be preferable to replace them with massive brick or stone piers. The choice will also depend on how it is intended to handle the landscaping of the garden in front of the porch.

A five bedroom version of this design is called the Maine, reference 82151.

Design Number 83151

Floor Area (exc. garage)	1447 sq. ft.	134 sq. m.
Dimensions overall	61'3" x 41'9"	18.6 x 12.7
Lounge	18'0" x 18'6"	5.48 x 5.64
Dining	11'0" x 19'2"	3.35 x 5.84
Kitchen	11'10" x 10'0"	3.60 x 3.05
Utility	7'0" x 10'0"	2.14 x 3.05
Garage	20'0" x 21'4"	6.10 x 6.50
Master Bed	14'0" x 12'2"	4.26 x 3.70
Bed 2	11'0" x 11'0"	3.35 x 3.35
Bed 3	11'0" x 9'0"	3.35 x 2.74

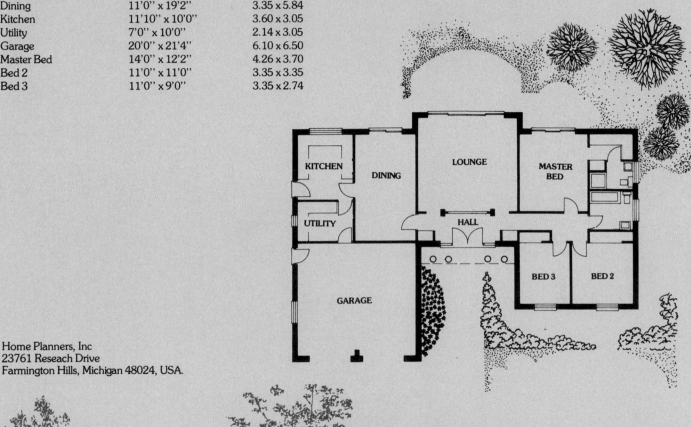

Home Planners, Inc
23761 Reseach Drive
Farmington Hills, Michigan 48024, USA.

151

CONNECTICUT

This is another typical American design, and is one that gets a great deal of character and interest in a layout that can suit a plot only 60 ft. wide — although it must be said that it will look its best with a lot more room around it. It looks complex and expensive; in fact it is not. All the three main roofs are at the same span, and the valley arrangements are simple and straight-forward. Shuttered windows to the garage match those in the living accommodation, and help to make the bungalow seem even larger than it is. The full depth bow window in the dining room rounds it off.

The dovecote above the garage doors is a fanciful feature — or is it? In the last century this sort of thing was commonplace, adding interest and character to a building. Then, for some reason, it was considered an architectural extravagance. Now the human values are reasserting themselves, and a good thing too.

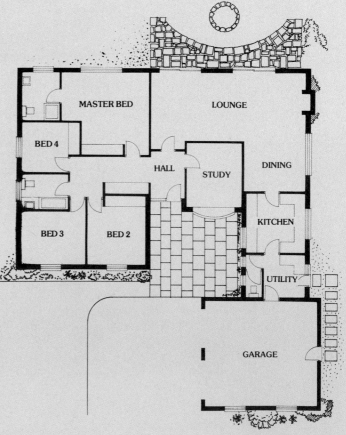

Design Number 83152

Area (exc. garage)	1767 sq. ft.	164 sq.m.
Dimensions overall	55'1" x 63'7"	16.8 x 19.3
Lounge	13'0" x 29'0"	3.96 x 8.85
Dining Area	11'6" x 9'4"	3.50 x 2.85
Kitchen	11'0" x 11'0"	3.35 x 3.35
Study	12'0" x 12'0"	3.65 x 3.65
Utility	7'0" x 6'6"	2.13 x 1.98
Garage	20'0" x 21'0"	6.10 x 6.40
Master Bed (overall)	16'6" x 15'6"	5.03 x 4.75
Bed 2	11'0" x 13'0"	3.35 x 3.96
Bed 3	12'0" x 10'0"	3.65 x 3.05
Bed 4	10'10" x 9'4"	3.30 x 2.85

Home Planners, Inc
23761 Reseach Drive
Farmington Hills, Michigan 48024, USA.

DEANSGATE

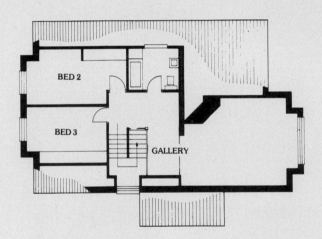

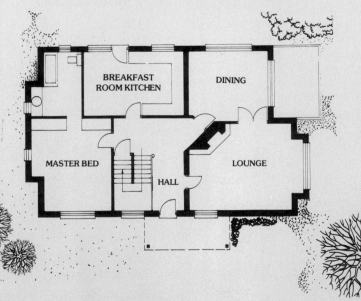

This is another American design by Home Plans Inc of Michigan which cleverly combines a traditional exterior with excitingly different floor plans. The idea of the internal arrangement takes some getting used to; the lounge has a sloping ceiling the full height of the house, overlooked by a minstrel gallery which is also the first floor landing. At the other end of the room is a massive floor to ceiling window which projects forward in a window wall, and which is shown here with a traditional stone surround. The master bedroom suite is on the ground floor and two other bedrooms and a bathroom above.

All this is in a floor area of under 1700 sq.ft., and can be accommodated on a fairly narrow plot if required. Unit building costs for this design are high, but this is a home that is an investment that will always keep well ahead of the market.

Incidentally this design can also be built with a gable porch to the front entrance, and in a suburban situation this would probably be preferable.

Design Number 83153

Floor Area	1661 sq.ft.	154 sq.m.
Dimensions overall	45'1'' x 33'0''	13.7 x 10.0
Lounge (overall)	17'6'' x 15'0''	5.32 x 4.55
Dining	13'6'' x 12'0''	4.13 x 3.65
Breakfast Kitchen	16'10'' x 11'6''	5.15 x 3.35
Master Bed (overall)	13'6'' x 16'0''	4.13 x 4.87
Bed 2	17'0'' x 9'4''	5.20 x 2.85
Bed 3	13'6'' x 9'6''	4.13 x 2.90

Home Planners, Inc
23761 Reseach Drive
Farmington Hills, Michigan 48024, USA.

OLLERTON

This bungalow was designed by Scattergood and Woodhams of Worksop, and has a distinctive appearance with an attractive balance between the wide glazed screen to the hall and the run of smaller windows on each side. To be seen at its best it needs a setting where the whole bungalow is in view, set well back in a large garden. A very interesting design.

Design Number 83154

Floor Area		
(exc. garage)	1270 sq. ft.	118 sq. m.
Overall dimensions	64'8" x 32'7½"	19.7 x 9.46
Lounge	16'1" x 20'0"	4.90 x 6.10
Dining	15'5" x 9'0"	4.70 x 2.75
Kitchen	11'10" x 11'10"	3.60 x 3.60
Utility	5'11" x 9'6"	1.80 x 2.90
Bed 1	13'6" x 10'10"	4.10 x 3.30
Bed 2	11'10" x 9'10"	3.60 x 3.00
Bed 3 (overall)	8'10" x 13'6"	2.70 x 4.10

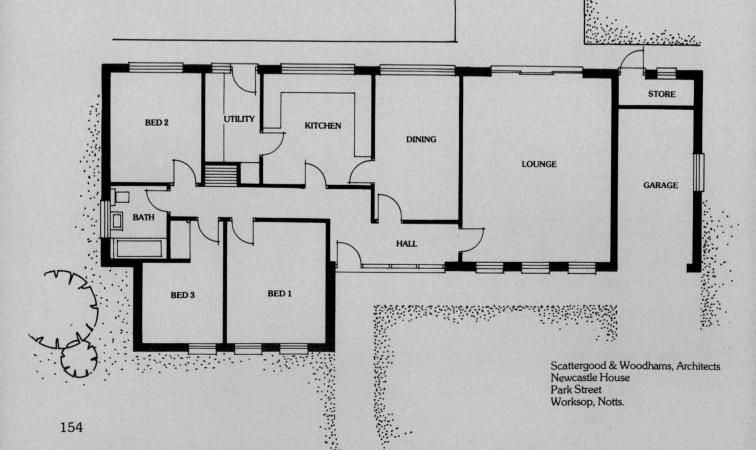

Scattergood & Woodhams, Architects
Newcastle House
Park Street
Worksop, Notts.

CHILTERN

This large 3 bedroomed bungalow has a layout to suit sites with a view to the rear. The large window in the lounge looks out to the back of the property, and another window or pair of french windows can be put in the gable end wall if required. As shown it has the lounge and dining room open-plan, but the internal walls can be re-arranged to divide them into separate rooms if required.

The cylinder cupboard is shown in the kitchen: This is a modern approach, based on the idea that the ironing will probably be done in the kitchen anyway, and that this is the most convenient place for the airing cupboard. This is a very individual sort of choice, and there are lots of alternative arrangements which can be made.

We are often asked for plans for this bungalow to be built with a patio window or french doors in the gable end wall of the lounge. There are no problems at all with this, but to meet building regulation requirements the size of the main window may have to be reduced slightly: we will advise on this when we know exactly what is required.

Design Number 83155

Area	1060 sq.ft.	99 sq.m.
Overall	47'11" x 25'1"	14.61 x 7.64
Lounge	19'9" x 11'0"	6.01 x 3.36
Dining	12'1" x 8'11"	3.68 x 2.72
Kitchen	12'1 x 10'6"	3.68 x 3.19
Bed 1	13'10" x 10'7"	4.23 x 3.24
Bed 2	10'7" x 10'1"	3.24 x 3.07
Bed 3	10'1" x 10'0"	3.07 x 3.05

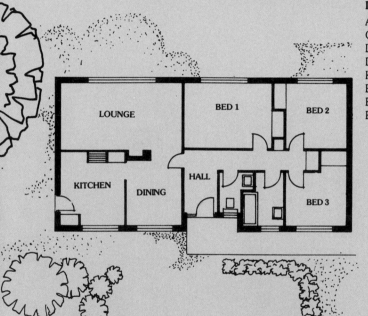

BATTLEBRIDGE

This is another Irish design of the maximum size which qualifies for the Irish Government grant. Unfortunately the Dublin Government does not pay this to those who build this bungalow in Britain, but it is a very good design anyway, well suited to life in a rural area

Note that there are two doors into the bathroom, one from the hall, and a sliding door leading from the master bedroom. There is lots of storage space in this design, and one particularly attractive feature is the small window set in a run of wardrobes in the main bedroom.

As with so many of our designs which were first drawn for a site in Eire, there is a fireplace in the dining room. This need not be built if it is not required, in which case there is space for a pair of double doors between the lounge and the dining room.

Design Number 83156

Floor Area
(exc. garage)	1296 sq.ft.	120 sq.m.
Overall	52'10½'' x 32'2½''	16.11 x 9.81
Lounge	18'2'' x 12'0''	5.35 x 3.66
Dining	16'0'' x 12'3''	4.88 x 3.74
Kitchen	19'1'' x 12'3''	5.80 x 3.74
Utility (overall)	7'6'' x 9'2''	2.29 x 2.80
Master Bedroom	14'3'' x 10'0''	4.35 x 3.05
Bed 2	12'2'' x 10'0''	3.71 x 3.05
Bed 3	10'3½'' x 7'9''	3.14 x 2.35

A four bedroom version of the Battlebridge is called the Donegal, reference 82156.

Fergus Murray, Architect
Moatlands, Navan, Eire.

CROSSHAVEN

This large and impressive bungalow was originally designed for a rural site in Southern Ireland, where round arches are a common theme in new homes. As originally built the lounge was sunk two steps below the floor level everywhere else, so that the windowsills were at shoulder level. This was deliberately contrived to distract from an unsatisfactory view to the front, and to make the fireplace the focal point in the room, with the eye led up to the dining room and its patio door through to the garden beyond. An interesting approach, and one that worked very well. The architect was Fergus Murray, who works in Co. Meath.

Design Number 83157

Area (exc. garage)	2030 sq.ft.	188 sq.m.
Dimensions overall	73'3'' x 32'2''	22.3 x 9.8
Lounge	23'9'' x 18'0''	7.25 x 5.48
Dining	14'0'' x 12'0''	4.26 x 3.65
Kitchen	12'0'' x 13'0''	3.65 x 3.96
Study	12'4'' x 8'0''	3.75 x 2.43
Utility	6'0'' x 12'0''	1.82 x 3.65
Breakfast Room	12'0'' x 9'6''	3.65 x 2.89
Master Bed	14'0'' x 10'2''	4.25 x 3.10
Bed 2	12'0'' x 12'0''	3.65 x 3.65
Bed 3	12'0'' x 11'6''	3.65 x 3.50
Bed 4	9'6'' x 14'3''	2.89 x 4.35

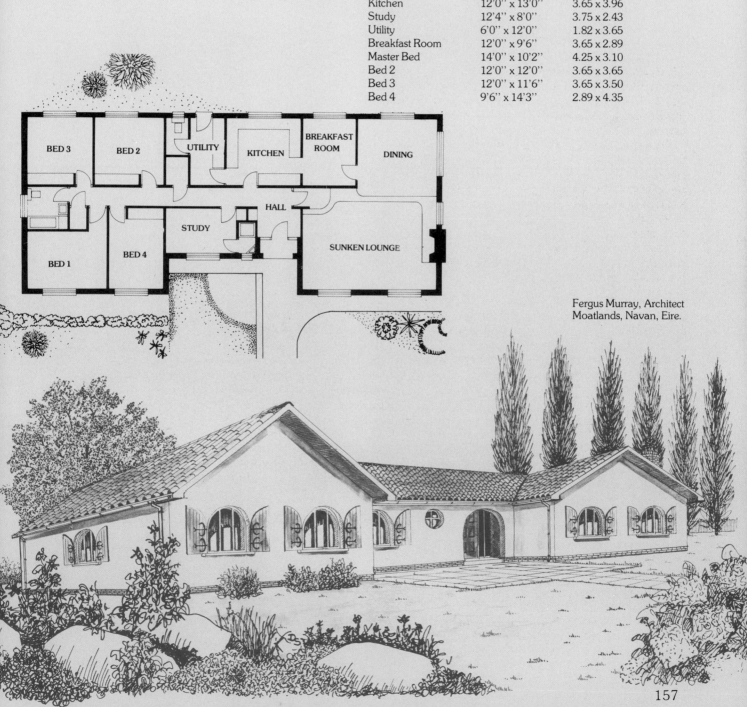

Fergus Murray, Architect
Moatlands, Navan, Eire.

HASLEMERE

ASCOT

Design Number 83158

Floor Area		
(exc. garage)	2948 sq. ft.	273 sq.m.
Dimensions overall	89'1" x 75'5½"	27.1 x 23.0
Lounge	15'11" x 23'7"	4.86 x 7.20
Dining	14'10" x 15'6"	4.52 x 4.74
Kitchen	16'1" x 14'1"	4.90 x 4.30
Study	14'10½" x 15'6"	4.53 x 4.74
Utility	9'10" x 11'10"	3.00 x 3.60
Garage	19'0" x 28'7"	5.79 x 8.71
Master Bed	16'0" x 15'6"	4.86 x 4.74
Bed 2	14'9" x 15'6"	4.50 x 4.74
Bed 3	12'3" x 14'9"	3.73 x 4.47
Bed 4	12'3" x 14'9"	3.73 x 4.47

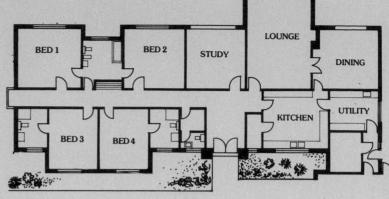

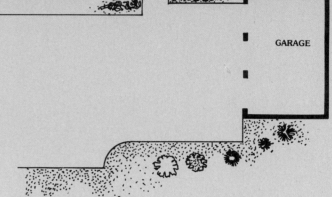

This is a design for sites where a large ranch style bungalow is wanted by the client, and where lots of gables are demanded by the planners!

Two bedrooms have en suite bathrooms, and as drawn the other two each have a door to the third bathroom. If this arrangement is not wanted it can easily be changed. The large store by the back door has been variously fitted out as a gun room, as a shower room on a stud farm, and as an office and drug store on a large dairy farm.

The window at the end of the long bedroom corridor deserves to be a feature, and can be either glazed to a low level sill or built as a little bay with a window seat.

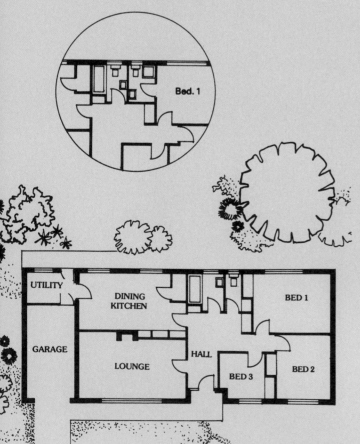

This big 3 bedroomed bungalow of 1060 square feet features the large kitchen/family room which is particularly popular with those who live and work in the country. There are built-in wardrobes to every bedroom, a cloaks cupboard and a broom cupboard in the hall, with an airing cupboard and a big walk-in larder in the kitchen. To match this generous storage with a feeling of size this bungalow is sometimes built with a glazed screen between the lounge and the hall, making both rooms feel even larger.

The Ascot is often built with the WC turned into a second bathroom serving the main bedroom, and the inset sketch shows how this is usually arranged.

The kitchen and utility room can be omitted, and this is often done when the bungalow is built on a farm where the car and landrover are parked elsewhere. In this case a porch is often built at the back door.

The 4 bedroomed version of this design is the Midhurst on page 114

Design Number 83159

Area	1060 sq. ft.	99 sq. m.
Overall	47'11" x 25'1"	14.61 x 7.64
Lounge	19'9" x 12'6"	6.01 x 3.81
Dining Kitchen	19'9" x 10'7"	6.01 x 3.23
Bed 1	14'4" x 10'11"	4.37 x 3.33
Bed 2	12'2" x 10'1"	3.71 x 3.07
Bed 3	8'10" x 8'1"	2.70 x 2.47

BANBURY

HYTHE

160

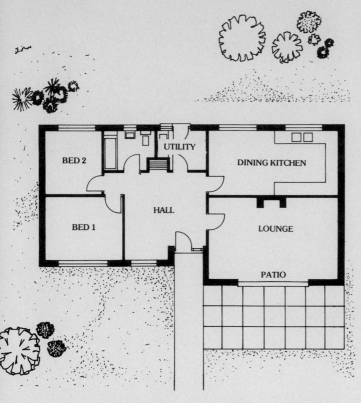

This attractive bungalow was originally designed for a Cotswold farmer as a bungalow for his retirement, and the design brief was that there should be a 20ft by 13ft lounge, a "decent sized hall", a kitchen big enough to take meals in, with everything else as compact as possible. The Banbury design resulted and has become very popular.

There is no provision for built-in furniture, but this can easily be arranged. Remember that most proprietary cupboard fronts are made to a 600mm module and as the dimensions on drawings are masonry dimensions before plastering, care has to be taken in working out exactly where cupboards can be fitted in. It is generally better to allow for a makeup piece on a run of cupboards than to plan to fill up a space exactly with doors.

The sketch shows this bungalow built in stone — as the original was — but it also looks very well with a rendered finish.

A three bedroom version of this bungalow is the Abingdon, reference number 82160.

Design Number 83160

Area (exc. garage)	994 sq.ft.	92 sq.m.
Lounge	20'6" x 13'1"	6.24 x 3.99
Dining/Kitchen	20'6" x 10'0"	3.19 x 3.05
Utility	7'8" x 6'3"	2.38 x 1.90
Master Bed	10'2" x 12'1"	3.09 x 3.69
Bed 2	10'0" x 9'0"	3.04 x 2.74

This is another design to take advantage of a site where the outlook is to the rear, and it is illustrated here built in rendered insulating blocks with stone features. This style is very popular in some areas, and particulary in West Wales. It is important to ensure that the stone stands well proud of the rendered walling, and when discussing this with the bricklayer remember to allow for the thickness of the render.

In the inset plan we show an arrangement for an integral garage for this design, giving a porch at the back door, with the garage door recessed. This arrangement looks well, is very practical, — and we are at a loss to know why it is not more popular!

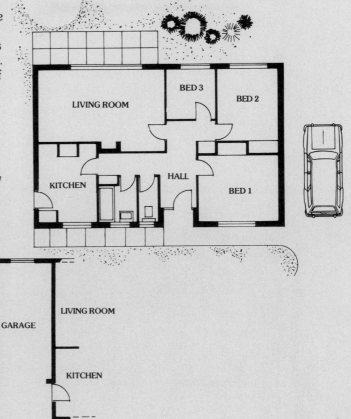

Design Number 83161

Area	840 sq.ft.	79 sq.m.
Overall	38'4" x 25'1"	11.69 x 7.64
Living Room	19'4" x 11'0"	5.90 x 3.36
Kitchen	12'0" x 9'0"	3.68 x 2.75
Bed 1	12'4" x 10'1"	3.76 x 3.08
Bed 2	11'0" x 9'2"	3.36 x 2.80
Bed 3	7'9" x 7'6"	2.36 x 2.29

RINGWOOD

We are often asked for drawings for a bungalow with a garage below the living accommodation and without any stairway to give access to it from inside the building. This saves space and minimizes costs. The Ringwood design meets these requirements, and is based on a bungalow built in Lincolnshire where the site had an old clay pit in the middle of it. This pit just fitted the garage, and everything else went on top. If you want this arrangement remember that there has to be a minimum of 8ft of difference in height between the garage floor level and the floor above it.

Design Number 83162

Floor Area

(exc. garage)	1470 sq.ft.	136 sq.m.
Dimensions overall	59'2'' x 27'5''	18.0 x 8.3
Lounge	18'0½'' x 13'5''	5.50 x 4.09
Dining	11'10'' x 11'10''	3.60 x 3.60
Kitchen	11'11½'' x 11'10''	3.64 x 3.60
Utility	9'9½'' x 5'8½''	2.99 x 1.74
Garage	25'6½'' x 17'8½''	7.79 x 5.40
Master Bed	13'5½'' x 11'10''	4.10 x 3.60
Bed 2	11'10'' x 11'10''	3.60 x 3.60
Bed 3	11'10'' x 9'9½''	3.60 x 2.99
Bed 4 (overall)	12'2½'' x 9'9½''	3.72 x 2.99

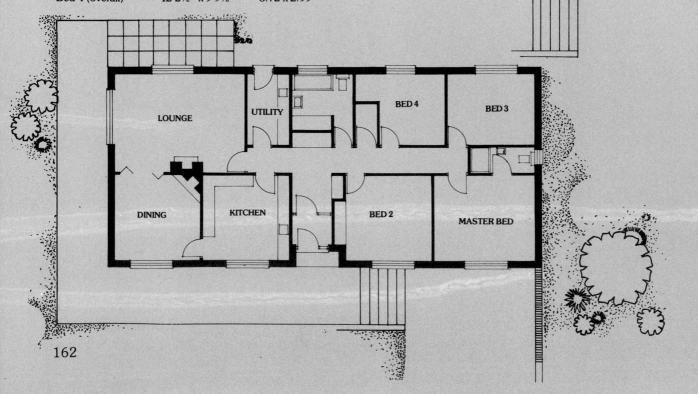

WHEATLEY

The planners loved this design when it was first drawn for a very sensitive site in 1980. It takes a moments thought to appreciate the internal arrangement. The front door leads into a very high hall, lit by windows above the entrance screen. From this hall there are two separate flights of stairs, one leading discretely up left to the bedrooms, while the other goes to a gallery leading to the living area. This is one of the most impressive entrances in any of our designs, and provides a marvellous setting for period furniture.

Although it is particularly well suited to a sloping site, this design can be built on level ground if care is given to landscaping, and soil can be obtained to build up the garden level around the single storey wing.

Note that there are three doors from the garage — into the hall, into the utility room, and into a large work room or store. The utility room is a long way from the kitchen, but the latter is large enough to avoid this being a problem.

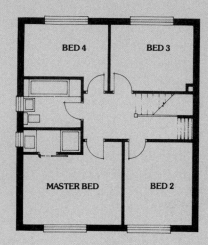

Design Number 83163

Floor Area (exc. garage)	1640 sq.ft.	152 sq.m.
Dimensions Overall	59'7" x 29'8"	18.16 x 9.05
Lounge	19'11" x 13'1"	6.06 x 3.99
Dining/		
Kitchen (overall)	10'0" x 23'6"	3.04 x 7.16
Workroom	12'0" x 9'2"	3.65 x 2.79
Utility	11'1" x 9'2"	3.39 x 2.79
Garage	23'5" x 18'4"	7.14 x 5.59
Master Bed (overall)	11'9" x 13'10"	3.59 x 4.22
Bed 2	11'9" x 9'3"	3.59 x 2.81
Bed 3	11'1" x 9'2"	3.39 x 2.79
Bed 4	12'0" x 7'3"	3.65 x 2.19

LAMBOURNE

A dream design in a dream setting, though not a figment of our architect's imagination, but a home that has been built and looks every bit as attractive as the drawing.

This is a big bungalow, and it must be emphasised that in many parts of the country the planners will suggest that our architectural tradition is that a home of this size is built as a two storey house. However, if it is built as part of a complex of single storey farm buildings, or integrated well into the landscape, the planning application should not be too much real trouble.

One of the advantages of a 'U' shaped design is that different parts of the house can be kept quite separate. The lounge/family room/dining room are grouped around the main entrance, the bedroom wing is quite separate, and the garage/farm office/farm kitchen form the third unit. Perhaps this is the ultimate modern farm bungalow.

The Plumpton design is a four bedroom version of this bungalow. The reference no. is 82164.

Design Number 83164

Floor Area (exc. garage) 2950 sq.ft.		273 sq.m.
Dimensions overall	62'2'' x 76'4''	18.9 x 23.2
Lounge	21'3'' x 18'3''	6.46 x 5.56
Dining	21'3'' x 14'9''	6.46 x 4.50
Kitchen	21'3'' x 17'8''	6.46 x 5.39
Study	12'0'' x 14'10''	3.65 x 4.52
Utility (overall)	9'6'' x 12'2''	2.88 x 3.70
Garage	15'9'' x 16'1''	4.80 x 4.90
Master Bed	21'3'' x 12'0''	6.46 x 3.65
Bed 2	16'11'' x 12'0''	5.16 x 3.65
Bed 3	16'11'' x 9'10''	5.16 x 3.00

NORMANBY

This traditionally styled bungalow was originally drawn for a site in Shropshire and has many unusual features. The deep verandah outside the principal rooms, the traditional purlin roof, and the style of the porch at the front door are all reminiscent of the 20's and of the leisurely living that went with them. Not a budget home, but a very interesting one.

Design Number 83165

Floor Area (exc. garage)	2000 sq.ft.	185 sq.m.
Dimensions overall	51'5'' x 62'9''	15.6 x 19.1
Lounge	20'4'' x 14'0''	6.19 x 4.26
Dining	14'0'' x 14'0''	4.26 x 4.26
Kitchen	15'0'' x 11'0''	4.57 x 3.35
Utility	13'0'' x 8'0''	3.97 x 2.43
Garage	20'0'' x 16'0''	6.09 x 4.87
Sun Lounge	14'0'' x 11'6''	4.26 x 3.50
Master Bed	15'7'' x 12'0''	4.74 x 3.65
Bed 2	14'0'' x 9'8''	4.26 x 2.94
Bed 3	10'9'' x 9'0''	3.26 x 2.74

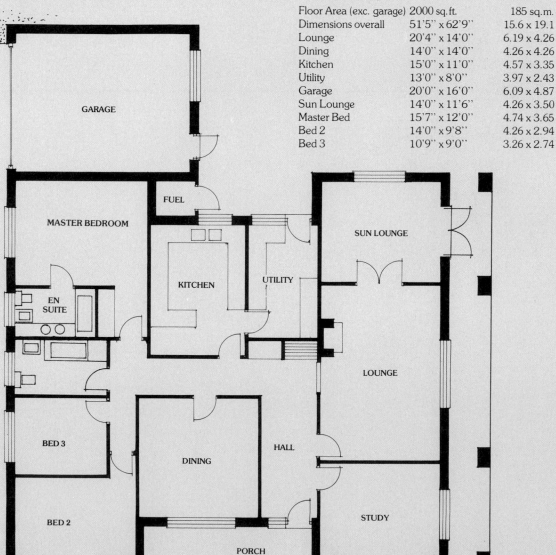

SHANNON

WATERBEACH

This large bungalow is another Irish design by Fergus Murray, and suits a site with a gentle slope. There is no direct access from the garage to the house, and this simplifies the structural design and reduces cost. However, there is plenty of room to re-arrange the layout to allow for stairs down to the garage if required, and we can provide drawings that show this. The actual arrangement depends on the position of the garage doors, which have to suit the access and the slope of the site.

This bungalow has been built on a level site in flat country with distant views, with the expense of the under-building to the bedrooms being justified by the commanding appearance of the structure. It all suited the site very well. Soil was brought in to build up the garden as appropriate, and this approach sometimes merits consideration on other sites.

Here the garage is approached from the side, and is sited under the forward projection of the lounge and family room, as shown on the inset plan.

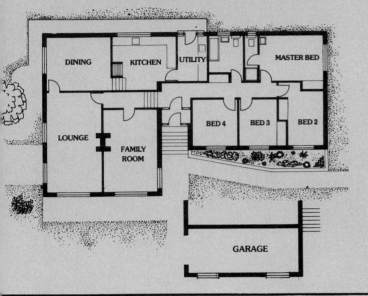

Design Number 83166

Floor Area (exc. garage)	1674 sq. ft.	155 sq.m.
Dimensions Overall	62'6'' x 36'1½''	19.06 x 11.01
Lounge	21'8'' x 12'0''	6.59 x 3.65
Dining	14'0'' x 12'4''	4.27 x 3.76
Kitchen	13'7'' x 12'4''	4.15 x 3.76
Utility	10'0'' x 6'6''	3.05 x 1.98
Garage	24'4'' x 9'2''	7.41 x 2.80
Family Room	17'11'' x 12'0'	5.47 x 3.65
Master Bed	14'0'' x 10'0''	4.27 x 3.05
Bed 2	12'0'' x 8'0''	3.66 x 2.44
Bed 3	8'0'' x 10'3½''	2.44 x 3.14
Bed 4	10'2'' x 10'3½''	3.09 x 3.14

Fergus Murray, Architect
Moatlands, Navan, Eire.

Arches to the front of the veranda which runs the whole length of the building are very popular with clients, but less so with the planners. Still, this design has been built on a number of occasions in Britain, and is very popular in Ireland. If the arches are in either brick or stone then the detailing of the masonry is most important, particularly at the point where the arch springs from the pillars. We always provide a drawing showing this particular feature, but there are many ways of doing it and often local practice is best. Discuss this with your builder or bricklayer.

Inside the bungalow the layout is orthodox, with a very large lounge. To suit the veranda outside the height of the rooms is nine feet, which gives a feeling of space and quality to the home.

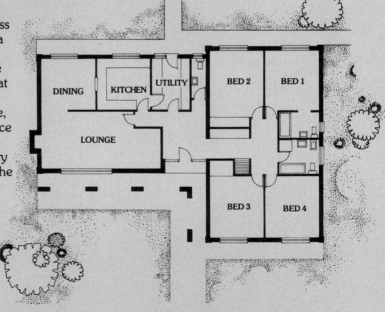

Design Number 83167

Floor Area		
(exc. garage)	1750 sq. ft.	162 sq. m.
Dimensions Overall	61'5'' x 41'6''	18.71 x 12.65
Lounge	25'7½'' x 12'1½''	7.81 x 3.70
Dining	11'10'' x 10'11½''	3.60 x 3.34
Kitchen	11'6'' x 10'11½''	3.50 x 3.34
Utility	8'1'' x 10'11½''	2.46 x 3.34
Master Bed	12'7½'' x 11'7½''	3.85 x 3.54
Bed 2	14'1½'' x 11'6''	4.30 x 3.50
Bed 3	13'1½'' x 11'6''	4.00 x 3.50
Bed 4	13'1½'' x 11'7''	4.00 x 3.54

Fergus Murray, Architect
Moatlands, Navan, Eire.

167

CLEVEDON

This is a design with a self-contained flat for someone using a wheelchair who lives with the family — and it will all fit on a 51 ft. plot. There is a front porch with double doors which are easily managed, and then there are sliding doors into the flat, and all the doors inside the flat are opened in this way. When this design was originally built the three windows in the flat were constructed as narrow bays with very deep sills. The sills were fitted with lead trays as permanent window-boxes and the room had house plants in flower all the year round.

Design Number 83168

Floor Area (total)	1582 sq.ft.	147 sq.m.
Overall dimensions	44'4½'' x 56'3''	13.5 x 17.1
Main Dwelling:		
Lounge/Dining (overall)	23'5'' x 19'9''	7.14 x 6.01
Kitchen	10'6'' x 10'7''	3.20 x 3.24
Bed 1	10'7'' x 10'0''	3.24 x 3.05
Bed 2	12'5½'' x 10'0''	3.80 x 3.05
Bed 3	8'11'' x 12'1''	2.71 x 3.68
Annexe:		
Bedsitting Room		
(overall)	18'2½'' x 14'0''	5.55 x 4.26
Kitchen	10'0'' x 7'0''	3.05 x 2.13
Bath	9'5'' x 7'0''	2.87 x 2.13

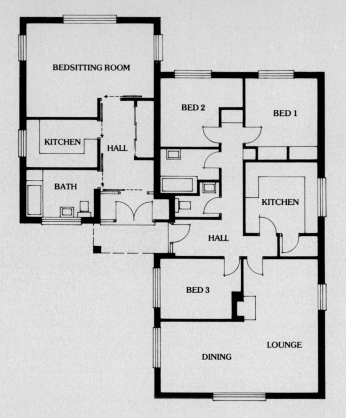

ALLINGTON

Design Number 83169

This is an alternative version of the Clevedon design with a special flat for someone living in a wheelchair, but has the main accommodation with the lounge at the rear instead of the front. The overall size and floor area are the same, although some of the room sizes vary.

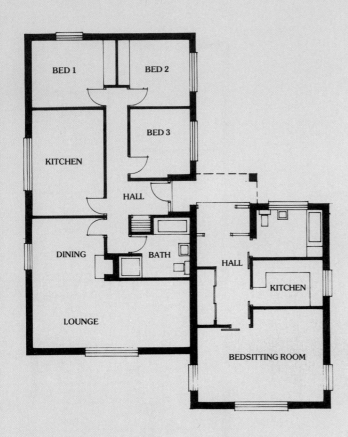

FOXTON

Many of those building a new home on their own land are building it as part of a business venture. In these cases sometimes they want integral office or shop accommodation as in this canal side bungalow with a boat chandlery. This same design has been built on two different occasions as the owners home on caravan sites, and the layout proved to be very practical.

Design Number 83170

Floor Area	1720 sq.ft.	160 sq.m.
Overall dimensions	59'2½'' x 50'5½''	18.0 x 15.3
Shop	16'0½'' x 15'1''	4.89 x 4.60
Store	16'0½'' x 8'10½''	4.89 x 2.70
Lounge	19'0'' x 12'7''	5.79 x 3.84
Dining	11'4'' x 10'10''	3.45 x 3.30
Kitchen	17'4'' x 10'6''	5.29 x 3.20
Master Bed	14'1'' x 12'11½''	4.30 x 3.95
Bed 2	12'9½'' x 9'0''	3.90 x 2.74
Bed 3	10'9'' x 9'0''	3.29 x 2.74

170

GLEN DUN

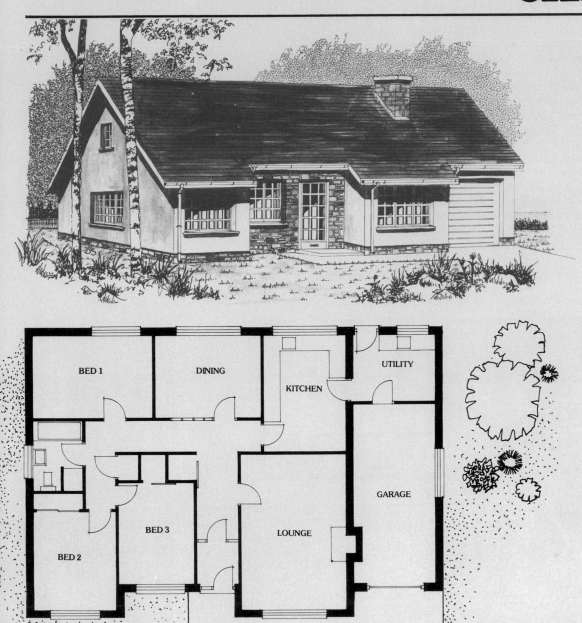

Design Number 83171

Floor Area

(exc. garage)	1555 sq. ft.	144 sq.m.
Dimensions overall	50'7½" x 35'1½"	15.4 x 10.7
Lounge	13'0" x 19'0"	3.96 x 5.79
Dining	13'0" x 10'0"	3.96 x 3.04
Kitchen	10'0" x 14'0"	3.04 x 4.26
Utility	10'0" x 8'0"	3.05 x 2.44
Garage	10'0" x 21'9½"	3.05 x 6.64
Master Bed	14'4½" x 10'0"	4.38 x 3.04
Bed 2	12'0" x 10'0"	3.65 x 3.04
Bed 3	12'6" x 9'1"	3.80 x 2.76

The Glen Dun bungalow by Prestoplan was specially designed for timber frame construction, and the timber frame structure is available from Prestoplan Ltd.

This bungalow and the nineteen other designs which follow were all specially designed for timber frame construction by Prestoplan Ltd., and the construction kits are available from that company as detailed earlier in the book.

The Glen Dun bungalow is available in two versions. We illustrate the Mk. I. The Mk. II has further accommodation in the roof, and details are available on request. As its name suggests, this bungalow is popular in Scotland where it is usually built with the rendered finish shown in the illustration.

DOUGLAS

The Douglas is the largest of the Prestoplan timber frame bungalows in this book, and includes just about every feature of luxury living anyone could ask for. The lounge/dining area has an island fireplace which can be built in almost any style to suit one of the super new fires for a central hearth. There is a family room which can be just that, or else used as a Granny Flat or a Nursery. There are four bedrooms, one with a dressing room and en suite bathoom — the Douglas has it all.

This is essentially a home for a site with all round views, If the ground falls away in the front then this bungalow can be built with the floor to the lounge and dining room dropped by a couple of feet, with feature stairs into the room. Another alternative is to build it with the boarded sloping ceiling and cathedral windows illustrated: the options are endless, and Prestoplan will certainly incorporate your own design ideas in their drawings if you wish.

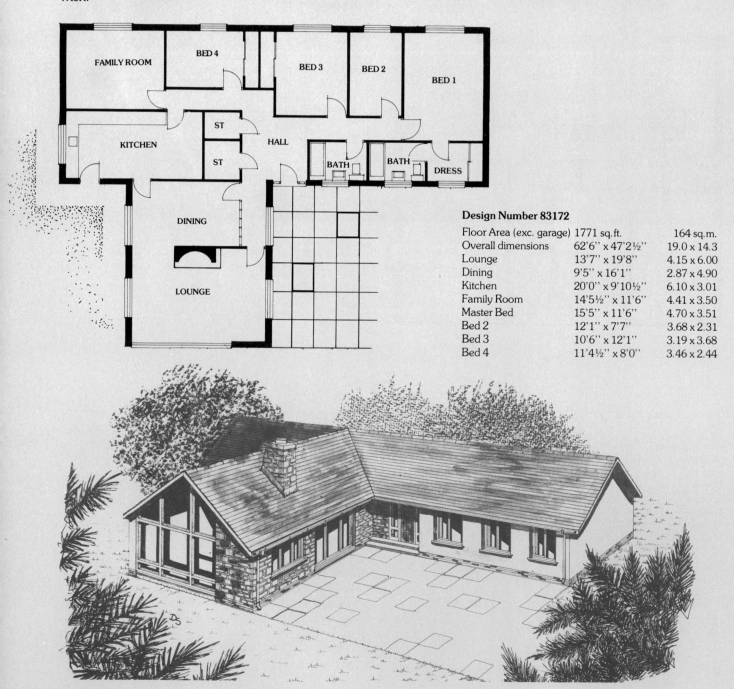

Design Number 83172

Floor Area (exc. garage)	1771 sq.ft.	164 sq.m.
Overall dimensions	62'6'' x 47'2½''	19.0 x 14.3
Lounge	13'7'' x 19'8''	4.15 x 6.00
Dining	9'5'' x 16'1''	2.87 x 4.90
Kitchen	20'0'' x 9'10½''	6.10 x 3.01
Family Room	14'5½'' x 11'6''	4.41 x 3.50
Master Bed	15'5'' x 11'6''	4.70 x 3.51
Bed 2	12'1'' x 7'7''	3.68 x 2.31
Bed 3	10'6'' x 12'1''	3.19 x 3.68
Bed 4	11'4½'' x 8'0''	3.46 x 2.44

ILKLEY

This is another Prestoplan design with a boarded sloping ceiling to the lounge and a matching cathedral window in the gable end. Although it is illustrated with a casement window in the side wall of the lounge, it is often built with a patio window in this position, making the lounge a splendid sun room.

Like all our Prestoplan designs, drawings and components for timber frame construction are available off the peg for this bungalow, and it is possible to re-position windows and make other alterations with the minimum of delay.

Design Number 83173

Floor Area (exc. garage)	1868 sq.ft.	173 sq.m.
Dimensions overall	41'0'' x 47'0''	12.5 x 14.3
Lounge	25'0'' x 12'9½''	7.60 x 3.90
Dining	13'5½'' x 12'6''	4.10 x 3.81
Kitchen	12'6'' x 11'2''	3.81 x 3.41
Master Bed	13'7'' x 10'6''	4.15 x 3.19
Bed 2	15'5½'' x 9'6½''	4.71 x 2.91
Bed 3	13'6'' x 9'10''	4.12 x 3.00
Bed 4	12'10'' x 9'5½''	3.92 x 2.88

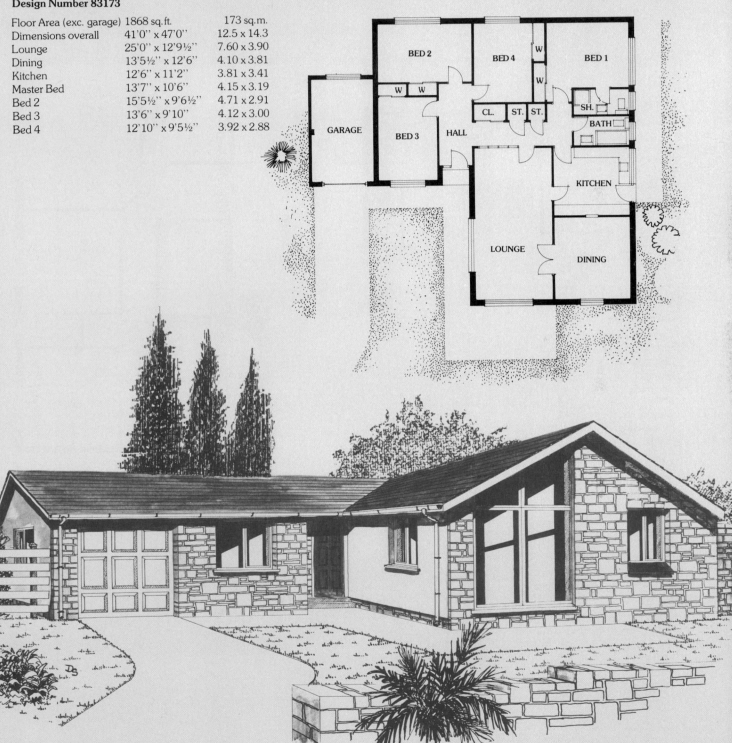

RICHMOND

This timber frame bungalow from Prestoplan has an interesting L shape layout with a hip roof that gives it a fashionable period appearance. The garage has a large recess for a workbench and connects with the utility room and kitchen via a useful lobby. The layout of all the rest of the accommodation shows a typical Prestoplan attention to detail — look at the angle corner of the lounge which gives space in the hall and adds interest to the lounge itself.

As with all our Prestoplan designs, a timber frame kit for this bungalow is available, together with the design calculations which will be required to support the building regulations application when you build in this way.

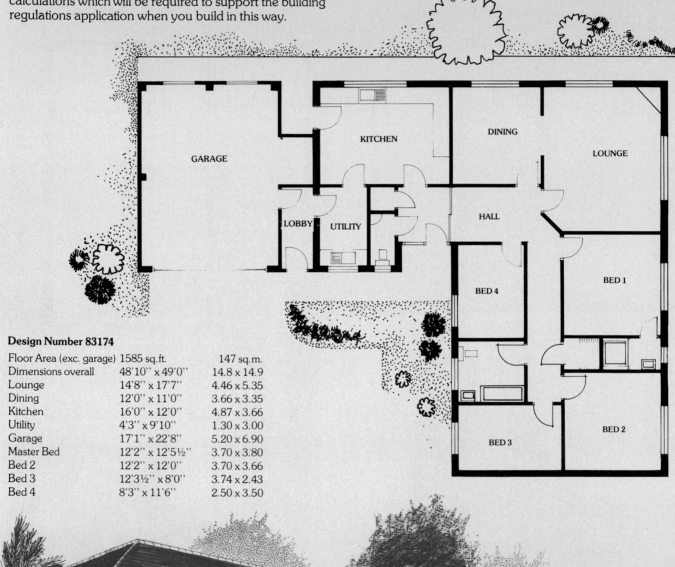

Design Number 83174

Floor Area (exc. garage)	1585 sq.ft.	147 sq.m.
Dimensions overall	48'10'' x 49'0''	14.8 x 14.9
Lounge	14'8'' x 17'7''	4.46 x 5.35
Dining	12'0'' x 11'0''	3.66 x 3.35
Kitchen	16'0'' x 12'0''	4.87 x 3.66
Utility	4'3'' x 9'10''	1.30 x 3.00
Garage	17'1'' x 22'8''	5.20 x 6.90
Master Bed	12'2'' x 12'5½''	3.70 x 3.80
Bed 2	12'2'' x 12'0''	3.70 x 3.66
Bed 3	12'3½'' x 8'0''	3.74 x 2.43
Bed 4	8'3'' x 11'6''	2.50 x 3.50

CHARNOCK

The Charnock is a very popular Prestoplan bungalow with a large study which makes it of particular interest to those who work from their homes. This room can also be used as a fourth bedroom, and as it is well separated from the other bedrooms this is popular with people who are building a home which they intend to share with an elderly relative.

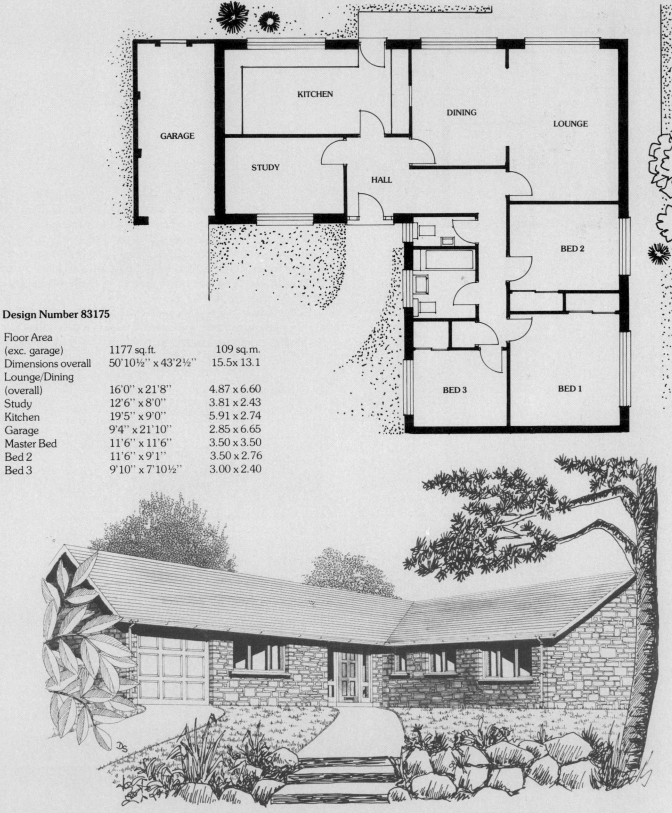

Design Number 83175

Floor Area		
(exc. garage)	1177 sq.ft.	109 sq.m.
Dimensions overall	50'10½" x 43'2½"	15.5 x 13.1
Lounge/Dining		
(overall)	16'0" x 21'8"	4.87 x 6.60
Study	12'6" x 8'0"	3.81 x 2.43
Kitchen	19'5" x 9'0"	5.91 x 2.74
Garage	9'4" x 21'10"	2.85 x 6.65
Master Bed	11'6" x 11'6"	3.50 x 3.50
Bed 2	11'6" x 9'1"	3.50 x 2.76
Bed 3	9'10" x 7'10½"	3.00 x 2.40

GLEN SHEE

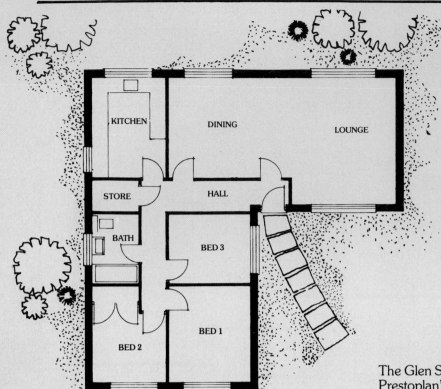

KITCHEN

DINING

LOUNGE

STORE

HALL

BATH

BED 3

BED 2

BED 1

The Glen Shee bungalow was designed in Scotland at Prestoplan's Strathaven office to give the maximum accommodation in just over a thousand square feet. With both wings at the same span of 21ft. 4'', the building is well proportioned and the massive stone window-sills shown in the sketch are typical Scottish features that always help a home to look impressive.

The store in the hall is very popular, and every time this bungalow is built it seems to be used in a different way — larder, cloakroom, gun room or simply a glory-hole!

Design Number 83176

Floor Area	1026 sq.ft.	95 sq.m.
Dimensions overall	39'3'' x 39'7''	11.9 x 12.0
Lounge/Dining (overall)	15'9'' x 28'3''	4.80 x 8.60
Kitchen	9'2'' x 12'5''	2.80 x 3.80
Master Bed	10'4'' x 12'0''	3.15 x 3.65
Bed 2	9'0'' x 12'0''	2.75 x 3.65
Bed 3	8'8'' x 10'4''	2.65 x 3.15

GLEN FARG

This is another of a series of designs which were specifically drawn for Scotland in Prestoplan's office in Strathaven, but it has proved popular elsewhere, and especially in N. Ireland. It is a very good example of a simple straight forward bungalow with an uncomplicated layout that is so well proportioned that it always looks bigger than it really is. The lounge is almost square; in an era when architects seem determined that all living rooms shall be rectangular it is a pleasant change, and is a deservedly popular feature.

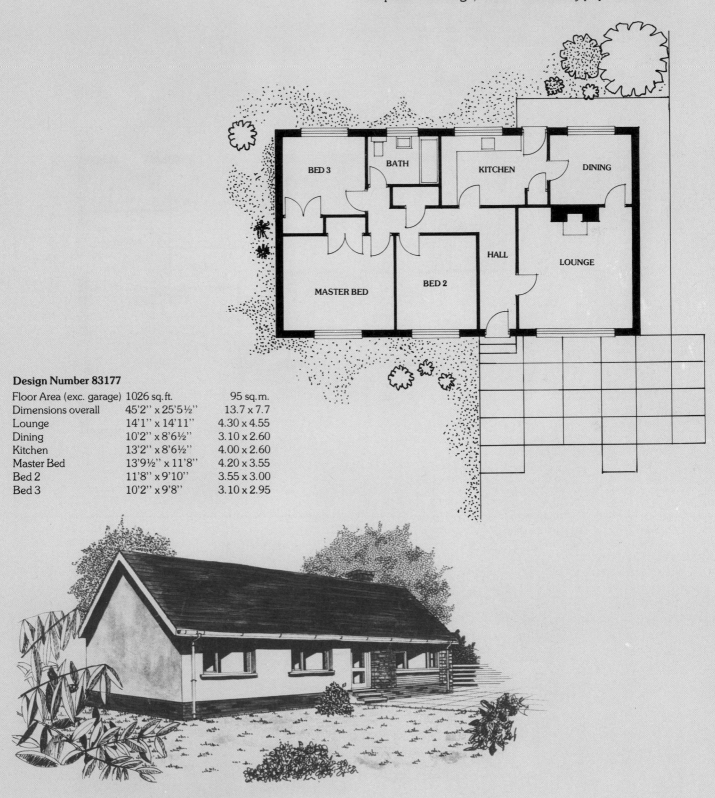

Design Number 83177

Floor Area (exc. garage)	1026 sq. ft.	95 sq. m.
Dimensions overall	45'2'' x 25'5½''	13.7 x 7.7
Lounge	14'1'' x 14'11''	4.30 x 4.55
Dining	10'2'' x 8'6½''	3.10 x 2.60
Kitchen	13'2'' x 8'6½''	4.00 x 2.60
Master Bed	13'9½'' x 11'8''	4.20 x 3.55
Bed 2	11'8'' x 9'10''	3.55 x 3.00
Bed 3	10'2'' x 9'8''	3.10 x 2.95

GLEN URQUHART

The Glen Urquhart is one of a series of homes which Prestoplan had specially designed to meet the demand in Scotland for simple bungalows with good proportions, good weather protection and sensible straight-forward layouts. This is one of the larger dwellings in this particular range and is deservedly popular.

The projection of the roof over the front door gives character to this design, and the treatment of the front porch is very important. Whether it is given a simple stanchion to support the roof with a dwarf wall below as shown, or whether it is a more elaborate feature, it must be designed to suit the building as a whole and to compliment the well balanced proportions

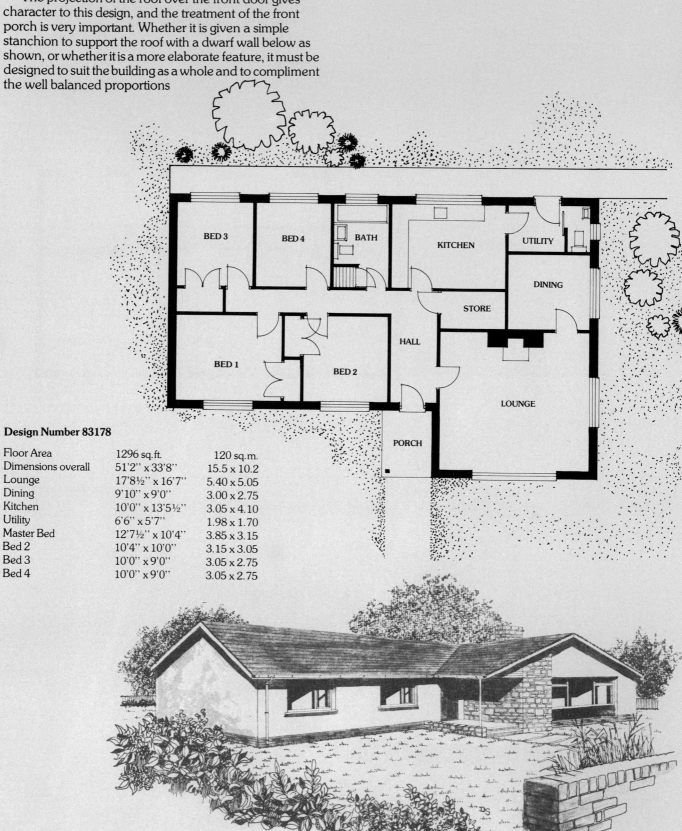

Design Number 83178

Floor Area	1296 sq.ft.	120 sq.m.
Dimensions overall	51'2'' x 33'8''	15.5 x 10.2
Lounge	17'8½'' x 16'7''	5.40 x 5.05
Dining	9'10'' x 9'0''	3.00 x 2.75
Kitchen	10'0'' x 13'5½''	3.05 x 4.10
Utility	6'6'' x 5'7''	1.98 x 1.70
Master Bed	12'7½'' x 10'4''	3.85 x 3.15
Bed 2	10'4'' x 10'0''	3.15 x 3.05
Bed 3	10'0'' x 9'0''	3.05 x 2.75
Bed 4	10'0'' x 9'0''	3.05 x 2.75

GLEN MORE

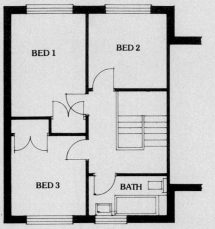

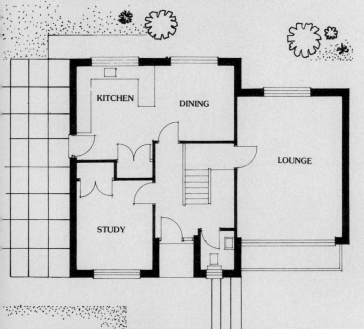

Another of the successful series of "Glen" designs from Prestoplan, with the split level accommodation and sloping ceiling to the lounge which are a feature of many Prestoplan designs. The highest point of the ceiling is over 12ft high, and slopes down to normal ceiling height. The rafters span the whole of the lounge and no beams are required to support them: however, if you are having a pine-boarded ceiling then you can incorporate a false beam to add to the character — the choice is yours. Whether the ceiling is boarded or plastered, it all gives enormous scope for imaginative decor and stunning lighting arrangements.

Design Number 83179

Floor Area (exc. garage)	1242 sq.ft.	115 sq.m.
Dimensions overall	27'4½'' x 35'9''	8.3 x 10.9
Lounge	13'5½'' x 17'9''	4.11 x 5.40
Kitchen/Dining (overall)	19'8'' x 12'0½''	6.00 x 3.67
Study	11'2'' x 9'6''	3.40 x 2.90
Garage	12'11½'' x 17'9''	3.95 x 5.40
Master Bed	12'0½'' x 9'6''	3.67 x 2.90
Bed 2	9'10'' x 9'9''	3.00 x 2.97
Bed 3	9'10'' x 9'6''	3.00 x 2.90

BALMORAL

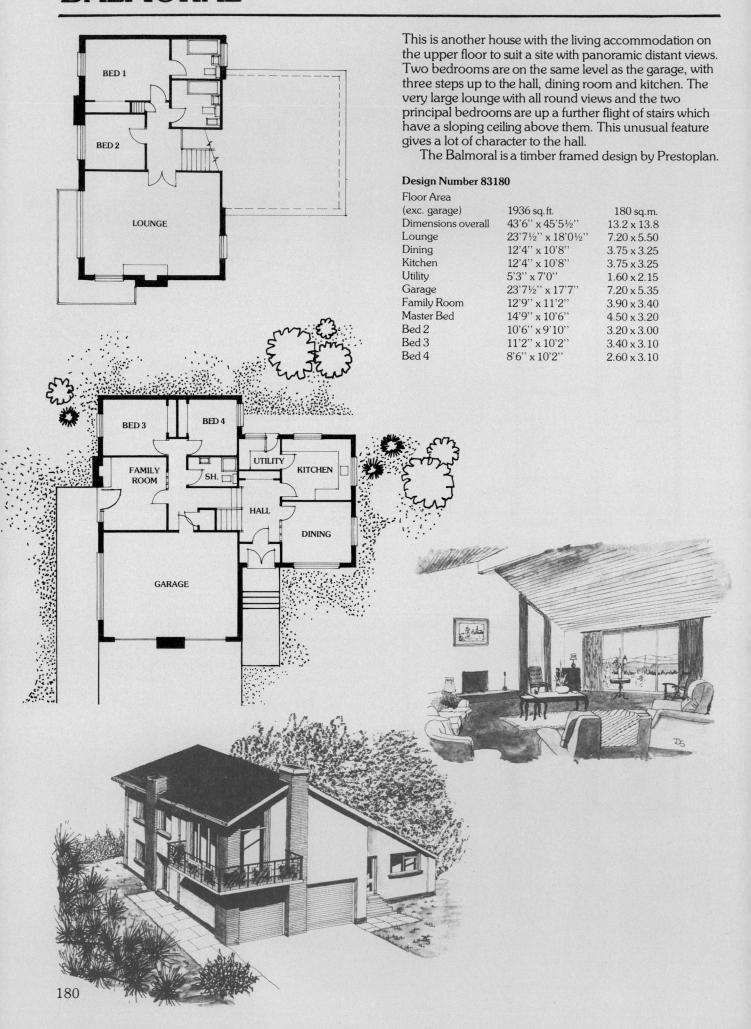

This is another house with the living accommodation on the upper floor to suit a site with panoramic distant views. Two bedrooms are on the same level as the garage, with three steps up to the hall, dining room and kitchen. The very large lounge with all round views and the two principal bedrooms are up a further flight of stairs which have a sloping ceiling above them. This unusual feature gives a lot of character to the hall.

The Balmoral is a timber framed design by Prestoplan.

Design Number 83180

Floor Area		
(exc. garage)	1936 sq.ft.	180 sq.m.
Dimensions overall	43'6'' x 45'5½''	13.2 x 13.8
Lounge	23'7½'' x 18'0½''	7.20 x 5.50
Dining	12'4'' x 10'8''	3.75 x 3.25
Kitchen	12'4'' x 10'8''	3.75 x 3.25
Utility	5'3'' x 7'0''	1.60 x 2.15
Garage	23'7½'' x 17'7''	7.20 x 5.35
Family Room	12'9'' x 11'2''	3.90 x 3.40
Master Bed	14'9'' x 10'6''	4.50 x 3.20
Bed 2	10'6'' x 9'10''	3.20 x 3.00
Bed 3	11'2'' x 10'2''	3.40 x 3.10
Bed 4	8'6'' x 10'2''	2.60 x 3.10

DUNVEGAN

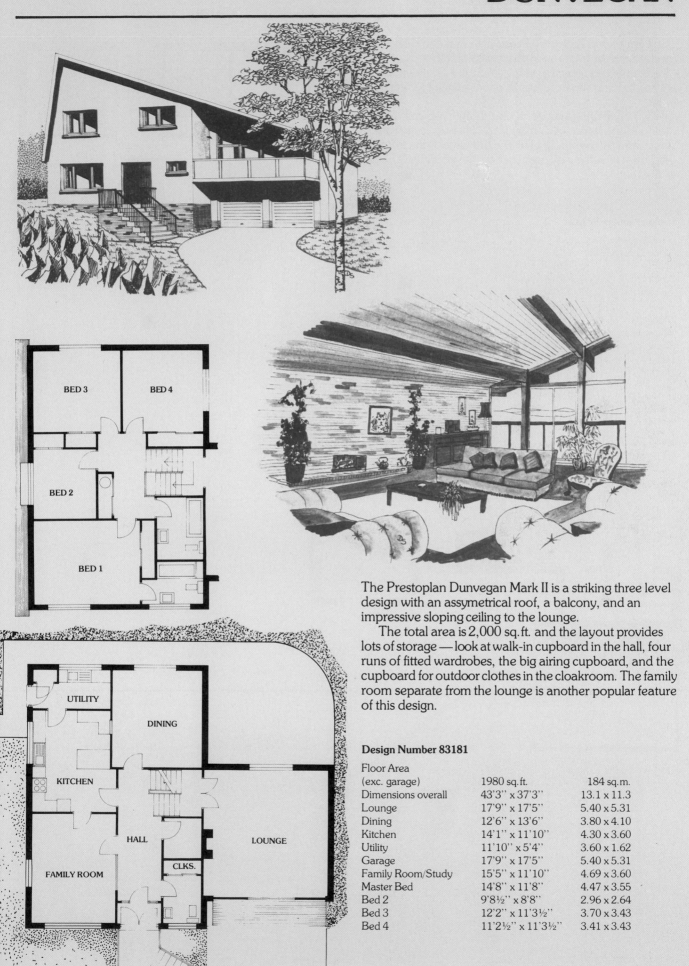

The Prestoplan Dunvegan Mark II is a striking three level design with an assymetrical roof, a balcony, and an impressive sloping ceiling to the lounge.

The total area is 2,000 sq. ft. and the layout provides lots of storage — look at walk-in cupboard in the hall, four runs of fitted wardrobes, the big airing cupboard, and the cupboard for outdoor clothes in the cloakroom. The family room separate from the lounge is another popular feature of this design.

Design Number 83181

Floor Area		
(exc. garage)	1980 sq. ft.	184 sq. m.
Dimensions overall	43'3'' x 37'3''	13.1 x 11.3
Lounge	17'9'' x 17'5''	5.40 x 5.31
Dining	12'6'' x 13'6''	3.80 x 4.10
Kitchen	14'1'' x 11'10''	4.30 x 3.60
Utility	11'10'' x 5'4''	3.60 x 1.62
Garage	17'9'' x 17'5''	5.40 x 5.31
Family Room/Study	15'5'' x 11'10''	4.69 x 3.60
Master Bed	14'8'' x 11'8''	4.47 x 3.55
Bed 2	9'8½'' x 8'8''	2.96 x 2.64
Bed 3	12'2'' x 11'3½''	3.70 x 3.43
Bed 4	11'2½'' x 11'3½''	3.41 x 3.43

HAMBLETON

The Hambleton design by Prestoplan makes it clear that modern timber frame construction can look as "traditional" as you can wish. Although it is shown here with a cladding of natural stone, it looks equally effective in brick.

Two interesting features to this design — a very large dining room, which can easily be divided up to give a study, and the grouping of all the drainage to the front of the house which is very useful when the ground falls away to the rear.

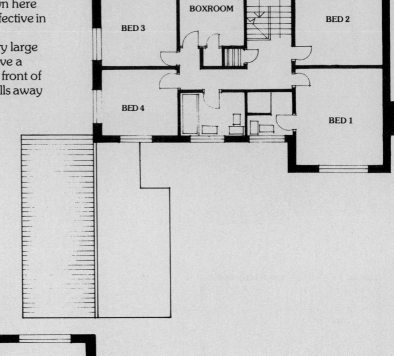

Design Number 83182

Floor Area (exc. garage)	1675 sq.ft.	155 sq.m.
Dimensions overall	45'10'' x 48'2''	13.9 x 14.6
Lounge	24'4'' x 12'4''	7.41 x 3.76
Dining	18'4'' x 11'0''	5.58 x 3.35
Kitchen	13'0'' x 9'0''	3.96 x 2.74
Utility	14'0'' x 6'6''	4.26 x 1.98
Garage	16'0'' x 17'0''	4.87 x 5.18
Master Bed	13'0'' x 12'4''	3.96 x 3.76
Bed 2	12'4'' x 11'0''	3.76 x 3.35
Bed 3	11'0'' x 10'0''	3.35 x 3.05
Bed 4	10'0'' x 9'0''	3.05 x 2.74
Boxroom/Bed 5	8'6'' x 8'0''	2.59 x 2.43

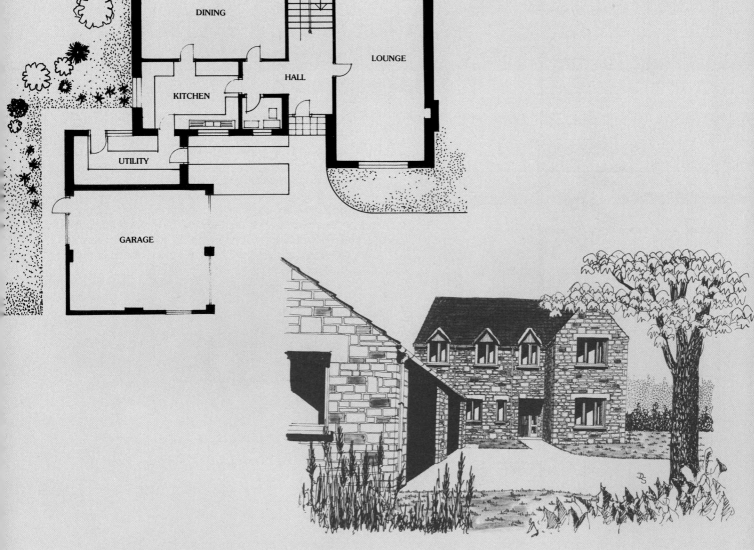

The Roundhay house by Prestoplan is a conventional executive home with an attractive Georgian style bow window to the lounge, and with matching french windows at the rear. The layout follows a well proven pattern and it shows clearly how well timber frame construction can adapt to traditional house styles.

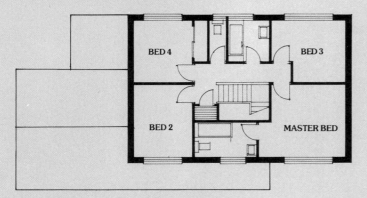

Design Number 83183

Floor Area (exc. garage)	1512 sq.ft.	140 sq.m.
Dimensions overall	52'3'' x 27'3''	15.9 x 8.3
Lounge/Dining (overall)	23'4'' x 21'8''	7.10 x 6.60
Kitchen	13'7'' x 9'10''	4.13 x 3.00
Study	7'9½'' x 9'10''	2.37 x 3.00
Utility	8'2'' x 7'5½''	2.50 x 2.27
Garage	16'8'' x 17'4½''	5.08 x 5.29
Master Bed	13'5½'' x 11'7''	4.10 x 3.54
Bed 2	11'7'' x 9'10''	3.54 x 3.00
Bed 3	11'6'' x 9'9''	3.50 x 2.97
Bed 4	9'10'' x 9'9''	3.00 x 2.97

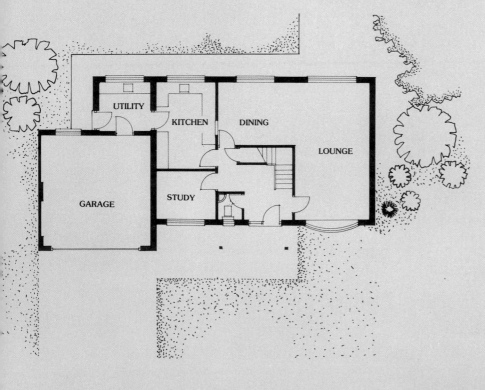

BEAUMONT

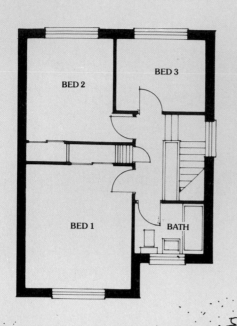

The Beaumont design by Prestoplan illustrates clearly how successfully a timber frame design can look completely traditional in every respect. This conventional house has a three bedroom layout that uses every last inch of floor area to the very best advantage, and still has room for a traditional larder — one reason why it is so often built as a farmhouse.

Note how the continuous run of cupboards between the master bedroom and the larger of the other two bedrooms is arranged to give the maximum of sound insulation.

Design Number 83184

Floor Area (exc. garage)	1026 sq.ft.	95 sq.m.
Dimensions overall	35'5'' x 29'5''	10.8 x 8.9
Lounge	11'10'' x 17'5''	3.60 x 5.31
Dining	9'10'' x 9'6½''	3.00 x 2.91
Kitchen (overall)	9'10'' x 9'10''	3.00 x 3.00
Garage (overall)	12'11½'' x 17'8½''	3.95 x 5.40
Master Bed	13'8'' x 11'10''	4.17 x 3.60
Bed 2	11'4'' x 9'6½''	3.45 x 2.91
Bed 3	9'10'' x 7'11''	3.00 x 2.40

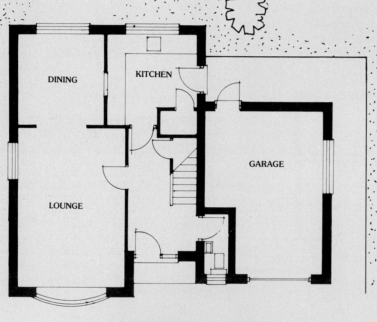

RIVINGTON

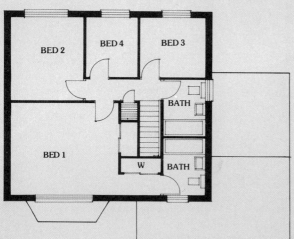

The Rivington Mk II house has a feature which many buying a new home feel they deserve but rarely find — a really big master bedroom with a dressing alcove and en suite bathroom in a house of only thirteen hundred square feet. If this is one of your priorities then this may be the design for you.

This is a Prestoplan design, and a timber frame kit is available for it. As with all timber frame homes it has a very high level of built in insulation.

Design Number 83185

Floor Area		
(exc. garage)	1328 sq.ft.	123 sq.m.
Dimensions overall	39'10" x 26'6"	12.1 x 8.0
Lounge	17'7½" x 12'9½"	5.37 x 3.90
Dining	10'8" x 11'6"	3.25 x 3.51
Kitchen	15'11" x 11'6"	4.86 x 3.51
Garage	21'8" x 10'8½"	6.60 x 3.26
Master Bed	15'0" x 12'9½"	4.58 x 3.90
Bed 2	11'6" x 10'1"	3.51 x 3.08
Bed 3	9'0" x 8'3"	2.74 x 2.52
Bed 4	8'3" x 7'2½"	2.52 x 2.20

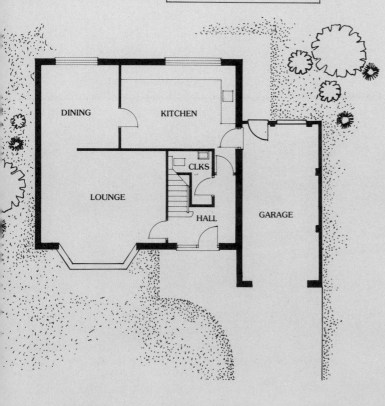

HAREWOOD

The Harewood is one of Prestoplan's larger houses, and follows a traditional design concept that is always popular. The large hall with its imposing staircase, the 25ft lounge, and the study placed well away from family distractions make it an ideal executive home, and it is a firm favourite as such. The first floor has plenty of cupboard space and generously sized bathrooms. It all adds up to the sort of home that is a top-of-the-market investment, always has been, and always will be.

Design Number 83186

Floor Area		
(exc. garage)	1620 sq.ft.	150 sq.m.
Dimensions overall	55'0'' x 27'5''	16.7 x 8.3
Lounge	13'9'' x 25'7''	4.20 x 7.80
Dining	11'6'' x 9'10''	3.50 x 3.00
Kitchen	9'4'' x 13'5½''	2.85 x 4.10
Study	9'4'' x 7'10½''	2.85 x 2.40
Utility	7'4½'' x 8'0''	2.25 x 2.43
Garage	18'0'' x 17'4½''	5.48 x 5.30
Master Bed	13'9'' x 13'5½''	4.20 x 4.10
Bed 2	9'4'' x 11'6''	2.85 x 3.50
Bed 3	13'9'' x 11'10''	4.20 x 3.60
Bed 4	9'4'' x 9'10''	2.85 x 3.00

GRANTLEY

This Prestoplan design follows a popular and successful formula for getting a four bedroomed house with an integral garage on a site with an overall width of only 50ft. The two gable windows of the larger bedrooms help to give the Earlswood the appearance of being larger than it really is, as do the twin windows in the lounge.

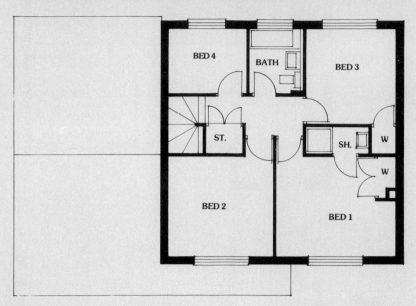

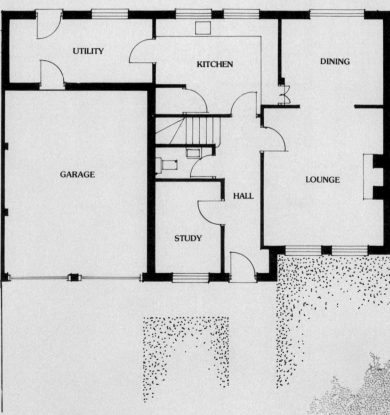

Design Number 83187

Floor Area (exc. garage)	1400 sq. ft.	130 sq.m.
Dimensions overall	43'0'' x 29'8½''	13.1 x 9.0
Lounge	15'1'' x 13'0''	4.60 x 3.96
Dining	9'6'' x 11'4''	2.90 x 3.45
Kitchen	13'6'' x 10'6''	4.10 x 3.20
Study	10'0'' x 7'0''	3.05 x 2.13
Utility	7'0'' x 15'9''	2.13 x 4.80
Garage	20'0'' x 15'9''	6.10 x 4.80
Master Bed	11'0'' x 13'0''	3.35 x 3.96
Bed 2	11'6'' x 11'0''	3.50 x 3.35
Bed 3	10'4'' x 9'10''	3.15 x 3.00
Bed 4	8'6'' x 7'3''	2.60 x 2.20

MILFORD

The Milford house is a Prestoplan design that incorporates projecting first floor bay windows that are now so much in fashion. The ground floor layout is straight-forward, with a larger study than usual which will appeal to those who work at home. On the first floor the room over the study has a large "walk-in" wardrobe which can be fitted out as a second en-suite bathroom if required. This arrangement is popular when a Grandparent shares a home with a family.

Design Number 83188

Floor Area (exc. garage)	1836 sq.ft.	170 sq.m.
Dimensions overall	62'8'' x 33'5''	19.1 x 10.1
Lounge	22'0'' x 13'0''	6.70 x 3.96
Dining	14'0'' x 12'0''	4.26 x 3.65
Kitchen	12'6'' x 10'6''	3.81 x 3.20
Study	11'0'' x 10'6''	3.35 x 3.20
Utility	10'0'' x 6'6''	3.05 x 1.98
Garage	17'0'' x 18'6''	5.18 x 5.64
Master Bed	14'0'' x 12'0''	4.26 x 3.65
Bed 2	13'0'' x 11'0''	3.96 x 3.35
Bed 3	12'9'' x 9'6''	3.88 x 2.89
Bed 4	12'9'' x 10'6''	3.88 x 3.20

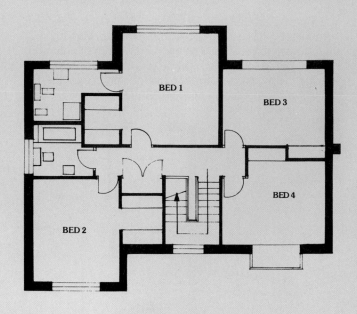

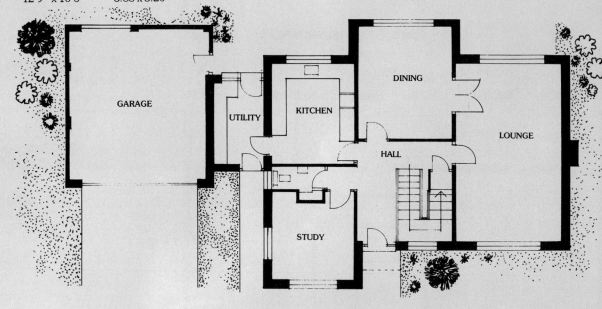

INVERNESS

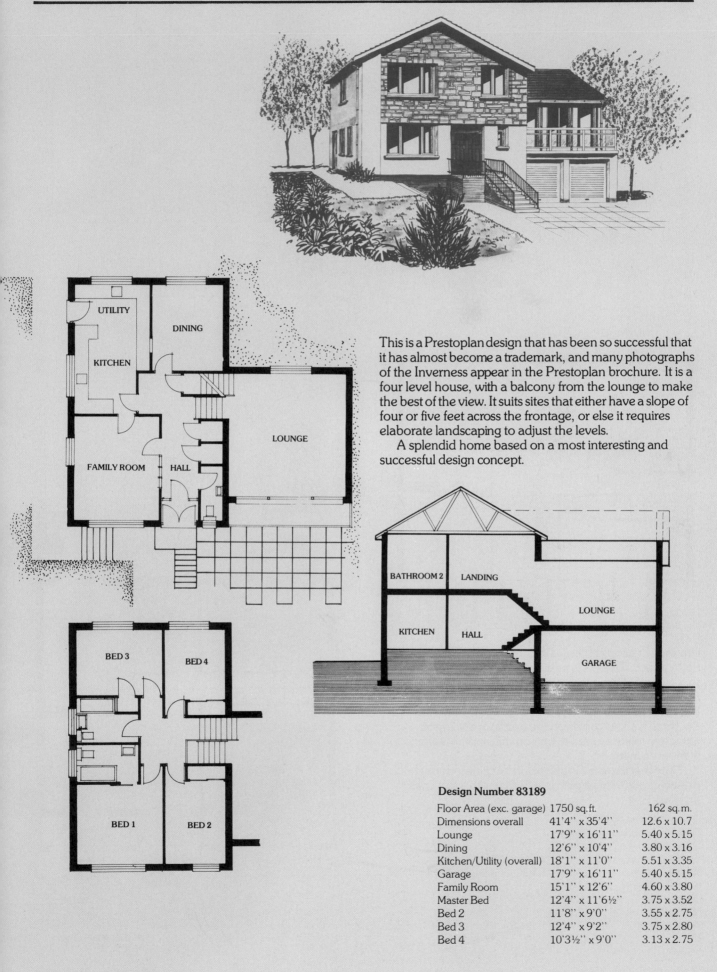

This is a Prestoplan design that has been so successful that it has almost become a trademark, and many photographs of the Inverness appear in the Prestoplan brochure. It is a four level house, with a balcony from the lounge to make the best of the view. It suits sites that either have a slope of four or five feet across the frontage, or else it requires elaborate landscaping to adjust the levels.

A splendid home based on a most interesting and successful design concept.

Design Number 83189

Floor Area (exc. garage)	1750 sq. ft.	162 sq. m.
Dimensions overall	41'4'' x 35'4''	12.6 x 10.7
Lounge	17'9'' x 16'11''	5.40 x 5.15
Dining	12'6'' x 10'4''	3.80 x 3.16
Kitchen/Utility (overall)	18'1'' x 11'0''	5.51 x 3.35
Garage	17'9'' x 16'11''	5.40 x 5.15
Family Room	15'1'' x 12'6''	4.60 x 3.80
Master Bed	12'4'' x 11'6½''	3.75 x 3.52
Bed 2	11'8'' x 9'0''	3.55 x 2.75
Bed 3	12'4'' x 9'2''	3.75 x 2.80
Bed 4	10'3½'' x 9'0''	3.13 x 2.75

BARDSEY

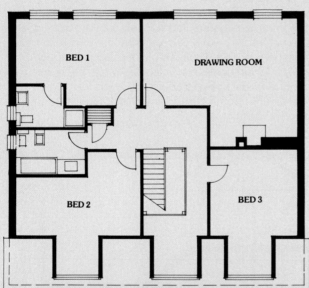

Another Prestoplan design with a thoroughly traditional appearance. This is a house for a site where the views are to the back of the home, and has the lounge/dining room, the kitchen, the first floor drawing room and the master bedroom all looking out to the rear. On the front elevation the three walk-in gables on the first floor are a most attractive feature, and the one on the landing is almost a little room in itself.

Note that there are fireplaces in both the lounge and the drawing room: this is our only design with a first floor fireplace!

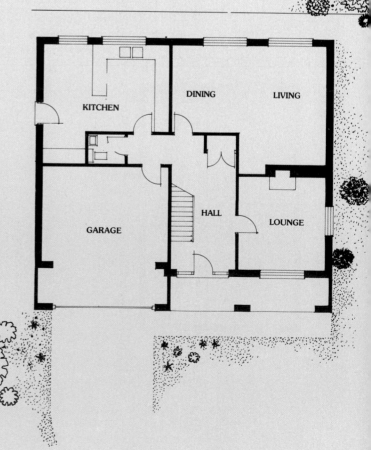

Design Number 83190

Floor Area (exc. garage)	2106 sq.ft.	195 sq.m.
Dimensions overall	40'2½'' x 37'3''	12.2 x 11.3
Lounge/Dining (overall)	21'1'' x 17'5''	6.41 x 5.30
Kitchen	17'1'' x 11'10''	5.20 x 3.60
Study	11'8'' x 12'7½''	3.55 x 3.85
Garage	17'1'' x 18'9''	5.20 x 5.70
Master Bed (overall)	17'1'' x 11'10''	5.20 x 3.60
Bed 2 (overall)	17'1'' x 11'4''	5.20 x 3.45
Bed 3	11'10'' x 11'4''	3.60 x 3.45
Drawing Room (overall)	21'1'' x 17'5''	6.41 x 5.30

STAFFORD

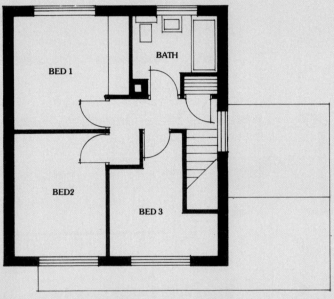

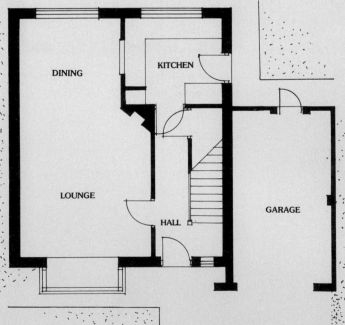

This compact Tudor style house has a lot of character and many features of a far larger home, with the corner fireplace and the bay window providing the potential for a really attractive period lounge decor. The half timbering suits either roughcast render or herringbone brick infill to the first floor walls, and there are many other options available to give this home exactly the regional style that suits a particular site.

Design Number 83191

Floor Area (exc. garage)	925 sq. ft.	86 sq. m.
Overall dimensions		
(inc. garage)	27'7'' x 31'8''	8.4 x 9.6
Lounge/Dining	23'5'' x 13'0''	7.14 x 3.96
Kitchen	9'6'' x 8'3''	2.89 x 2.51
Garage	17'0'' x 9'4''	5.18 x 2.85
Bed 1	11'2'' x 9'4''	3.40 x 2.85
Bed 2	9'0'' x 11'11½''	2.75 x 3.64
Bed 3 (overall)	10'6'' x 11'11½''	3.19 x 3.64

HUNTINGDON

This detached family house is particularly popular in country areas, and the porches at the doors, the corbelling under the eaves, and the pointed verges to the gables are features often called for by planners in rural situations, especially if there are older adjacent properties. As drawn here the Huntingdon requires a plot width of at least forty feet, but if the utility room is built at the back of the house, with the kitchen window in the side wall, it can be accommodated on a thirty-foot plot.

As with virtually all square designs with simple roofs, the roof can be turned so that there is a gable to the front, and in some infill situations this is very useful.

The internal layout is straightforward and practical, with a small hall that is lit from a window above the stairs which helps it to feel larger than it really is.

The Huntingdon is a particularly economical design, and has often been built at very low costs per square foot although there is nothing "budget" about it at all.

Design Number 83192

Area (exc. porch and utility which can be varied)	1036 sq.ft.	96 sq.m.
Overall (as illustrated)	33'11" x 25'0"	10.34 x 7.64
Lounge	14'5" x 11'6"	4.40 x 3.51
Dining	10'1" x 11'6"	3.07 x 3.50
Kitchen	12'0" x 11'6"	3.60 x 3.50
Bed 1	13'5" x 12'4"	4.08 x 3.75
Bed 2	12'4" x 10'8"	3.75 x 3.26
Bed 3	8'6" x 9'0"	2.59 x 2.75

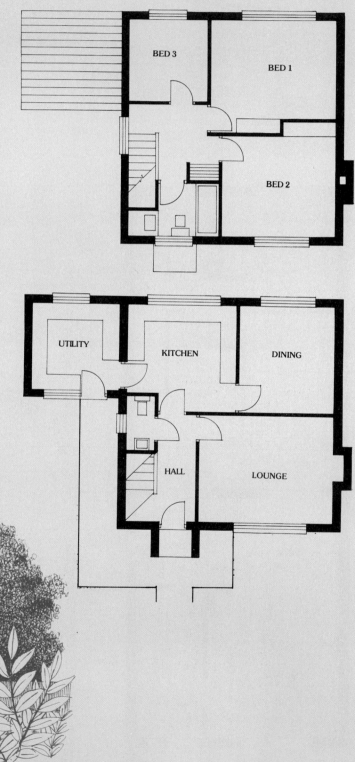

GRAFHAM

This is a very popular design in rural areas and combines a practical layout with low construction costs and a cottage appearance that goes down well with the Planners. It is shown here together with our garage type G.28, which is in the same style.

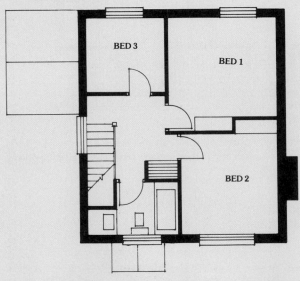

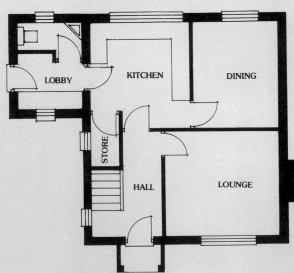

Design Number 83193

Floor Area	1011 sq.ft.	94 sq.m.
Overall dimensions	25'3'' x 30'2''	7.7 x 9.1
Lounge	12'6½'' x 11'7½''	3.82 x 3.54
Dining	9'0'' x 11'6''	2.74 x 3.50
Kitchen	11'0'' x 11'6''	3.35 x 3.50
Bed 1	11'5'' x 12'4''	3.48 x 3.75
Bed 2	10'4'' x 10'9½''	3.15 x 3.29
Bed 3	8'7'' x 8'6''	2.61 x 2.58

SHARNBROOK

Dormer bungalows are not nearly as popular now as they were twenty years ago, but the Sharnbrook is really more of a traditional Bedfordshire cottage than a bungalow. No cottage with a purlin roof and four gable windows is going to be built at a low unit cost, but this design does give a very effective way of getting less than 1100 sq.ft. of compact living accommodation on a minimum site width of only 32 feet.

The first floor landing is lit by a side window, which always has the effect of helping the home to look larger than it is. This is particularly true when the stairs are a feature of an interestingly shaped hall as in this case.

The Sharnbrook has been built as a farm cottage on occasion, with the utility room reduced in size to just a porch, giving the living room of a kitchen that suits people who work on the land. Another option would be to build an external utility room porch at the back door; we have never done this, but it would not present any problems.

Design Number 83194

Floor Area (exc. garage)	1004 sq.ft.	93 sq.m.
Dimensions overall	26'0'' x 29'2½''	7.92 x 8.90
Lounge		5.40 x 3.63
Dining		3.63 x 2.54
Kitchen		3.63 x 3.97
Master Bed		5.50 x 3.03
Bed 2		3.03 x 2.70

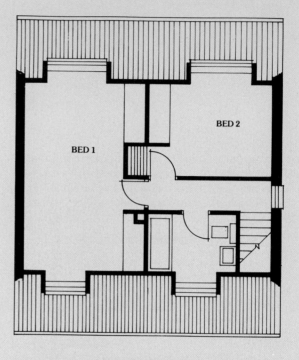

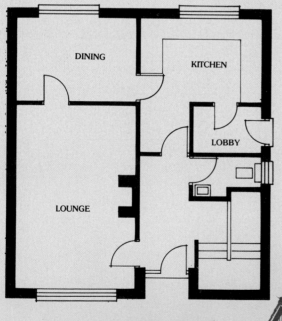

A three bedroom cottage with the same appearance and overall dimensions as the Sharnbrook is the Buckingham, reference 82194.

RUSHDEN

This useful design originated in a Bedfordshire village where the planners required gables above all first floor windows — there are three more gable windows on the rear elevation — with a complex roof line to fit in with neighbouring Victorian buildings.

The layout is particularly roomy for a three bedroomed design of only 1140 sq. ft. and has the feel of a much larger property. The hall is lit from a window on the half landing so the front door does not need a glazed screen — something that is often inescapable in compact designs, but which does not have the period feel of the Rushden house.

A shower or bidet can be fitted into the bathroom with only the minimum of alteration, and provided that the drains can be taken around the right hand side of the house, the drainage arrangements are economically grouped together. There are no significant windows in either side walls as far as the building regulations are concerned, and either wall can be built within three feet of a boundary.

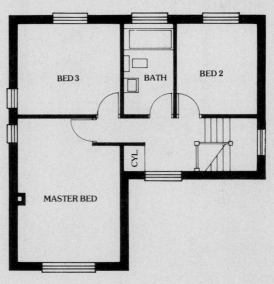

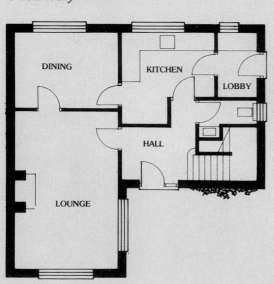

Design Number 83195

Floor Area	1130 sq.ft.	105 sq.m.
Dimensions overall	29'0'' x 28'7½''	8.82 x 8.72
Lounge	18'1½'' x 11'7''	5.52 x 3.54
Dining	11'7'' x 8'4''	3.54 x 2.54
Kitchen (overall)	10'3'' x 10'3½''	3.11 x 3.12
Master Bed	16'3'' x 11'7''	4.95 x 3.54
Bed 2	9'3'' x 10'3''	2.82 x 3.11
Bed 3	11'7'' x 10'3''	3.54 x 3.11

FAIRFORD

A neat compact house which looks equally well on a narrow site or when set in a large garden. The three different roof lines give it the appearance of a much larger property, and this is the sort of design which is always a very good investment in terms of the building cost/market value ratio.

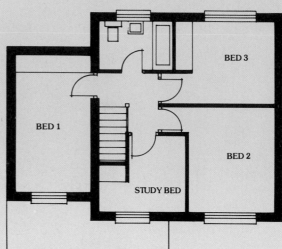

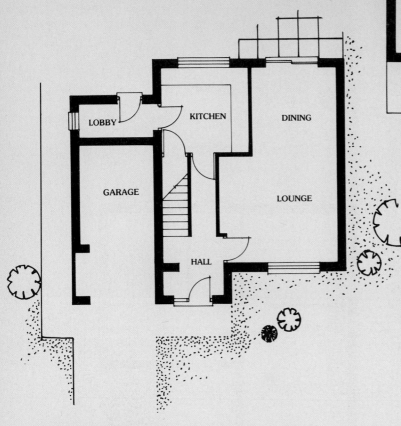

Design Number 83196

Floor Area (exc. garage)	1054 sq.ft.	98 sq.m.
Overall dimensions	25'6'' x 31'6''	7.7 x 9.6
Lounge/Dining (overall)	22'0'' x 13'6''	6.70 x 4.10
Kitchen	10'0'' x 9'8''	3.05 x 2.94
Lobby	4'1'' x 8'9''	1.24 x 2.67
Garage	17'0'' x 8'9''	5.18 x 2.67
Bed 1	15'10½'' x 8'9''	4.84 x 2.67
Bed 2	9'10'' x 12'0''	3.00 x 3.66
Bed 3	9'10'' x 9'8''	3.00 x 2.94
Study Bed (overall)	9'10'' x 8'9''	3.00 x 2.66

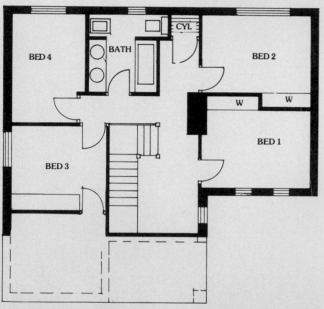

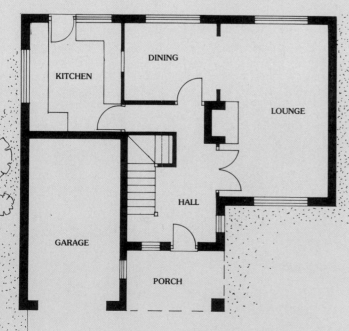

This two storey house has the look of a dormer bungalow, but it has a trussed rafter roof which keeps down costs. If it is to be built on a site of restricted width a dormer window may have to be put in the roof to light the third bedroom, but it can fit under the wallplate and avoids purlin construction.

The high window in the hall which extends up to the landing is a striking feature.

Design Number 83197

Floor Area	1097 sq.ft.	102 sq.m.
Overall dimensions	34'6'' x 31'6½''	10.5 x 9.6
Lounge	12'0'' x 19'0''	3.65 x 5.79
Dining	10'0'' x 8'8½''	3.05 x 2.65
Kitchen	12'0'' x 10'0''	3.65 x 3.05
Garage	17'0'' x 10'0''	5.18 x 3.05
Bed 1	12'0'' x 8'6''	3.65 x 2.59
Bed 2	12'0'' x 8'6''	3.65 x 2.59
Bed 3	10'6'' x 7'6½''	3.20 x 2.30
Bed 4	12'0'' x 8'0''	3.65 x 2.43

COTSWOLD

This design takes its name from the part of the country where it will be most at home, but it is in a style that is part of the tradition of all the English countryside. The original was built by a client of D & M Limited in 1982, in the Cotswolds, and was relatively cost effective in spite of the complex front elevation. One reason is that the span of 22ft 10'' is relatively modest, although the Architect did have to arrange for all the first floor walls between the bedrooms to be built in solid blockwork as this was part of the client's brief. Incidentally, the Planners were most enthusiastic about it.

There was a spiral staircase in the original design, although we have shown more conventional stairs in the plan on these pages. Whether you prefer this, or think winding stairs would be more fun, the staircase will certainly be a key feature and merits a great deal of thought. The hall is large enough to hold a number of pieces of furniture, and choice of staircase should really be made after considering how you intend to furnish the hall. An oak staircase to match a small oak refectory table would be a very appropriate combination.

The first floor arrangement is quite conventional, although some would wish to turn the en suite shower room into a larger bathroom at the expense of the fourth bedroom. A bigger cylinder cupboard may also be required by some, and there is room for this if the bathroom door is moved to the right.

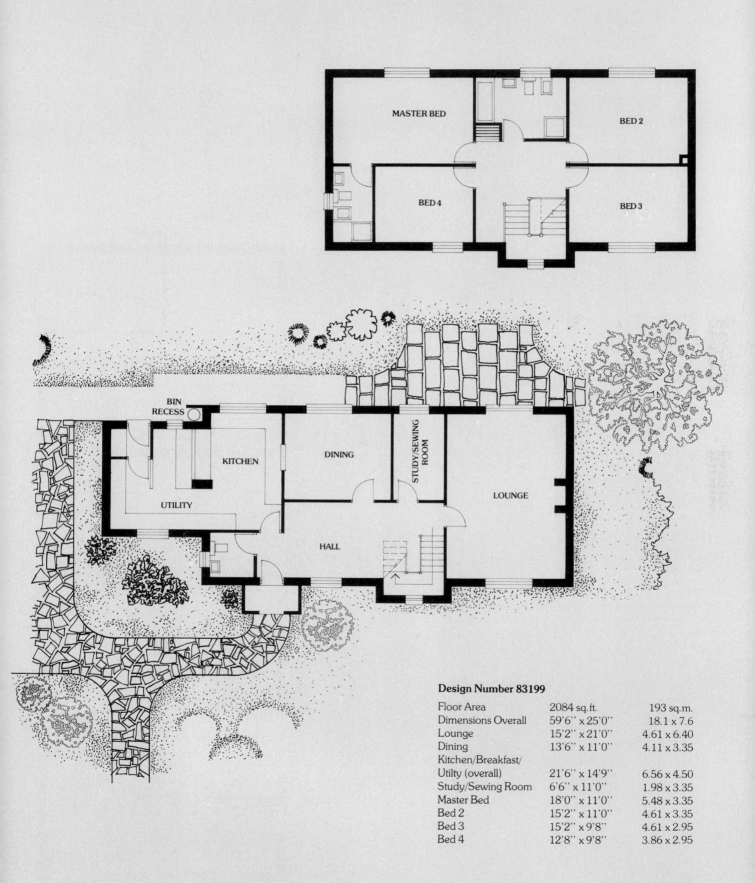

MASTER BED

BED 2

BED 4

BED 3

BIN
RECESS

KITCHEN

DINING

STUDY/SEWING
ROOM

LOUNGE

UTILITY

HALL

Design Number 83199

Floor Area	2084 sq.ft.	193 sq.m.
Dimensions Overall	59'6'' x 25'0''	18.1 x 7.6
Lounge	15'2'' x 21'0''	4.61 x 6.40
Dining	13'6'' x 11'0''	4.11 x 3.35
Kitchen/Breakfast/		
Utilty (overall)	21'6'' x 14'9''	6.56 x 4.50
Study/Sewing Room	6'6'' x 11'0''	1.98 x 3.35
Master Bed	18'0'' x 11'0''	5.48 x 3.35
Bed 2	15'2'' x 11'0''	4.61 x 3.35
Bed 3	15'2'' x 9'8''	4.61 x 2.95
Bed 4	12'8'' x 9'8''	3.86 x 2.95

PETERBOROUGH

The Peterborough house is a good example of a design concept that is useful on sites where the important views are to the sides and rear, and not to the front. With only two bedrooms in 1150 sq.ft. it has many features of a much larger home, with a very large 'L' shaped living area and a hall that is lit from a gallery window above.

The storage arrangements are very generous, with a cloakroom that has plenty of room for golf bags and the other things usually forgotten by those who design houses. There is also a big walk-in cylinder cupboard, large fitted wardrobes, and plenty of space in the utility room.

The bathroom has plenty of room for any combination of fittings.

Design Number 83200

Floor Area	1156 sq.ft.	107 sq.m.
Dimensions Overall	31'11'' x 25'3½''	9.73 x 7.70
Lounge	18'0'' x 11'0''	5.48 x 3.35
Dining	9'2'' x 12'1''	2.79 x 3.68
Kitchen/Breakfast	12'2'' x 12'1''	3.69 x 3.68
Utility	10'5'' x 7'7''	3.18 x 2.30
Master Bed	13'5'' x 11'5''	4.09 x 3.48
Bed 2	8'0'' x 9'9''	2.43 x 2.96

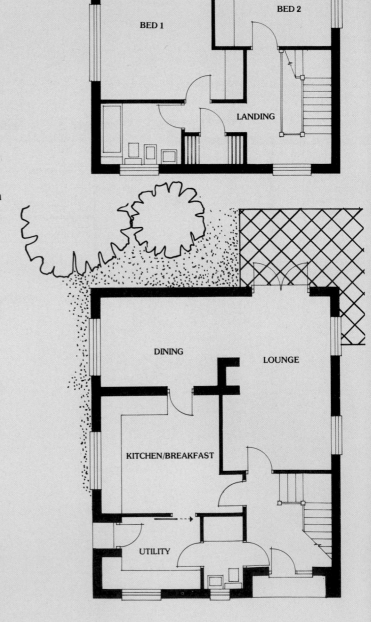

Design Number 83201

Floor Area (exc. garage)	1738 sq.ft.	161 sq.m.
Dimensions Overall	54'4'' x 35'8''	16.55 x 10.87
Lounge	23'4'' x 16'0''	7.11 x 4.90
Dining Hall	19'8'' x 11'6''	6.00 x 3.50
Kitchen/Breakfast	10'6'' x 23'4''	3.20 x 7.11
Utility	10'6'' x 7'8''	3.20 x 2.35
Garage (overall)	19'8'' x 23'4''	6.01 x 7.11
Master Bed	13'6'' x 11'5''	4.15 x 3.50
Bed 2	11'5'' x 11'6''	3.50 x 3.51
Bed 3	10'6'' x 15'5''	3.20 x 4.66

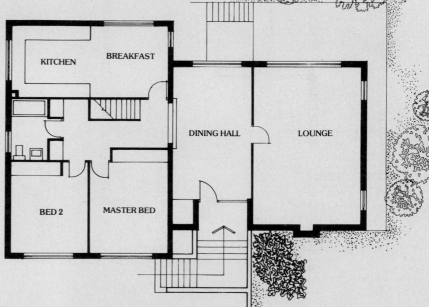

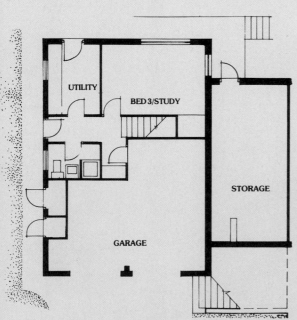

This design for a sloping site has a flight of steps leading up to the front door. It is most important that these should be as generous in width as possible, with the quarter landing carefully integrated into the landscaping.

The front door leads straight into a dining hall — a feature which is gaining popularity. There are two bedrooms on the upper floor, and a complete self contained study/bedroom, utility/kitchen and shower below. As originally designed this was accommodation for an au pair, but it can be put to many uses, including a granny flat if granny can manage the stairs.

OAKHILL

This is a design for a sloping site where there is at least 8ft. of difference in height between the garage floor level and the front door step.

In our illustration and the plan we have not shown any access onto the flat garage roof, which permits a much cheaper specification than is the case if it were to be used as a balcony. This is something that has to be cleared when a building regulation application is made, and an early decision has to be made whether or not you want french windows opening out onto the garage roof.

If you are building this house it is most important to make sure that the steps to the main entrance are really impressive so that the garage door does not dominate the front of the building. This is easily arranged, and can be quite economical.

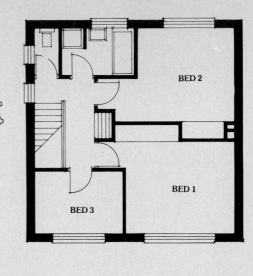

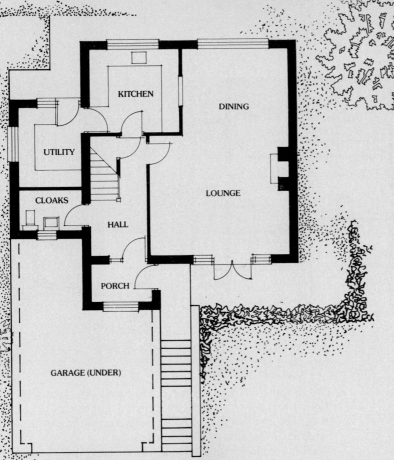

Design Number 83202

Floor Area (exc. garage)	1188 sq.ft.	110 sq.m.
Dimensions overall	50'2½'' x 33'0''	15.3 x 10.0
Lounge/Dining (overall)	15'9½'' x 23'5''	4.81 x 7.14
Kitchen	10'4½'' x 9'4''	3.15 x 2.90
Utility	7'3'' x 8'6''	2.21 x 2.59
Garage	19'0'' x 15'5½''	5.79 x 4.71
Master Bed	12'4½'' x 10'4''	3.76 x 3.14
Bed 2	11'1½'' x 10'10''	3.39 x 3.30
Bed 3	10'0'' x 7'0½''	3.04 x 2.15

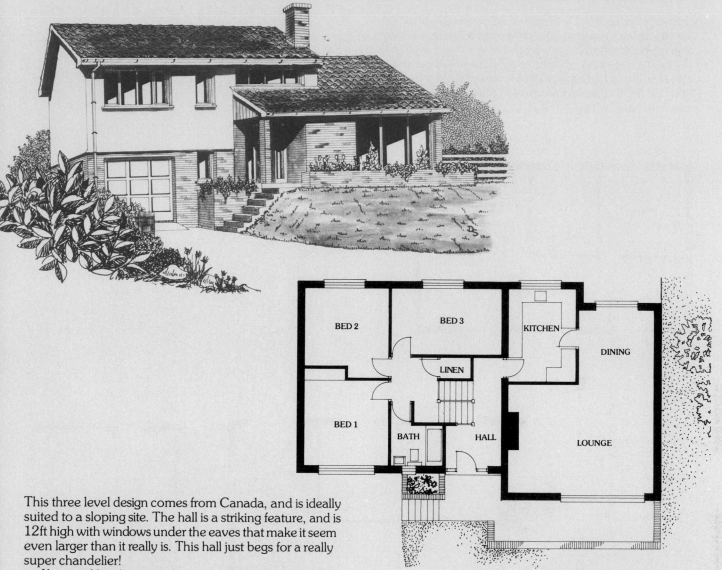

This three level design comes from Canada, and is ideally suited to a sloping site. The hall is a striking feature, and is 12ft high with windows under the eaves that make it seem even larger than it really is. This hall just begs for a really super chandelier!

If ground levels permit the store adjacent to the garage can have its own window and even become an extra bedroom, perhaps with the workshop as a second bathroom. This would be under the main bathroom, which gives an economical drainage arrangement. If you want to do this, it is important to discuss it all with us first, as some re-arrangement is necessary to meet fire regulations.

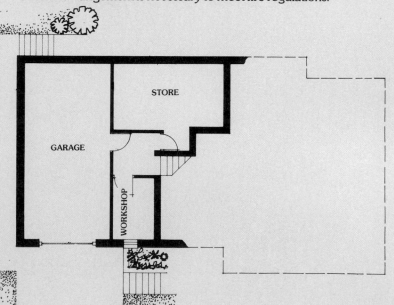

Design Number 83203

Floor Area (exc. garage)	1560 sq. ft.	145 sq. m.
Dimensions overall	50'5'' x 30'3''	15.3 x 9.2
Lounge/Dining (overall)	19'10'' x 25'6''	6.04 x 7.77
Kitchen	13'0'' x 9'6''	3.96 x 2.89
Playroom/Storage (overall)	15'6'' x 9'4''	4.72 x 2.85
Garage	25'3½'' x 12'0''	7.71 x 3.65
Workshop	6'0'' x 8'8''	1.83 x 2.65
Master Bed	12'0'' x 12'0''	3.65 x 3.65
Bed 2	12'0'' x 11'0''	3.65 x 3.35
Bed 3	15'6'' x 9'4''	4.72 x 2.85

QUEENSGATE

Some of the leading Development Companies claim that it was they who pioneered the return to traditional cottage styles, and that Architects followed where they had shown the way. True or not, this attractive cottage design was commissioned by Queensgate Homes of Maidenhead for their Boyn Hill development in 1978, and was a tremendous success.

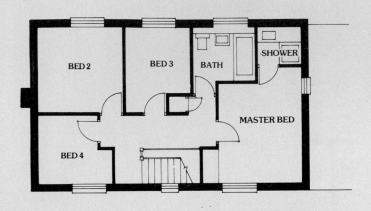

Design Number 83204

Floor Area (exc. garage)	1184 sq.ft.	110 sq.m.
Overall dimensions	54'4" x 19'9½"	16.5 x 6.0
Lounge	11'6" x 17'11"	3.50 x 5.47
Dining	8'9" x 10'10"	2.67 x 3.30
Kitchen	9'4" x 10'10"	2.85 x 3.30
Utility	5'11" x 8'5"	1.80 x 2.57
Workshop	5'11" x 8'9"	1.80 x 2.67
Garage	17'10" x 16'2½"	5.43 x 4.94
Master Bed (overall)	9'5" x 13'4"	2.87 x 4.07
Bed 2	9'10" x 9'10"	3.00 x 3.00
Bed 3	7'6" x 7'6"	2.29 x 2.30
Bed 4	7'10" x 8'6"	2.39 x 2.60

Queensgate Homes
Tectonic Place, Holyport Rd
Maidenhead, Berkshire SL6 3EZ.

CHEVINGTON

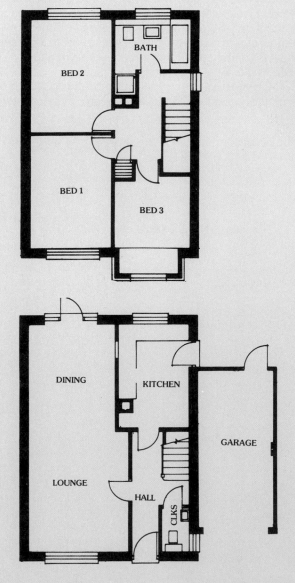

This interesting detached house was designed by architect Mike Wigmore of Kevin Neary Associates for the Pimblett Self-Build Housing Association in Hertfordshire, and has some very interesting features. The Housing Association members built their homes with provision in the roof for either one or two more bedrooms to be added at a later date. Roof lights, gable windows and appropriate floor joists were all built in ready for another staircase to be installed and the third floor fitted out whenever the owner wished.

Design Number 83205

Floor Area	936 sq. ft.	87 sq.m.
Dimensions overall	27'9'' x 28'6½''	8.45 x 8.7
Lounge/Dining (overall)	11'4'' x 25'11''	3.45 x 7.90
Kitchen	7'10½'' x 11'10''	2.40 x 3.60
Garage	17'11'' x 8'6''	5.46 x 2.60
Bed 1	9'0'' x 12'10''	2.74 x 3.90
Bed 2	9'0'' x 12'10''	2.74 x 3.90
Bed 3	8'2½'' x 8'6''	2.50 x 2.60

Michael J. Wigmore, Reg. Arch.
Kevin Neary Associates
Broadway North, Pitsea
Basildon, Essex SS13 3AY.

MALVERN

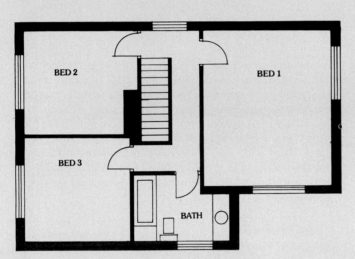

This interesting design is shown in a large garden, but is also very well suited to a narrow site. If necessary it can fit on a plot only 30ft. wide, in which case the bathroom window would be moved from the side wall to a position above the vanity unit. This sort of minor alteration is made to our plans as a matter of routine.

The layout dictates a small hall and landing, which permits an unusually large master bedroom for a house of this size.

A four bedroom version of this design is the Bromyard, reference 82206.

Design Number 83206

Floor Area	1160 sq.ft.	108 sq.m.
Overall dimensions	24'10'' x 35'5''	7.5 x 10.7
Lounge/Dining (overall)	23'0'' x 12'6''	7.01 x 3.80
Kitchen	7'0'' x 11'2''	2.13 x 3.40
Garage	17'0'' x 9'6''	5.18 x 2.89
Bed 1	17'4'' x 14'0''	5.27 x 4.25
Bed 2	11'4'' x 12'6''	3.45 x 3.80
Bed 3	11'4'' x 11'6''	3.45 x 3.50

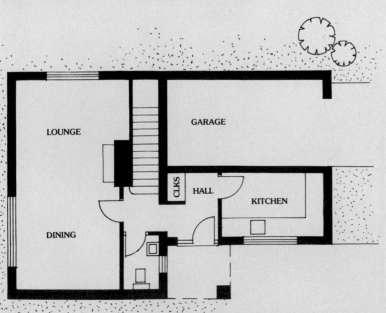

HALSTEAD

This three bedroom house has a square ground floor plan and can be built with an integral garage at either side. It is illustrated here with a window in the gable end to give light in the loft, and to add character to the design. This particular feature suits a house with a roof at a fairly steep pitch. If the roof pitch is dropped it is practicable to put the garage on the other side, as the garage roof ridge is then below the level of the landing window.

Design Number 83207

Floor Area (exc. garage)	1000 sq. ft.	93 sq. m.
Overall size		
(inc. garage)	43'6'' x 25'3''	13.2 x 7.7
Lounge/Dining	23'5'' x 12'4''	7.14 x 3.75
Kitchen	11'6'' x 7'10''	3.50 x 2.38
Garage	17'0'' x 18'6½''	5.18 x 5.65
Bed 1	11'6'' x 12'4''	3.50 x 3.75
Bed 2	9'11½'' x 11'0''	3.03 x 3.35
Bed 3	11'6'' x 7'10''	3.50 x 2.38

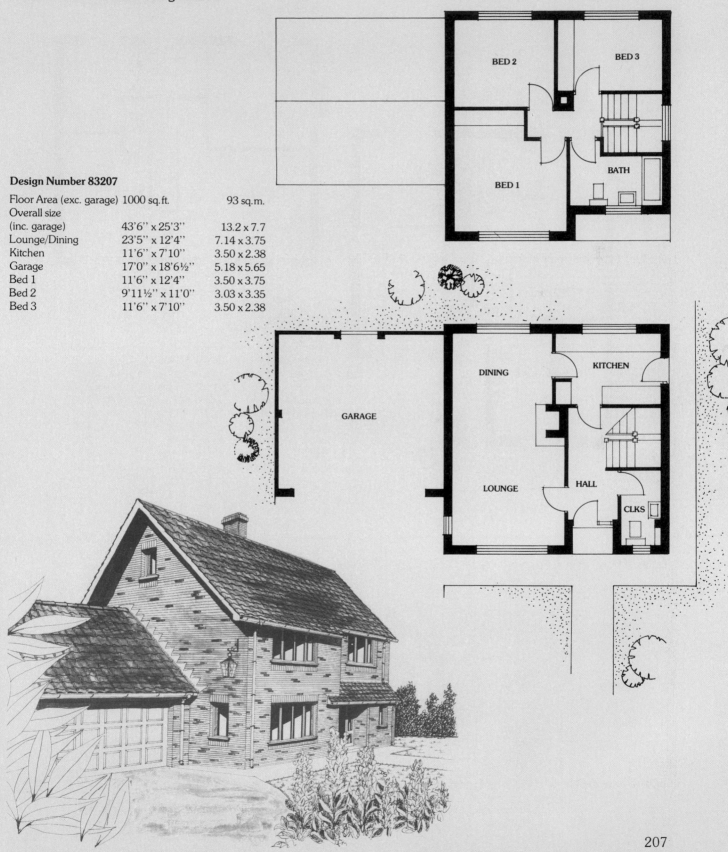

VENTNOR

It is surprising how often our clients insist that a new home should be designed with a large downstairs bedroom for an invalid or elderly parent. This design was drawn to meet this requirement and is shown with a bay window in the room in question. Alternatively, windows can be put in either of the side walls, and the whole of this bedroom accommodation can be re-arranged to suit particular requirements.

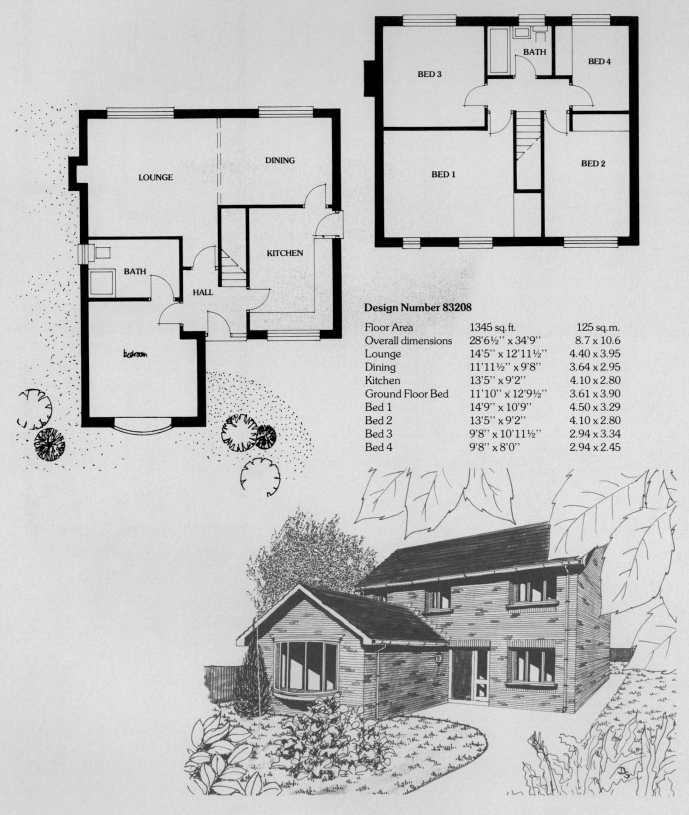

Design Number 83208

Floor Area	1345 sq.ft.	125 sq.m.
Overall dimensions	28'6½'' x 34'9''	8.7 x 10.6
Lounge	14'5'' x 12'11½''	4.40 x 3.95
Dining	11'11½'' x 9'8''	3.64 x 2.95
Kitchen	13'5'' x 9'2''	4.10 x 2.80
Ground Floor Bed	11'10'' x 12'9½''	3.61 x 3.90
Bed 1	14'9'' x 10'9''	4.50 x 3.29
Bed 2	13'5'' x 9'2''	4.10 x 2.80
Bed 3	9'8'' x 10'11½''	2.94 x 3.34
Bed 4	9'8'' x 8'0''	2.94 x 2.45

WHITTINGTON

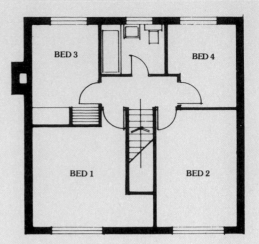

The Whittington house can be built on a site with a frontage of only thirty feet, although it would completely fill the plot and this may not be acceptable to the planners. It is a particularly valuable design where the actual plot is wider, but only a thirty foot strip of it can be built on.

The design is illustrated here with a flat roof and porch, and in most urban situations this is acceptable. If it is not, drawings are available for it to be built with a tiled garage roof.

The large lounge lends itself to many window arrangements, and if required it can be linked with the kitchen by an arch to give open-plan living. Fitting four sensibly sized bedrooms into this modest overall area means using a glazed area over a door to light the upstairs landing, and a storey height door casing is usually specified for the bathroom door for this purpose.

Design Number 83209

Area (inc. garage)	1200 sq. ft.	111 sq.m.
Overall	34'8'' x 25'1''	10.56 x 7.64
Lounge	23'5'' x 13'0''	7.14 x 3.96
Kitchen	13'5'' x 9'2''	4.10 x 2.80
Bed 1	11'6'' x 10'9''	3.50 x 3.29
Bed 2	13'5'' x 9'2''	4.10 x 2.80
Bed 3	9'8'' x 7'8''	2.94 x 2.34
Bed 4	9'8'' x 8'0''	2.94 x 2.45

KENMORE

Most detached houses of 1200 sq. ft. have four bedrooms, but there is a steady demand for three bedroomed houses of this size with larger-than-average rooms and generous bathrooms. The Kenmore design is one answer to this requirement. The layout provides a particularly large first floor landing, with room for a desk or sewing table at the landing window.

The prototype of this design was built at Tamworth by a client who used sub-contractors and managed the work himself. He achieved very low cost per square foot figures, and we have details of this particular job with a full cost breakdown available on request.

Design Number 83210

Floor Area (exc. garage)	1215 sq. ft.	113 sq.m.
Dimensions overall	48'11'' x 26'9''	14.9 x 8.1
Lounge	20'6'' x 11'4½''	6.24 x 3.47
Dining	11'1½'' x 9'0''	3.39 x 2.74
Kitchen	12'1½'' x 9'0''	3.69 x 2.75
Utility	7'0½'' x 5'11''	2.15 x 1.80
Garage	16'9½'' x 16'2''	5.11 x 4.92
Master Bed	13'1'' x 11'4½''	3.99 x 3.47
Bed 2	12'0'' x 9'0''	3.65 x 2.74
Bed 3	9'5'' x 7'0½''	2.87 x 2.15

ROSSENDALE

This design for a suburban house is only 1400 sq.ft. and has the appearance of being a much larger home. Note that there is no back door, and the window arrangements enable the Rossendale to be built close to the back boundary. There are two separate arrangements within this design concept: one has a downstairs bedroom with its own bathroom, which is a very suitable arrangement for an invalid or elderly person. Alternatively, the kitchen moves to the back of the house, with a utility room replacing the downstairs bathroom.

Design Number 83211

Floor Area	1400 sq.ft.	130 sq.m.
Dimensions overall	40'6'' x 23'0''	12.3 x 7.0
Lounge	17'10'' x 16'5''	5.44 x 5.00
Dining	11'7'' x 10'5''	3.54 x 3.18
Kitchen	13'1½'' x 9'2''	4.00 x 2.80
Master Bed	17'10'' x 13'1½''	5.44 x 4.00
Bed 2	16'8'' x 9'4''	5.08 x 2.84
Bed 3	13'1½'' x 9'6''	4.00 x 2.90

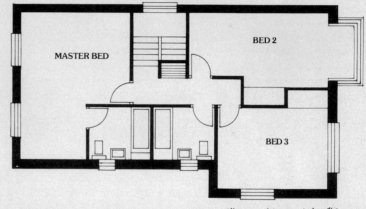

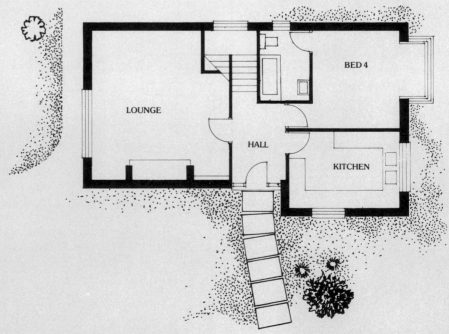

TONBRIDGE

Houses with all round views often have a lounge which runs from front to back, looking out in both directions. Here is a house with this advantage enjoyed by the kitchen as well. This feature, together with the utility room and cloakroom at the back door have made it very popular as a farmhouse.

The Tonbridge is illustrated here with a simple canopy porch to the front door, but this can be altered to conform to any local style, and of course, the house can be built with a gable roof instead of hips if this is more appropriate.

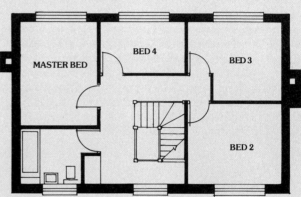

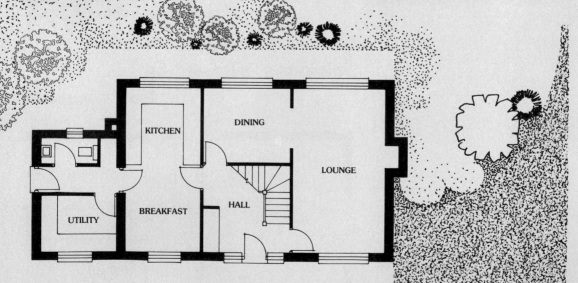

Design Number 83212

Floor Area	1285 sq.ft.	119 sq.m.
Dimensions overall	42'5'' x 20'10''	12.9 x 6.3
Lounge	19'3'' x 11'0''	5.79 x 3.35
Dining	10'0'' x 9'0''	3.04 x 2.74
Kitchen	9'0'' x 9'0''	2.74 x 2.74
Utility	9'0'' x 6'6''	2.74 x 1.98
Breakfast Room	9'0'' x 9'9''	2.74 x 2.98
Master Bed	12'0'' x 9'0''	3.65 x 2.74
Bed 2	11'0'' x 9'8''	3.35 x 2.94
Bed 3	11'0'' x 9'0''	3.35 x 2.74
Bed 4	10'0'' x 6'1''	3.04 x 1.84

FERNDALE

The Ferndale house has a very practical and cost effective layout for a wide site, and it can be built with either the gable roof shewn in the illustration, or with a hip roof. It is illustrated here in brick with render to part of the front elevation, but it can be built with any walling material.

If a fireplace is required the first floor layout restricts it to being positioned in the gable wall of the lounge.

A straightforward design that looks well in both rural and suburban settings.

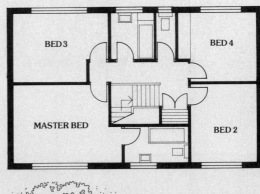

Design Number 83213

Floor Area (exc. garage)	1675 sq.ft.	155 sq.m.
Dimensions overall	54'10½'' x 30'5''	16.73 x 9.27
Lounge/Dining (overall)	21'7'' x 25'3''	6.59 x 7.78
Kitchen/Breakfast (overall)	13'5'' x 18'2''	4.09 x 5.54
Utility	8'8'' x 6'10''	2.65 x 2.70
Study	7'10½'' x 9'4½''	2.40 x 2.86
Garage	19'0'' x 16'11''	5.76 x 5.15
Master Bed	15'10'' x 11'5½''	4.84 x 3.49
Bed 2	11'5½'' x 9'4½''	3.49 x 2.86
Bed 3	13'11'' x 9'10''	4.24 x 3.00
Bed 4	9'4½'' x 9'10''	2.86 x 3.00

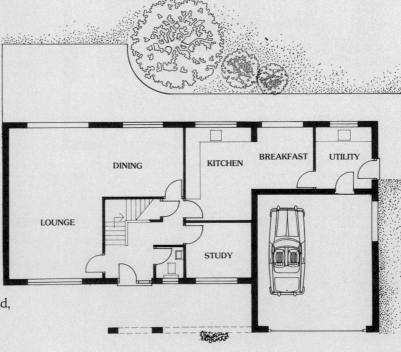

A five bedroom version of this design is the Lingfield, reference 82213.

ALDERWOOD

This is a house for those who want big rooms, and who are happy with a smaller hall and landing to make this possible in a home of only 1500 sq. ft. The bedrooms are exactly the same size as the rooms below, so that all the first floor walls are in solid blockwork with excellent sound insulation. A very solid house this, for solid citizens with a no-nonsense approach and a liking for generously proportioned rooms — all ceilings are 8'6'' high.

Design Number 83214

Floor Area (exc. garage)	1440 sq. ft.	134 sq. m.
Dimensions overall	43'3'' x 34'2½''	13.1 x 10.4
Lounge	13'0'' x 19'0''	3.96 x 5.80
Dining	13'0'' x 13'0''	3.96 x 3.96
Kitchen (overall)	16'5'' x 8'0''	5.00 x 2.43
Study	10'0'' x 8'6''	3.05 x 2.59
Garage	17'0'' x 11'2½''	5.18 x 3.41
Bed 1	13'0'' x 19'0''	3.96 x 5.80
Bed 2	13'0'' x 13'0''	3.96 x 3.96
Bed 3	10'0'' x 8'6''	3.05 x 2.59

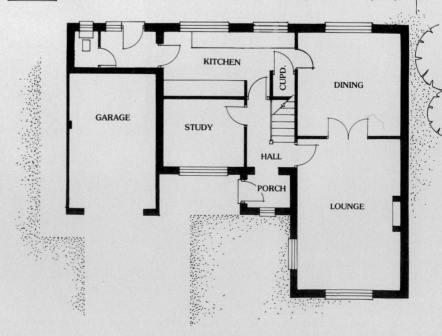

WESTBURY

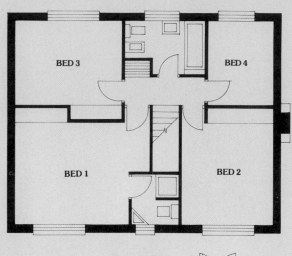

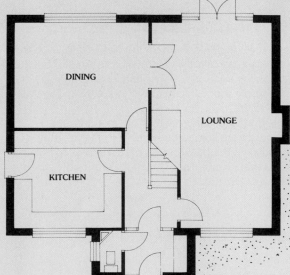

The Westbury design with its prominent gable features will suit many sites where the planners are looking for a strong traditional theme. Inside the house the layout is conventional, with an L-shaped lounge with double doors leading through to the large dining room. On the first floor there is a conventional four bedroom layout with a fully equipped bathroom as well as a small shower room which serves the master bedroom.

The gables can be roofed with either small plain tiles or with any of the flat interlocking tiles, but are not well suited to pantiles. However, in traditional pantile areas it would be normal practice to use pantiles on the main roof, with small plain tiles on the gables and vertical tile hanging above the gable windows.

This design would normally be built in brick, and in the right situation it will look well with plenty of traditional brick features. This sort of thing is illustrated over the front door in the sketch, and one of the joys of having a new house built for yourself is the fun of deciding the details of this sort of feature. In recent years it has become popular to build a discrete plaque with ones initials and the date into the walling above a gable end, and this is always a particularly happy feature of a new home.

Design Number 83215

Area	1410 sq.ft.	131 sq.m.
Overall dimensions	31'2'' x 30'2½''	9.5 x 9.2
Lounge	13'7½'' x 23'5''	4.15 x 7.14
Dining	15'4½'' x 12'0''	4.69 x 3.65
Kitchen	11'1'' x 12'5''	3.38 x 3.79
Master Bed	11'7½'' x 13'1''	3.54 x 3.99
Bed 2	10'4'' x 11'7½''	3.15 x 3.54
Bed 3	12'3'' x 9'10''	3.74 x 3.00
Bed 4	7'3'' x 9'10''	2.20 x 3.00

MEDWAY

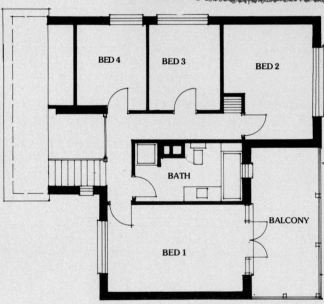

This design was originally built on the Kent coast, with the balcony looking out over the Medway estuary. It is built in local stock bricks under a roof of plain tiles, and looks splendid. The big roof coming down to the front door is typical of the area.

The chimney-breast above the Inglenook fireplace can also take a flue from a solid fuel cooker in the kitchen. It carries through to the bathroom where it serves to box in the shower recess, or, if a shower is not required, to locate a large airing cupboard.

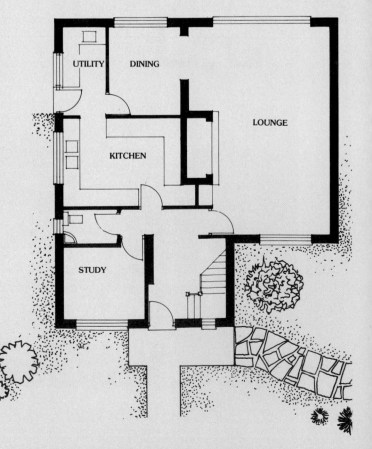

Design Number 83216

Floor Area (exc. garage)	1300 sq.ft.	120 sq.m.
Dimensions overall	34'10'' x 31'11''	10.6 x 9.7
Lounge	23'5'' x 16'1½''	7.14 x 4.91
Dining	10'0½'' x 8'0''	3.06 x 2.43
Kitchen	13'1½'' x 9'9''	4.00 x 2.97
Study	9'2'' x 8'3½''	2.80 x 2.52
Utility	10'0½'' x 4'10''	3.06 x 1.46
Master Bed	15'4'' x 9'9''	4.67 x 2.96
Bed 2	13'2'' x 10'0½''	4.00 x 3.06
Bed 3	9'10'' x 8'0''	3.00 x 2.43
Bed 4	9'10'' x 8'0''	3.00 x 2.43

STORRINGTON

This design has the complex roof line and contrasting levels of roof so popular with the planners for infill sites in villages and on farms, and yet is only 1300 sq. ft.

The master bedroom suite is isolated from the rest of the first floor accommodation by an 11" wall, and this is a feature which is deservedly popular. In our plan we show the back door right at the back of the house, but it can easily be moved to the side, or even into the front elevation where it would open into the utility room.

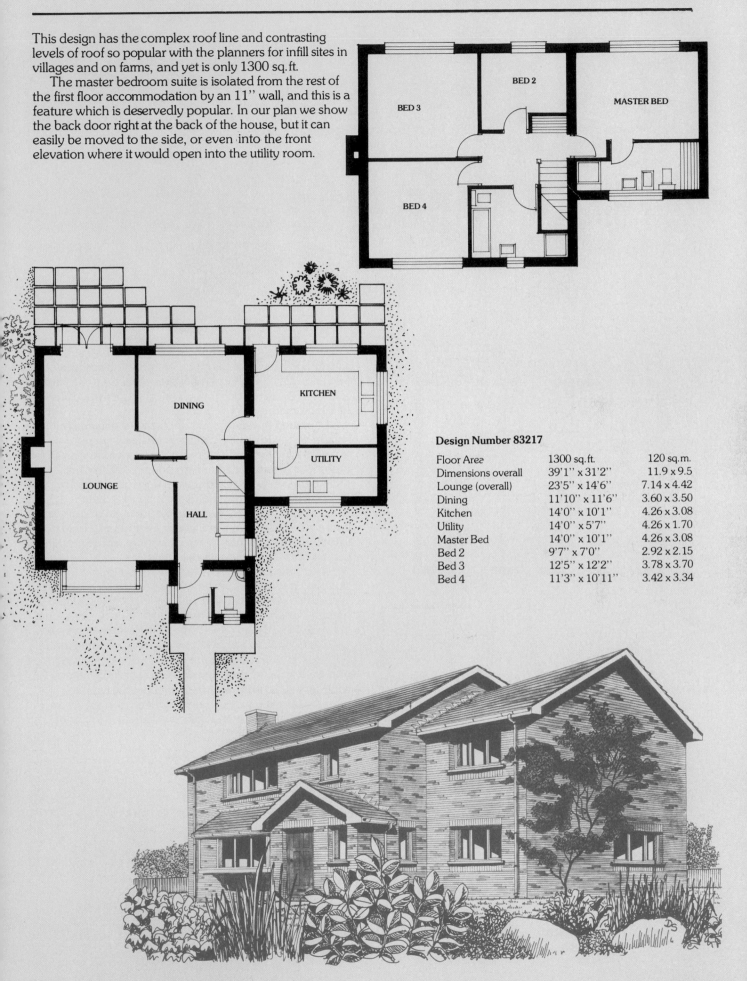

Design Number 83217

Floor Area	1300 sq. ft.	120 sq. m.
Dimensions overall	39'1" x 31'2"	11.9 x 9.5
Lounge (overall)	23'5" x 14'6"	7.14 x 4.42
Dining	11'10" x 11'6"	3.60 x 3.50
Kitchen	14'0" x 10'1"	4.26 x 3.08
Utility	14'0" x 5'7"	4.26 x 1.70
Master Bed	14'0" x 10'1"	4.26 x 3.08
Bed 2	9'7" x 7'0"	2.92 x 2.15
Bed 3	12'5" x 12'2"	3.78 x 3.70
Bed 4	11'3" x 10'11"	3.42 x 3.34

CHELTENHAM

This simple straight forward Georgian style design is as simple and effective as its nineteenth century predecessor, and although the hip roof is not as cost effective as a gable roof, it is cheap to build and will always appreciate ahead of the market.

If required the study can become a utility room as shown on the inset plan. All the drainage is very economically grouped at the back, except for the en suite bathroom. If saving had to be made this bathroom can be fitted out later, being used as a sewing room or study before it is turned into a bathroom. If this is done remember that the drainage stack pipe must be built in when the house is built, as it will be troublesome to put this in later. Everything else is easy, as the water connections can be taken from the cylinder cupboard.

The portico illustrated is typical of the many prefabricated timber and fibreglass porticos on the market. These are usually available with matching bay window heads — which must be constructed so they do not sound like a drum in heavy rain. Some fibreglass window heads used to do that; most have now got this problem sorted out. Incidentally, do not think you are doing anything non-traditional by buying ready made porticos and window heads; in the eighteen twenties the builders merchants catalogues were full of them, and are studied carefully by todays manufacturers who use the original designs.

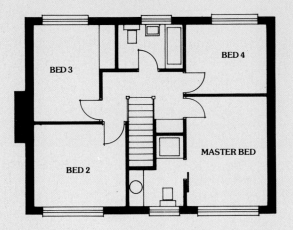

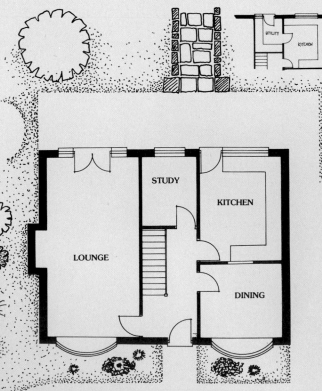

Design Number 83218

Floor Area	1415 sq. ft.	131 sq.m.
Dimensions overall	25'3'' x 32'0''	7.7 x 9.7
Lounge	23'5'' x 12'0''	7.14 x 3.65
Dining	9'6'' x 10'6''	2.89 x 3.20
Kitchen	10'6'' x 13'7''	3.20 x 4.14
Study	7'0'' x 8'6''	2.13 x 2.60
Master Bed	10'6'' x 14'3''	3.20 x 4.34
Bed 2	12'0'' x 10'6''	3.65 x 3.20
Bed 3	12'7'' x 8'8½''	3.84 x 2.65
Bed 4	10'6'' x 8'10''	3.20 x 2.70

WESTWOOD

The Westwood is a design for a narrow plot, and provides 1360 sq. ft. of accommodation in a conventional layout. The plan shows the back door at the rear, but it can be moved into the side wall provided attention is paid to various aspects of the building regulations. We will advise on this.

The illustration shows slate facing to the walls around the front door. This is popular in West and Central Wales, and to set it off to the best advantage it requires a really crisp rendered finish to the rest of the house. The slate should be slightly recessed to enable the render to be carried proud of it, with a pronounced drip above: we have tried to show this in the illustration.

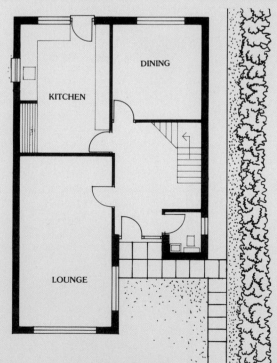

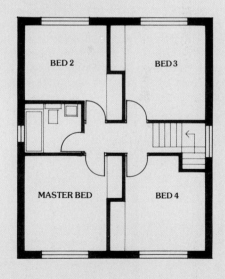

Design Number 83219

Floor Area	1360 sq.ft.	126 sq.m.
Dimensions overall	40'0'' x 24'3''	12.20 x 7.40
Lounge	21'7'' x 11'8''	6.57 x 3.54
Dining	12'0'' x 11'0''	3.65 x 3.34
Kitchen	16'4'' x 11'2''	4.96 x 3.40
Master Bed	12'0'' x 10'2''	3.65 x 3.10
Bed 2	9'9'' x 10'2''	2.96 x 3.10
Bed 3	12'0'' x 10'0''	3.65 x 3.04
Bed 4	12'0'' x 10'0''	3.65 x 3.04

HINDHEAD

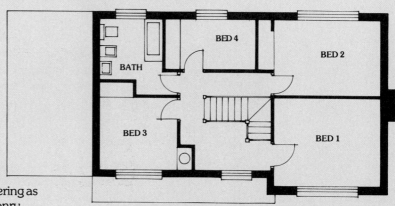

A classic four bedroom house of 1400 sq.feet, the
Hindhead design can be built with Tudor half timbering as
shown, or with plain brick or stone walls and masonry
pillars to the porch.

The garage need not be built if it is not required, and
without it the overall width is under 40ft, which makes this
a useful design for suburban infill sites.

A very cost effective design, with the feel of a much
larger property.

Design Number 83220

Floor Area		
(exc. garage)	1400 sq.ft.	130 sq.m.
Overall dimensions	48'3½'' x 22'10''	14.7 x 6.9
Lounge	21'0'' x 13'6''	6.40 x 4.11
Dining	11'6'' x 9'6''	3.50 x 2.89
Kitchen	10'0'' x 9'6''	3.05 x 2.89
Study	6'8'' x 9'0''	2.03 x 2.73
Garage	19'6½'' x 10'5½''	5.97 x 3.19
Bed 1	13'6'' x 11'2''	4.11 x 3.40
Bed 2	13'6'' x 9'6''	4.11 x 2.89
Bed 3	10'0'' x 9'0''	3.05 x 2.73
Bed 4	9'4'' x 6'3''	2.85 x 1.89

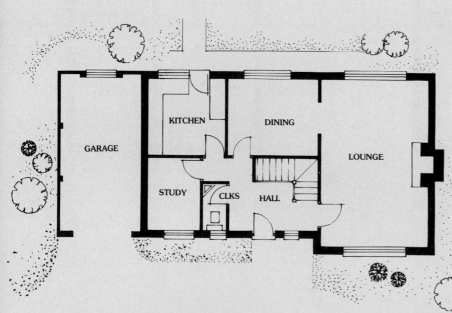

KNEBWORTH

This straight-forward Tudor style home meets the requirements of those who want three large bedrooms in a house of just over 1100 sq. ft. instead of the four bedrooms which are more usual in a property of this size. The layout is simple and cost effective, and without any windows to the side it can be fitted easily into a fairly narrow suburban plot. If it is to be built in the country then all sorts of re-arrangements of the windows are possible.

The winding stairs with a window half way up are a period feature to suit the style of the Knebworth, and if possible the stairs should be made in hardwood. The windows in this design are well suited to leaded lights, and of course, these should be double glazed sealed units.

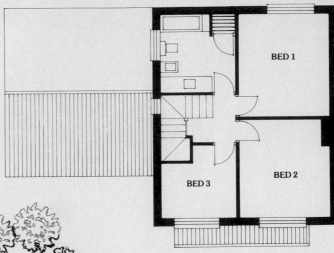

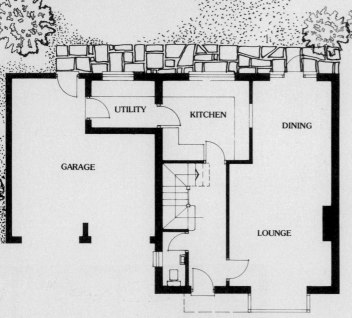

Design Number 83221

Floor Area (exc. garage)	1134 sq. ft.	105 sq. m.
Dimensions overall	42'0'' x 27'8''	12.7 x 8.4
Lounge	13'0'' x 15'6''	3.96 x 4.73
Dining	10'4'' x 10'0''	3.15 x 3.05
Kitchen	10'0'' x 11'0''	3.05 x 3.35
Utility	8'0'' x 6'0''	2.43 x 1.83
Garage (overall)	20'0'' x 18'0''	6.10 x 5.48
Master Bed	11'6'' x 13'0''	3.50 x 3.96
Bed 2	12'6'' x 11'6''	3.81 x 3.50
Bed 3	9'6'' x 9'2''	2.90 x 2.80

APPLETON

The Appleton is another design with a complex shape and roof line in today's cottage style, carefully arranged in a way to keep down unit costs. Note how all the changes of roof lines are above load bearing walls, without any valleys or other expensive features. It is a D & M design that has been built in a number of different parts of the country, and which looks best with a fairly steep roof pitch.

The illustration shows a double garage door: if funds and the site allow, it would be preferable to stretch the garage by another two feet and have two single doors. In some situations these would look best as old fashioned side hung doors with strap hinges.

Inside the room arrangement is simple and logical, and the way in which the master bedroom is away from the rest of the first floor accommodation is always very popular.

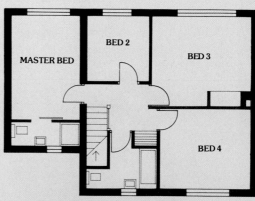

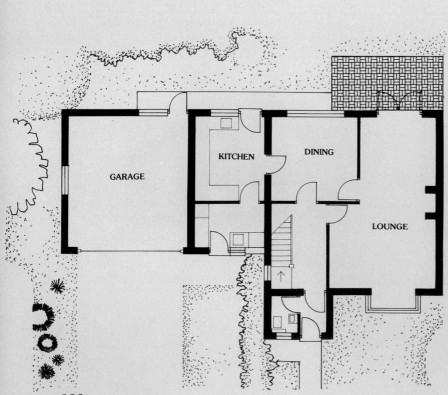

Design Number 83222

Floor Area (exc. garage)	1404 sq.ft.	130 sq.m.
Dimensions Overall	51'5'' x 31'1½''	15.67 x 9.49
Lounge (overall)	14'6'' x 23'5''	4.42 x 7.14
Dining	12'0'' x 11'6''	3.60 x 3.50
Kitchen	9'6'' x 11'6''	2.90 x 3.50
Utility	5'9'' x 9'6''	1.74 x 2.90
Garage	16'7'' x 17'6''	5.06 x 5.34
Master Bed (exc. shower room)	9'6'' x 13'11''	2.90 x 4.24
Bed 2	8'7'' x 9'0''	2.61 x 2.75
Bed 3	13'5'' x 12'4''	4.08 x 3.75
Bed 4	10'10'' x 12'4''	3.29 x 3.75

FOSSEBRIDGE

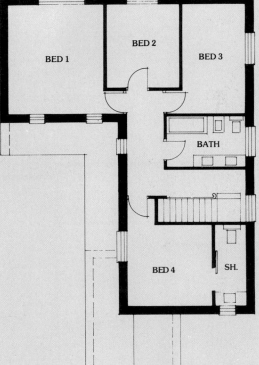

This interesting design of 1570 sq. ft. requires only 40ft. of plot width to meet building regulations, although it is certainly too large for a site with a total width of this size. However, where only a 40ft. width of a larger plot can be used for a building, because of some limitation to the use of the rest of the site, this design comes into its own.

The bedroom layout is unusual as the shower room is en suite with the guest room. This is very convenient when this room is occupied by an older person living with the family.

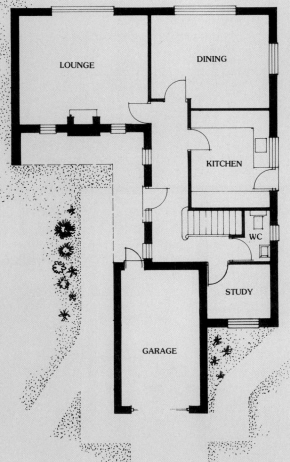

Design Number 83223

Floor Area (exc. garage)	1570 sq. ft.	146 sq. m.
Dimensions overall	33'7'' x 51'3''	10.2 x 15.6
Lounge	16'5'' x 14'0''	5.00 x 4.26
Dining	15'0'' x 12'0''	4.57 x 3.65
Kitchen	12'0'' x 10'0''	3.65 x 3.05
Study	7'0'' x 8'0''	2.13 x 2.43
Garage	17'6'' x 10'0''	5.33 x 3.05
Master Bed	14'1'' x 14'0''	4.29 x 4.26
Bed 2	10'8'' x 9'0''	3.26 x 2.74
Bed 3	14'0'' x 8'0''	4.26 x 2.43
Bed 4 Guest Room	10'9'' x 10'4''	3.27 x 3.15

TWYFORD

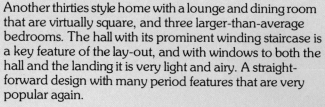

Another thirties style home with a lounge and dining room that are virtually square, and three larger-than-average bedrooms. The hall with its prominent winding staircase is a key feature of the lay-out, and with windows to both the hall and the landing it is very light and airy. A straight-forward design with many period features that are very popular again.

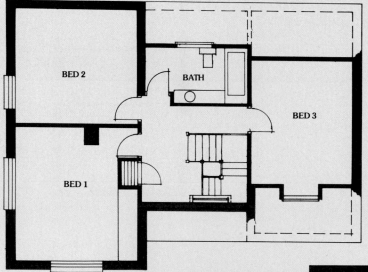

Design Number 83224

Floor Area	1452 sq. ft.	135 sq. m.
Dimensions overall	39'0'' x 30'2''	11.8 x 9.1
Lounge	14'0'' x 15'0''	4.26 x 4.57
Dining	14'0'' x 13'0''	4.26 x 3.96
Kitchen		
(inc. breakfast area)	11'6'' x 13'7½''	3.50 x 4.15
Garage	10'6'' x 17'0''	3.20 x 5.18
Bed 1	12'0'' x 15'0''	3.66 x 4.57
Bed 2	14'0'' x 13'0''	4.26 x 3.96
Bed 3	11'0'' x 13'10''	3.35 x 4.20

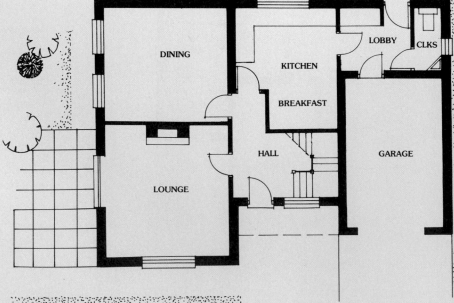

BROCKENHURST

The Brockenhurst design was originally drawn to meet the planners requirements in a conservation area where a new house had to have a complex shape and roof line to conform to the local architectural idiom, and it has since been used on a number of other sites. There is very little waste space in this layout, and it has the advantage of a kitchen with views in all directions.

The complex roof and the unusual shape do not help with building costs, but it is a remarkably attractive house and looks particularly well when built in rustic brick under a pantile roof.

Remember that both the appearance of the house and the feel of the individual rooms can be altered by moving windows around.

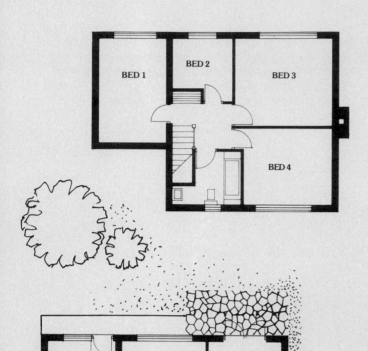

Design Number 83225

Area	1357 sq.ft.	126 sq.m.
Overall	34'3'' x 31'0''	10.45 x 9.44
Lounge	23'5'' x 14'6''	7.14 x 4.42
Kitchen	14'7'' x 9'6''	4.44 x 2.90
Dining	12'0'' x 11'6''	3.60 x 3.50
Bed 1	14'7'' x 9'6''	4.44 x 2.90
Bed 2	8'7'' x 7'0''	2.61 x 2.15
Bed 3	13'5'' x 12'4''	4.08 x 3.75
Bed 4	12'4'' x 10'9''	3.75 x 3.29

A three bedroom version of this design is available and is called the Northwich. The reference number is 82225.

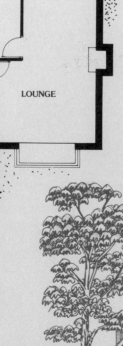

AYLESBURY

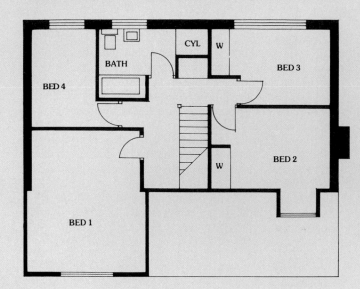

The Aylesbury design has all the cottage features that are the essentials of todays traditional housing style, yet inside there is a practical modern layout without an inch of wasted space.

There are no windows in side walls so this house can be built on plots down to 40ft. in width, while if there is more room it is possible to move the windows round to suit the view.

Drawings are available for this design to be built with an open plan lounge/dining room and a separate family room. This re-arrangement also includes providing an en-suite bathroom to the master bedroom. The relevant drawings are indexed as Wendlebury, reference 82226.

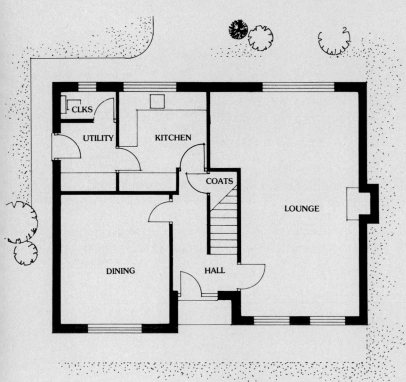

Design Number 83226

Floor Area	1506 sq.ft.	140 sq.m.
Overall size	34'7½'' x 28'4''	10.5 x 8.6
Lounge	13'0'' x 24'5½''	3.96 x 7.45
Dining	12'0'' x 14'1''	3.65 x 4.30
Kitchen	9'10'' x 11'0''	3.00 x 3.35
Utility	6'0'' x 7'8½''	1.83 x 2.35
Bed 1	12'0'' x 15'7''	3.65 x 4.75
Bed 2	13'0'' x 8'10''	3.96 x 2.70
Bed 3	13'0'' x 8'2½''	3.96 x 2.50
Bed 4	7'0'' x 11'0''	2.13 x 3.35

WENTWORTH

This attractive family house has both the lounge and kitchen windows to the rear, suiting a North aspect site. The dining room can either be completey separate from the lounge, or it can be connected to it with an arch as shown, giving scope for imaginative decor. There is a large utility room, and we have shown a WC at the far end of it. This need not be built if it is not required.

The cloakroom area can be rearranged with access off the porch to give a larger hall at the expense of storage room in the cloakroom. Alternatively, the outer door and screen to the storm porch need not be built at all, or can be put in at a later date.

The Wentworth can be built with a single garage replacing the double garage illustrated. Note that the pergola shown on our drawing is a suggested landscaping feature, and is not part of the structural design.

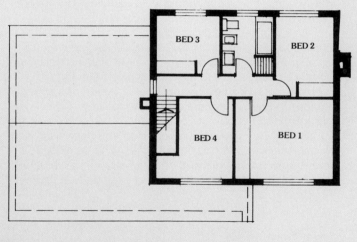

Design Number 83227

Area (inc. garage)	1560 sq.ft.	145 sq.m.
Overall	47'11'' x 28'9''	14.16 x 8.75
Lounge	14'5'' x 14'5''	4.39 x 4.39
Dining	13'2'' x 9'0''	4.02 x 2.74
Kitchen	11'5'' x 10'11''	3.49 x 3.31
Bed 1	14'1'' x 11'0''	4.30 x 3.35
Bed 2	12'1'' x 8'8''	3.69 x 2.63
Bed 3	9'0'' x 8'6''	2.74 x 2.59
Bed 4	11'0'' x 7'11''	3.35 x 2.41

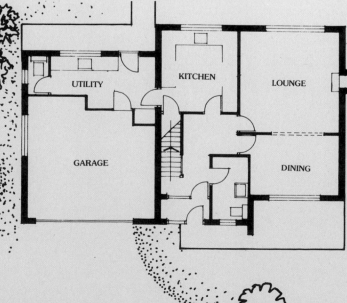

Plans are available for this home with a self-contained flat in place of the garage, with the option of turning the flat into a garage at a later date. This design is called the Corsham, reference 82227.

STAMFORD

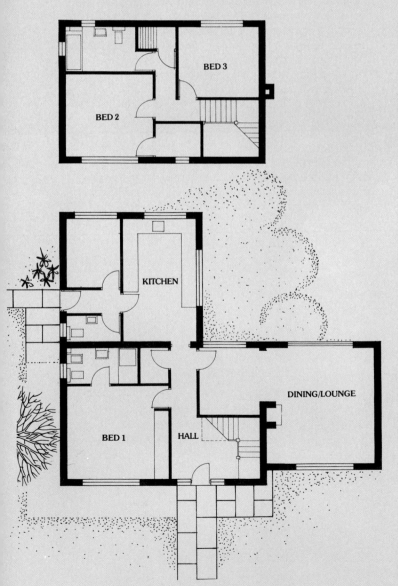

This design was drawn to meet a situation where a bedroom is required on the ground floor of a 3 bedroomed house, and by designing 2 separate single storey wings this has been achieved in a way that avoids the structure looking like a bungalow with a first floor extension. It is particularly useful in situations where the planners are insisting on a house rather than a bungalow, but where our clients must have a ground floor bedroom.

The hall is particularly well laid out and the stairs with 2 quarter landings gives the feel of a much larger property once one enters the front door. In the sketch it is drawn as built in a cottage style to meet the typical planning requirements for a farmhouse, but the same basic layout can be modified to give the executive look appropriate to a pery-urban situation.

The "spare" room at the back door has been built as a farm office, as a shower room and WC on a stock farm, and simply as a hobbies room. Alternatively the whole of this wing can be redesigned to meet a clients own special requirements.

Design Number 83228

Area	1523 sq.ft.	141 sq.m.
Overall dimensions	37'10"x 44'6½"	11.5 x 13.5
Lounge	16'1" x 14'8"	4.90 x 4.47
Dining	9'10" x 8'6"	3.00 x 2.60
Kitchen	10'5" x 16'11"	3.16 x 5.15
Utility	6'6" x 7'7"	1.97 x 2.30
Master Bed	14'8" x 13'0"	4.46 x 3.96
Bed 2	12'2" x 11'8"	3.70 x 3.56
Bed 3	11'4" x 9'10"	3.46 x 3.00

STOWMARKET

This 3 bedroomed house of just under 1600 square feet was originally designed as a farmhouse, and the accommodation is laid out to suit the working farmer. In many ways it reflects traditional ideas — a large hall, lit from above with winding stairs: a square lounge: solid masonry walls to the master bedroom to give total sound insulation and all rooms of a generous size.

The front door is tight in the angle between the two wings of the house, and when this is an inescapable feature of the layout — as it is in this case — it is essential that it is given a strong character to identify it as a focal point. In this case this is achieved by a really massive gallows bracket to the porch roof, and this should be backed up with very careful landscaping.

Design Number 83229

Area	1555 sq.ft.	144 sq.m.
Overall dimensions	32'10" x 39'9"	10.0 x 12.1
Lounge	16'0" x 15'11"	4.88 x 4.84
Dining	10'0" x 10'0"	3.04 x 3.04
Kitchen	16'2" x 10'8"	4.93 x 3.25
Study	10'0" x 8'0"	3.04 x 2.43
Utility	7'0" x 10'8"	2.13 x 3.25
Master Bed	13'1" x 10'8"	3.97 x 3.25
Bed 2	11'1" x 10'8"	3.38 x 3.25
Bed 3	10'0" x 11'1"	3.04 x 3.38

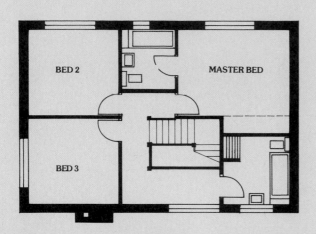

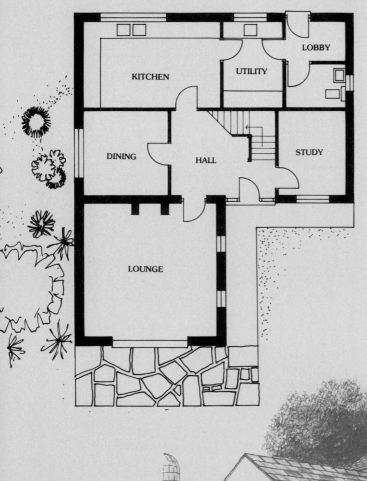

SOUTHWELL

The Southwell house has an unusual layout with a large study: it was originally built for a Doctor who wanted a study door adjacent to the front door. Note the box room on the first floor: a Victorian design feature that can be very useful in today's busy world.

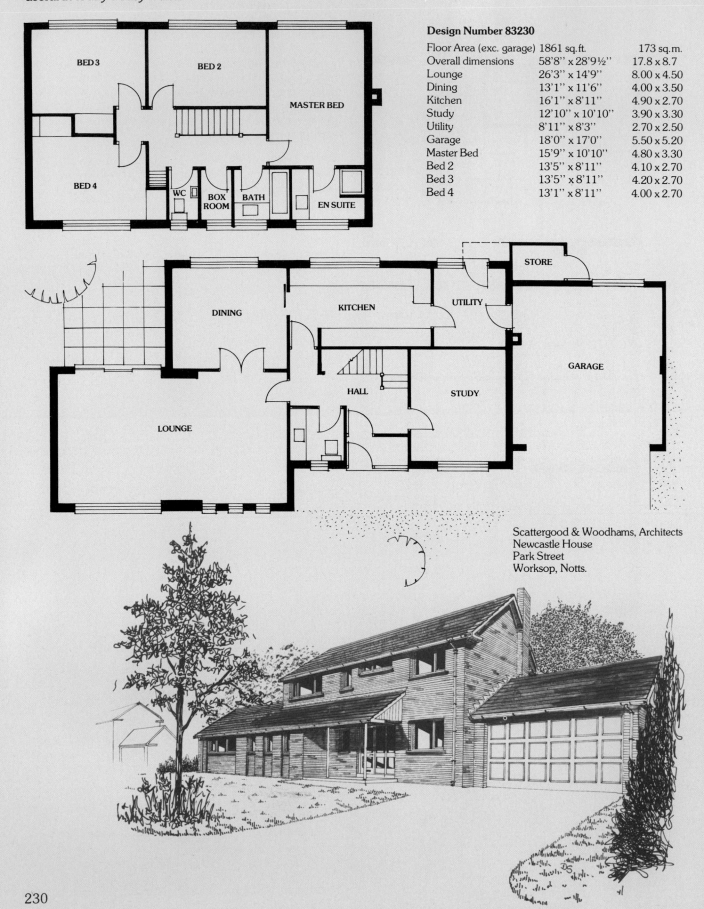

Design Number 83230

Floor Area (exc. garage)	1861 sq.ft.	173 sq.m.
Overall dimensions	58'8" x 28'9½"	17.8 x 8.7
Lounge	26'3" x 14'9"	8.00 x 4.50
Dining	13'1" x 11'6"	4.00 x 3.50
Kitchen	16'1" x 8'11"	4.90 x 2.70
Study	12'10" x 10'10"	3.90 x 3.30
Utility	8'11" x 8'3"	2.70 x 2.50
Garage	18'0" x 17'0"	5.50 x 5.20
Master Bed	15'9" x 10'10"	4.80 x 3.30
Bed 2	13'5" x 8'11"	4.10 x 2.70
Bed 3	13'5" x 8'11"	4.20 x 2.70
Bed 4	13'1" x 8'11"	4.00 x 2.70

Scattergood & Woodhams, Architects
Newcastle House
Park Street
Worksop, Notts.

230

EASTWOOD

Another Scattergood & Woodhams design, this one originally drawn for a prestige site in a South Yorkshire village. The large hall and landing were very popular features of the Eastwood when it was built speculatively, and it is sure to be just as much a favourite with those choosing a design for a site of their own.

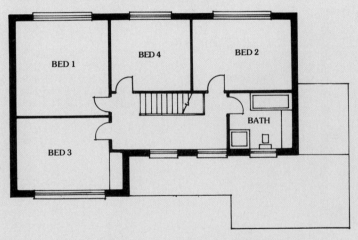

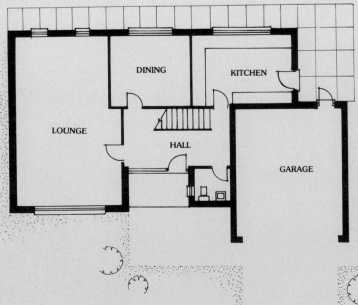

Design Number 83231

Floor Area (exc. garage)	1442 sq.ft.	134 sq.m.
Overall dimensions	47'9½'' x 29'6''	14.5 x 8.9
Lounge	23'0'' x 15'0''	7.01 x 4.57
Dining	11'0'' x 10'0''	3.35 x 3.05
Kitchen	13'9'' x 10'0''	4.19 x 3.05
Garage	15'9'' x 17'0''	4.80 x 5.18
Bed 1	13'3'' x 13'0''	4.03 x 3.96
Bed 2	13'9'' x 10'0''	4.19 x 3.05
Bed 3	13'3'' x 10'0''	4.03 x 3.05
Bed 4	11'0'' x 10'0''	3.35 x 3.05

Scattergood & Woodhams, Architects
Newcastle House
Park Street
Worksop, Notts.

LUDLOW

The Ludlow design with its gable roof and solid appearance suits a rural site, and is popular in Wales and the Midlands. It has a very traditional layout with two separate bathrooms instead of the more modern en suite arrangement, and the two larger bedrooms are well above average size. Essentially a design for a site with views at the back of the house.

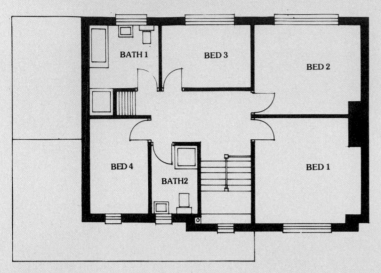

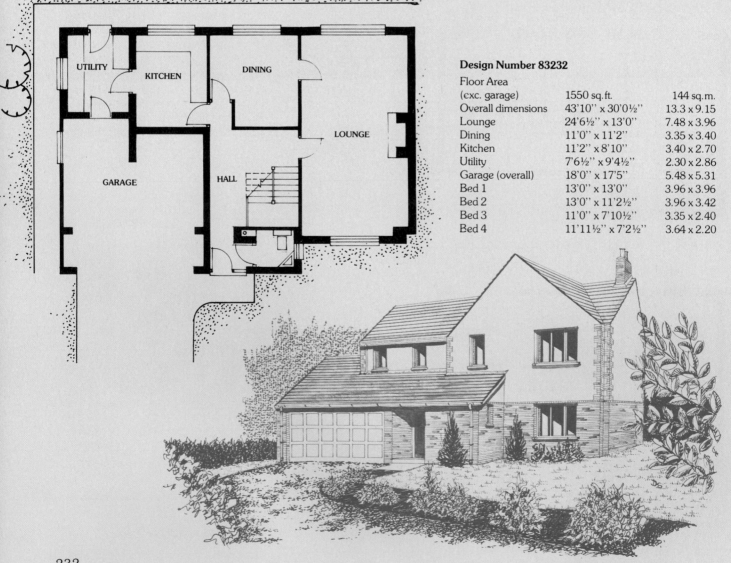

Design Number 83232

Floor Area		
(exc. garage)	1550 sq. ft.	144 sq. m.
Overall dimensions	43'10'' x 30'0½''	13.3 x 9.15
Lounge	24'6½'' x 13'0''	7.48 x 3.96
Dining	11'0'' x 11'2''	3.35 x 3.40
Kitchen	11'2'' x 8'10''	3.40 x 2.70
Utility	7'6½'' x 9'4½''	2.30 x 2.86
Garage (overall)	18'0'' x 17'5''	5.48 x 5.31
Bed 1	13'0'' x 13'0''	3.96 x 3.96
Bed 2	13'0'' x 11'2½''	3.96 x 3.42
Bed 3	11'0'' x 7'10½''	3.35 x 2.40
Bed 4	11'11½'' x 7'2½''	3.64 x 2.20

GRANCHESTER

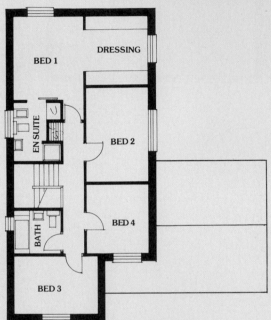

This original and imposing house was designed by D & M for a site near Cambridge and in spite of the complex roof line it was remarkably economical to build. This comes from all the separate elements in the roof being independent of each other: the result looks involved but is very easy to build.

The huge open plan kitchen/breakfast room/dining area, with stairs set in one corner, may not suit everyone and if it is not your taste then dividing walls can be built between the different rooms. However, it was first built exactly as it is drawn here, and is much admired: open plan arrangements where the lounge is at the centre of things are common enough, but the idea of a private lounge and a separate open plan living area elsewhere is unusual.

The dressing area in the main bedroom, with its double row of wardrobes, is another feature that attracts much favourable comment.

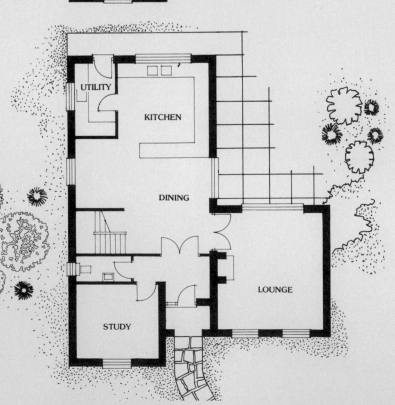

Design Number 83233

Floor Area (exc. garage)	1825 sq. ft.	169 sq. m.
Dimensions overall	45'0'' x 37'7''	13.7 x 11.4
Lounge	17'4'' x 15'3½''	5.28 x 4.66
Dining/Kitchen (overall)	27'9'' x 13'3½''	8.46 x 4.05
Study	11'0'' x 12'2''	3.35 x 3.70
Utility	10'4'' x 5'11''	3.15 x 1.80
Master Bed	12'0'' x 10'3''	3.65 x 3.12
Bed 2	13'8'' x 9'0''	4.16 x 2.73
Bed 3	12'2'' x 8'6''	3.70 x 2.59
Bed 4	10'0'' x 9'0''	3.04 x 2.73

SUNNINGDALE

The Sunningdale house follows a very popular design concept that you will find in every book of plans. There are only a limited number of ways in which 4 bedroomed accommodation with an integral double garage can be offered in a total of only 1560 square feet, and this is certainly the most popular.

Within the design concept we have aimed for the most practical layout for a no-frills family house, with lots of storage space, a large bathroom, a good kitchen, and a really cost-effective design.

The double garage can be reduced in size if required, and the WC behind it need not be built if it is not appropriate. The storm porch can also be omitted, or left to a later stage.

The Sunningdale suits a site with views to the front. Where the principal view is to the rear, or where there are views in all directions, see the Wentworth design which is a variant of the Sunningdale.

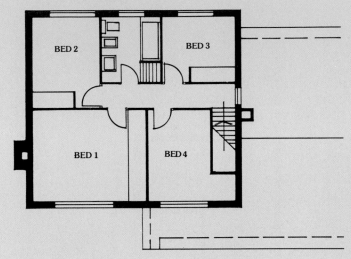

Design Number 83234

Area (inc. garage)	1560 sq.ft.	145 sq.m.
Overall	47'11'' x 28'9''	14.16 x 8.75
Lounge	18'5'' x 12'4''	5.61 x 3.76
Dining	10'9'' x 10'6''	3.27 x 3.20
Kitchen	14'10'' x 10'9''	4.51 x 3.27
Bed 1	14'1'' x 11'0''	4.30 x 3.35
Bed 2	12'1'' x 8'8''	3.69 x 2.63
Bed 3	9'0'' x 8'6''	2.74 x 2.59
Bed 4	11'0'' x 7'11''	3.35 x 2.41

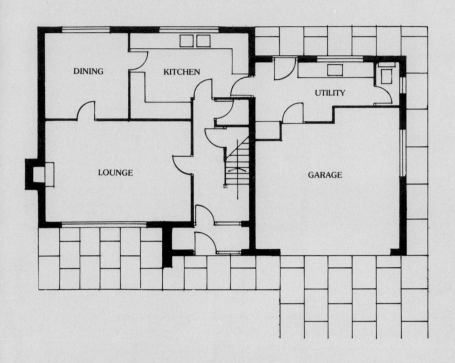

BEVERLEY

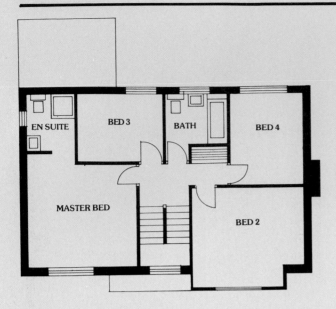

This is another design with the projecting bedroom wall which is so popular in the South of the country. There are no significant windows in the side walls, so it can be built on a plot of restricted width if required, although this is a style of home that certainly looks at its best in a large garden.

The study need not be built if it is not required, or alternatively it can be left until a later stage. Another option is to extend it as a granny flat

Design Number 83236

Floor Area	1614 sq. ft.	150 sq.m.
Overall dimensions	32'9'' x 38'9½''	9.9 x 11.8
Lounge (overall)	22'0'' x 14'0''	6.70 x 4.26
Dining	11'10'' x 10'6''	3.60 x 3.20
Kitchen	11'0'' x 10'6''	3.35 x 3.20
Utility	7'0'' x 10'6''	2.13 x 3.20
Study	10'6'' x 8'0''	3.20 x 2.43
Master Bed	13'9'' x 13'2''	4.20 x 4.01
Bed 2 (overall)	12'6'' x 14'0''	3.80 x 4.26
Bed 3	8'6'' x 10'9''	2.59 x 3.27
Bed 4	9'0'' x 11'9½''	2.75 x 3.59
Granny Annexe:		
Bedsitting	13'0'' x 10'6''	3.96 x 3.20
Kitchen	6'0'' x 7'0''	1,83 x 2.13

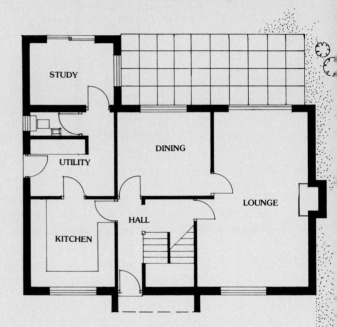

DEREHAM

This is another 1700 sq. ft. house with three large bedrooms instead of four smaller ones. Some of the space saved has gone into an impressive hall, the dining room is much larger than usual and will accommodate a table for a dozen diners.

The study can have its door moved to open into the kitchen, and becomes a utility room or laundry if required.

Design Number 83237

Floor Area (exc. garage)	1700 sq. ft.	158 sq. m.
Dimensions overall	38'9" x 30'11"	11.8 x 9.4
Lounge	20'0" x 13'0"	6.10 x 3.96
Dining	11'0" x 15'9"	3.35 x 4.80
Kitchen	13'0" x 14'3½"	3.96 x 4.35
Study	9'0" x 8'0"	2.74 x 2.43
Master Bed	14'6" x 13'0"	4.42 x 3.96
Bed 2	14'3½" x 13'0"	4.35 x 3.96
Bed 3	14'3½" x 10'6"	4.35 x 3.20

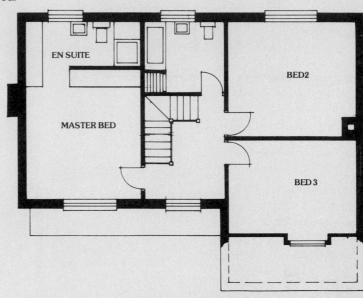

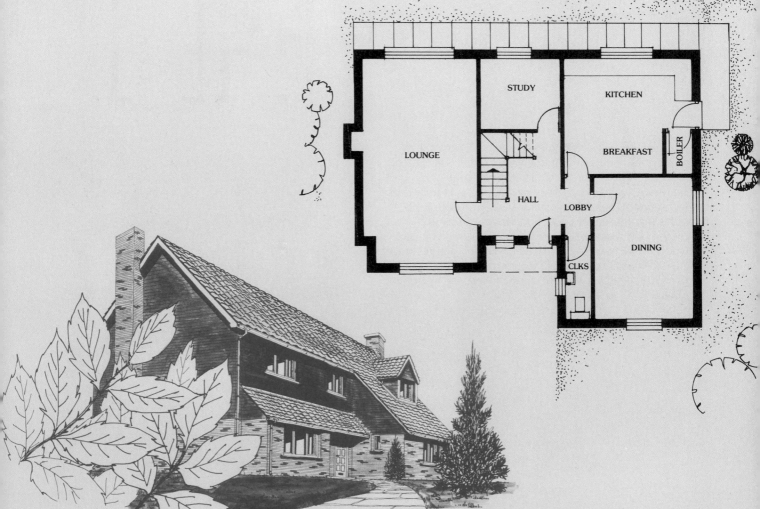

WINCHELSEA

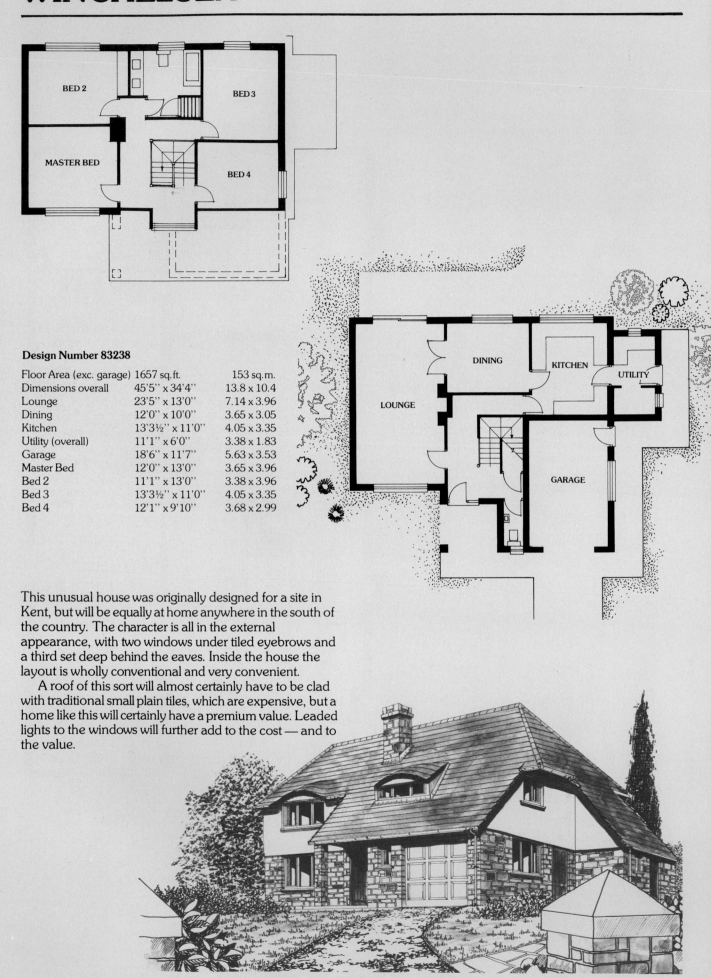

Design Number 83238

Floor Area (exc. garage)	1657 sq.ft.	153 sq.m.
Dimensions overall	45'5'' x 34'4''	13.8 x 10.4
Lounge	23'5'' x 13'0''	7.14 x 3.96
Dining	12'0'' x 10'0''	3.65 x 3.05
Kitchen	13'3½'' x 11'0''	4.05 x 3.35
Utility (overall)	11'1'' x 6'0''	3.38 x 1.83
Garage	18'6'' x 11'7''	5.63 x 3.53
Master Bed	12'0'' x 13'0''	3.65 x 3.96
Bed 2	11'1'' x 13'0''	3.38 x 3.96
Bed 3	13'3½'' x 11'0''	4.05 x 3.35
Bed 4	12'1'' x 9'10''	3.68 x 2.99

This unusual house was originally designed for a site in Kent, but will be equally at home anywhere in the south of the country. The character is all in the external appearance, with two windows under tiled eyebrows and a third set deep behind the eaves. Inside the house the layout is wholly conventional and very convenient.

A roof of this sort will almost certainly have to be clad with traditional small plain tiles, which are expensive, but a home like this will certainly have a premium value. Leaded lights to the windows will further add to the cost — and to the value.

PETERSFIELD

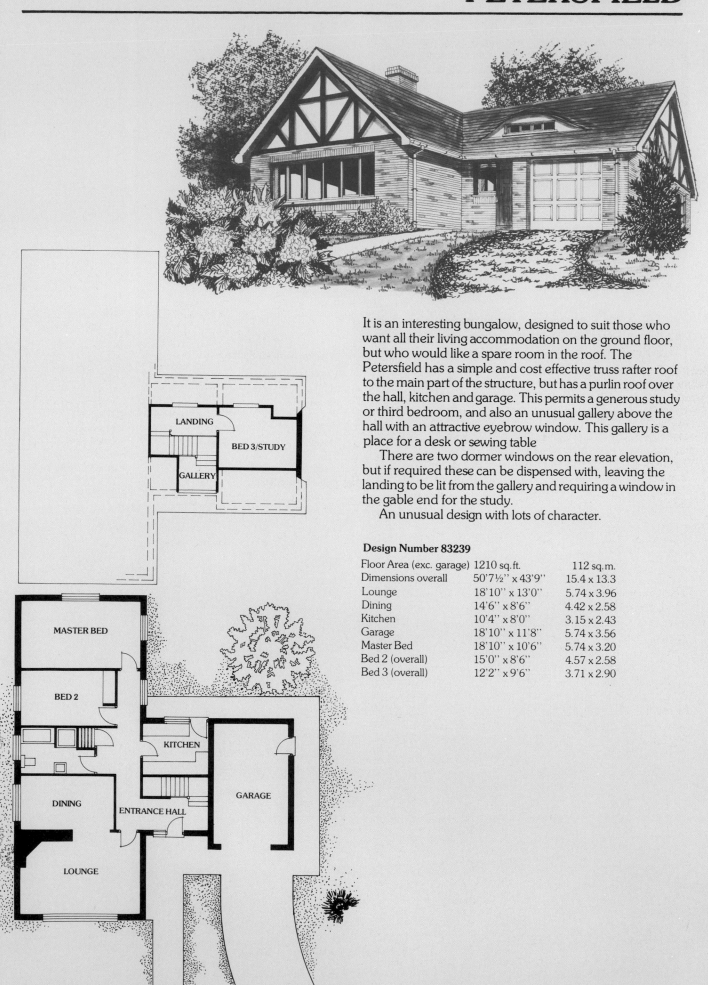

It is an interesting bungalow, designed to suit those who want all their living accommodation on the ground floor, but who would like a spare room in the roof. The Petersfield has a simple and cost effective truss rafter roof to the main part of the structure, but has a purlin roof over the hall, kitchen and garage. This permits a generous study or third bedroom, and also an unusual gallery above the hall with an attractive eyebrow window. This gallery is a place for a desk or sewing table

There are two dormer windows on the rear elevation, but if required these can be dispensed with, leaving the landing to be lit from the gallery and requiring a window in the gable end for the study.

An unusual design with lots of character.

Design Number 83239

Floor Area (exc. garage)	1210 sq.ft.	112 sq.m.
Dimensions overall	50'7½'' x 43'9''	15.4 x 13.3
Lounge	18'10'' x 13'0''	5.74 x 3.96
Dining	14'6'' x 8'6''	4.42 x 2.58
Kitchen	10'4'' x 8'0''	3.15 x 2.43
Garage	18'10'' x 11'8''	5.74 x 3.56
Master Bed	18'10'' x 10'6''	5.74 x 3.20
Bed 2 (overall)	15'0'' x 8'6''	4.57 x 2.58
Bed 3 (overall)	12'2'' x 9'6''	3.71 x 2.90

LANDING

BED 3/STUDY

GALLERY

MASTER BED

BED 2

KITCHEN

DINING

ENTRANCE HALL

GARAGE

LOUNGE

BLYTH

The Blyth house is our most popular 4 bedroomed house design, and has been built in one style or another in well over a hundred times. It always looks well, whether built with landscape windows with a generous eaves overhang or with casement windows and a roof to a steeper pitch to suit a planning requirement in a rural area.

   The plan shows a large patio window in the lounge rear wall. This can be moved into the side wall if appropriate, and the chimney can be moved to suit. This house is frequently built with the chimney as a feature built out from the lounge gable wall. Either of the screens to the storm porch can be omitted if required, thus giving a larger hall, or a recessed doorway.

   The double garage is often reduced to a single garage, or given an extra 2 feet of width to suit a pair of 7 foot garage doors. The utility room behind can be built with a WC at the far end, while on farms it sometimes becomes a porch with a farm office.

A version of the Blyth design with the garage redesigned as a self-contained flat is called the Letwell, reference 82240.

Design Number 83240

Area (exc. garage)	1695 sq.ft.	157 sq.m.
Overall	53'0'' x 25'0''	16.15 x 7.64
Lounge	23'5'' x 13'10''	7.14 x 4.21
Dining	13'10'' x 10'10''	4.22 x 3.31
Kitchen	13'0'' x 10'10''	3.94 x 3.31
Bed 1	13'10'' x 11'10''	4.21 x 3.60
Bed 2	10'11'' x 10'9''	3.32 x 3.27
Bed 3	10'9'' x 10'1''	3.27 x 3.07
Bed 4	10'3'' x 9'2''	3.12 x 2.79
Garage	18'4'' x 17'7''	5.60 x 5.37
Utility	15'1'' x 7'4''	4.60 x 2.22

LOUNGE

KITCHEN

UTILITY

DINING

GARAGE

BED 4

BED 2

BED 1

BED 3

ANSTON

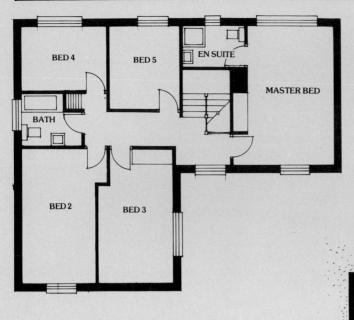

This is one of the few designs in "Home Plans For The Eighties" which has five bedrooms as well as a study, and yet the total area, excluding the garage, is under 1700 sq. ft. The dividing wall between the two car spaces in the garage is essential to keep down construction costs, and although this is an unusual feature one quickly gets used to it.

Although shown with a hip roof, this house can also be built with gables, and lends itself to many different alterations to suit a special site.

Design Number 83242

Floor Area		
(exc. garages)	1668 sq.ft.	155 sq.m.
Overall dimensions	42'0" x 34'9"	12.8 x 10.5
Lounge (overall)	18'0" x 13'0"	5.48 x 3.96
Dining	9'0" x 10'10"	2.74 x 3.30
Kitchen	11'0" x 9'6"	3.35 x 2.90
Study	8'0" x 5'3"	2.43 x 1.60
Garages (each)	17'0" x 9'8"	5.18 x 2.95
Master Bed (overall)	18'0" x 13'0"	5.48 x 3.96
Bed 2	9'8" x 17'0"	2.95 x 5.18
Bed 3	9'8" x 17'0"	2.95 x 5.18
Bed 4	11'0" x 8'2½"	3.35 x 2.50
Bed 5	9'0" x 10'10"	2.74 x 3.30

EASTGATE

An interesting design with a half hip roof. The roof above the kitchen and utility room is an extension of the rear slope of the garage roof: an unusual arrangement which gives a lot of character to the back of the house.

The fourth bedroom is small for a house of this size and would probably be used as a box room or sewing room. Alternatively, bedrooms 3 and 4 can be combined to make one very large and interestingly shaped room with two windows in one wall.

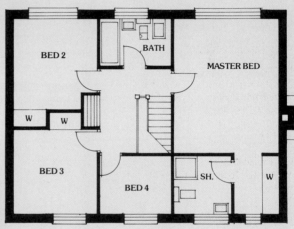

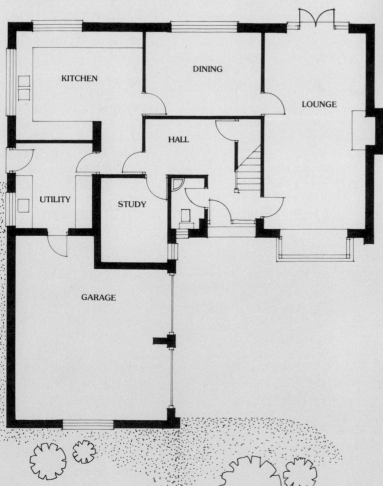

Design Number 83243

Floor Area (exc. garage)	1750 sq.ft.	162 sq.m.
Dimensions overall	44'1½" x 48'0"	13.4 x 14.6
Lounge	23'5" x 12'4"	7.14 x 3.76
Dining	14'4" x 10'0"	4.37 x 3.04
Kitchen/Breakfast	14'11" x 13'2"	4.55 x 4.00
Study	10'0" x 8'1"	3.04 x 2.47
Utility	10'7" x 9'0"	3.21 x 2.75
Garage (overall)	21'10" x 18'0"	6.66 x 5.50
Master Bed	16'2" x 12'4"	4.94 x 3.76
Bed 2	10'10" x 10'0"	3.30 x 3.04
Bed 3	10'3½" x 10'0"	3.14 x 3.04
Bed 4	9'4" x 6'11"	2.84 x 2.10

MEADOWFIELD

In many ways this is the ideal farmhouse. It not only looks the part, but it has a practical layout that is relevant to the lifestyle of today's working farmers — and their wives!

There are various different versions of this design. One of the most popular is to extend the garage to provide a utility room and W.C. at the kitchen door and this is shown in the inset diagram.

Provision has been made for an Aga or similar solid fuel cooker in the kitchen. If this is not required then the chimney at the left of the building need not be built.

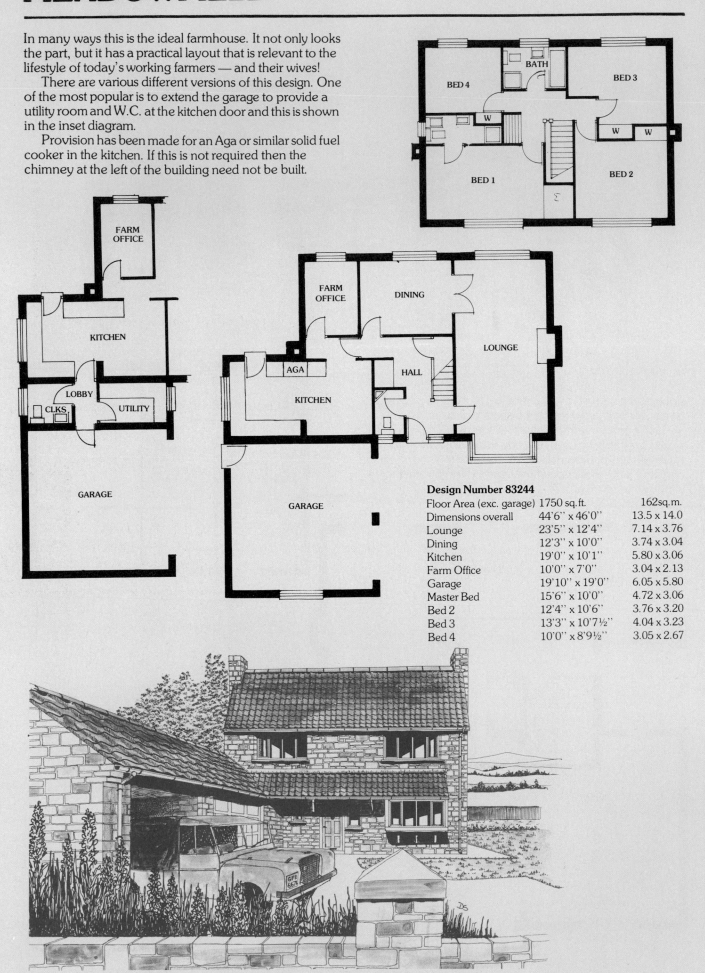

Design Number 83244

Floor Area (exc. garage)	1750 sq.ft.	162sq.m.
Dimensions overall	44'6'' x 46'0''	13.5 x 14.0
Lounge	23'5'' x 12'4''	7.14 x 3.76
Dining	12'3'' x 10'0''	3.74 x 3.04
Kitchen	19'0'' x 10'1''	5.80 x 3.06
Farm Office	10'0'' x 7'0''	3.04 x 2.13
Garage	19'10'' x 19'0''	6.05 x 5.80
Master Bed	15'6'' x 10'0''	4.72 x 3.06
Bed 2	12'4'' x 10'6''	3.76 x 3.20
Bed 3	13'3'' x 10'7½''	4.04 x 3.23
Bed 4	10'0'' x 8'9½''	3.05 x 2.67

THIRSK

This large home was designed as a farmhouse for a client who farms in the North Yorks National Park, and has the massive look and stone features that the Park Planning Board requires.

As far as layout is concerned, it has just about every feature which we have learned that farmers want: somewhere at the back door for the dog to sleep, room for a table and chairs just inside a very large kitchen, a very large hall where two or three large men can linger over their farewells, a study or farm office near the front door, and a lounge as far away from the mud at the back door as possible!

The original was built with an oak open tread staircase and the stairwell was big enough for an antique candelabra, but if this is beyond your pocket, don't despair: ask that the drawings show a pine staircase that is fastened to the walls but structurally independant of them, and know that when you want your luxury staircase you will be able to have it fitted with the minimum of disruption. This idea of making provision for changes in the future is always important with a new home.

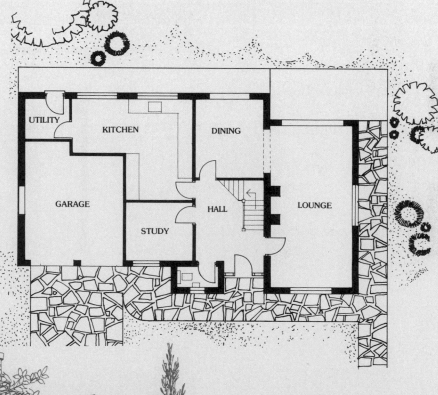

Design Number 83245

Floor Area (exc. garage)	1738 sq. ft.	161 sq. m.
Dimensions overall	49'3'' x 27'3½''	15.0 x 8.3
Lounge	23'5'' x 12'0''	7.14 x 3.65
Dining	9'11'' x 11'6''	3.02 x 3.50
Kitchen (overall)	17'6'' x 14'9''	5.32 x 4.50
Study	8'4'' x 9'10''	2.54 x 2.99
Utility	6'7'' x 5'11''	2.00 x 1.80
Garage (overall)	17'2'' x 14'2''	5.24 x 4.32
Master Bed	14'2'' x 15'1''	4.32 x 4.60
Bed 2	9'11'' x 11'6''	3.02 x 3.50
Bed 3	9'10'' x 8'0''	2.99 x 2.44
Bed 4	8'0'' x 7'11''	2.44 x 2.42

A five bedroom version of the Thirsk is the Skipton, reference 82245.

KENILWORTH

This large Georgian home has an imposing front entrance which leads into a hall that is lit by a window to the landing in the traditional way. It is illustrated here with a large inglenook fireplace in the lounge and a corner fireplace in the dining room. This is unusual: it is simply how it was built by the client who originally commissioned this design, and of course these features can be changed.

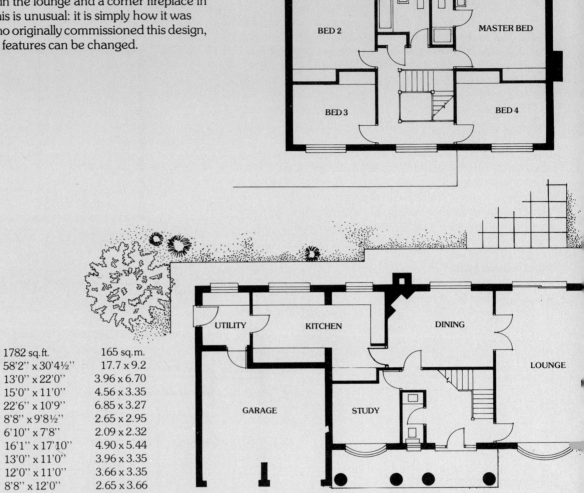

Design Number 83246

Floor Area (exc. garage)	1782 sq.ft.	165 sq.m.
Dimensions overall	58'2'' x 30'4½''	17.7 x 9.2
Lounge	13'0'' x 22'0''	3.96 x 6.70
Dining	15'0'' x 11'0''	4.56 x 3.35
Kitchen (overall)	22'6'' x 10'9''	6.85 x 3.27
Study	8'8'' x 9'8½''	2.65 x 2.95
Utility	6'10'' x 7'8''	2.09 x 2.32
Garage	16'1'' x 17'10''	4.90 x 5.44
Master Bed	13'0'' x 11'0''	3.96 x 3.35
Bed 2	12'0'' x 11'0''	3.66 x 3.35
Bed 3	8'8'' x 12'0''	2.65 x 3.66
Bed 4	8'8'' x 13'0''	2.65 x 3.96

246

FORDCOMBE

This large house of nearly 2,000 sq. ft. has larger-than-average rooms downstairs and four double bedrooms on the first floor. The arrangement of the study and cloakroom enable it to be used as an extra ground floor bedroom with its own bathroom if required.

This is a home to build in a formal setting, and the terrace shown in the sketch suits it perfectly. A good design for a prestige suburban site.

Design Number 83247

Floor Area		
(exc. garage)	1998 sq. ft.	185 sq. m.
Dimensions overall	38'3'' x 31'4½''	11.6 x 9.5
Lounge/Dining		
(overall, exc. bay)	25'10½'' x 18'2½''	7.88 x 5.55
Kitchen	12'0'' x 13'0''	3.65 x 3.96
Study (overall)	13'6'' x 11'4''	4.11 x 3.45
Utility	6'6'' x 6'8''	1.98 x 2.03
Master Bed	17'4½'' x 12'6½''	5.30 x 3.82
Bed 2	10'0'' x 13'0''	3.05 x 3.96
Bed 3	10'0'' x 12'6½''	3.05 x 3.82
Bed 4 (overall)	11'0'' x 13'0''	3.35 x 3.96

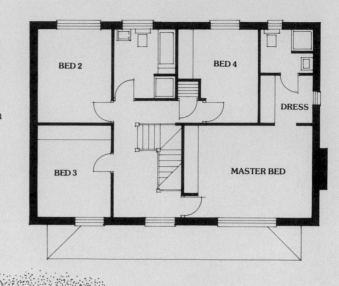

SHERBORNE

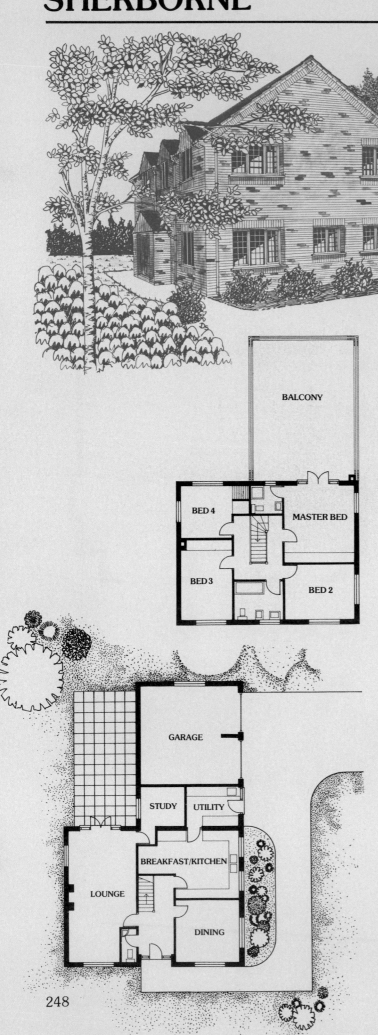

BALCONY

BED 4

MASTER BED

BED 3

BED 2

GARAGE

STUDY   UTILITY

BREAKFAST/KITCHEN

LOUNGE

DINING

This impressive house was originally built by a lady client of D & M Ltd, as her own new home. When it was completed, circumstances had changed and she did not want to move in, so she sold it, and made a huge profit This started her off on a career as a successful one-woman development company!

The prototype "Sherborne" was built in Butterley Grey Minster bricks, but it would also look well in stone. The leaded lights are double glazed and there are two ways of doing this. One is to have traditional lead strips bonded to the outside of sealed double glazing units, and the other is to have spacers simulating lead in the cavity between the two panes of glass. If you are interested in having leaded lights, then do make a decision between these two systems after seeing them actually installed in a house, and not from sample panes. In a house they look quite different.

The balcony is a major feature of this design, and the decision on the balustrading is most important. There are many choices, and they must be considered in relation to the site, to the use to be made of the balcony, and to the design of any garden furniture to be left up there.

Design Number 83248

Floor Area (exc. garage)	1836 sq.ft.	170 sq.m.
Overall dimensions	34'9'' x 55'2''	10.6 x 16.8
Lounge	25'8'' x 13'1''	7.81 x 3.99
Dining	12'4'' x 12'0''	3.77 x 3.65
Kitchen/Breakfast (overall)	13'4'' x 19'6''	4.05 x 5.95
Study	9'0'' x 8'0''	2.74 x 2.43
Utility	10'0'' x 8'0''	3.05 x 2.43
Garage	19'0'' x 18'2''	5.80 x 5.52
Master Bed	15'0'' x 13'0''	4.58 x 3.96
Bed 2	13'0'' x 10'3½''	3.96 x 3.13
Bed 3	13'4'' x 9'10''	4.06 x 2.99
Bed 4	10'0'' x 10'0''	3.05 x 3.05

WESTBURTON

This interesting house has French windows opening from the first floor landing onto a large balcony. It is shown here with a garage and workshop annexe at the rear and a large utility room, but the whole of this area can be re-designed to give a separate family room if required. Upstairs there is a very large bathroom with room for a corner bath and all the other luxury fittings that you can imagine.

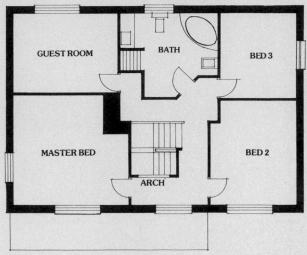

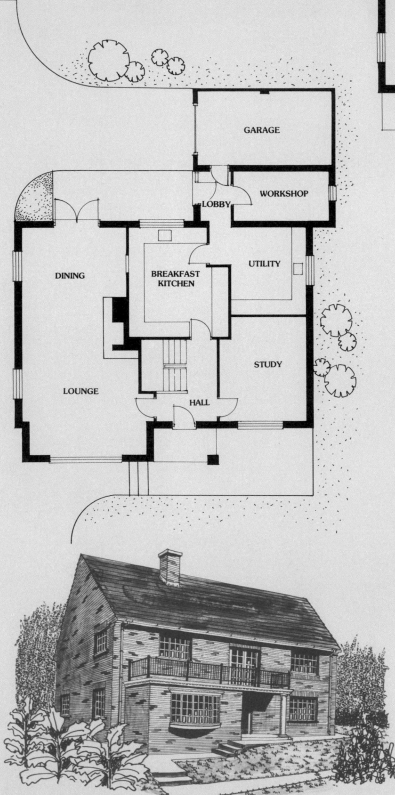

Design Number 83249

Floor Area (exc. garage)	2152 sq.ft.	200 sq.m.
Dimensions overall	52'0'' x 42'11''	15.8 x 13.0
Lounge/Dining (overall)	32'0'' x 15'6''	9.75 x 4.72
Breakfast/Kitchen	14'9'' x 13'6''	4.49 x 4.11
Study	14'0'' x 11'6''	4.26 x 3.50
Utility	11'8'' x 10'0''	3.55 x 3.05
Garage	18'0'' x 10'0''	5.48 x 3.05
Workshop	7'0'' x 12'9''	2.13 x 3.88
Master Bed (overall)	15'6'' x 14'8''	4.72 x 4.47
Bed 2	14'0'' x 11'6''	4.26 x 3.50
Bed 3	11'8'' x 10'0'''	3.55 x 3.05
Bed 4	14'0'' x 11'0''	4.26 x 3.35

WINDSOR

Another traditional house which was designed with the Home Counties in mind, but which has been just as popular in other parts of the country. Our illustration shows contrasting tile hanging above ground floor brickwork, but it can also be built in many other materials.

Note the generous covered porch at the back door. If required, a door can be put in the garage wall to open into this covered area.

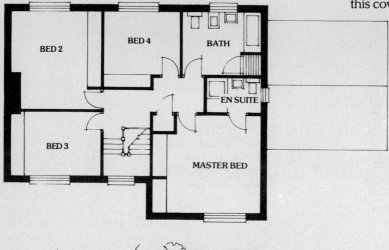

Design Number 83250

Floor Area (exc. garage)	1872 sq.ft.	174 sq.m.
Overall dimensions	53'8½'' x 30'5''	16.3 x 9.2
Lounge	23'5'' x 13'0''	7.14 x 3.96
Dining	11'0'' x 9'0''	3.35 x 2.74
Kitchen	11'0'' x 9'0''	3.35 x 2.74
Study	13'9'' x 10'0''	4.20 x 3.05
Utility	6'0'' x 8'6''	1.83 x 2.60
Garage (overall)	17'0'' x 10'5½''	5.18 x 3.19
Master Bed	13'3'' x 13'9''	4.03 x 4.20
Bed 2	11'0½'' x 14'3''	3.36 x 4.34
Bed 3	8'10'' x 11'0½''	2.69 x 3.36
Bed 4	11'0'' x 9'0''	3.35 x 2.74

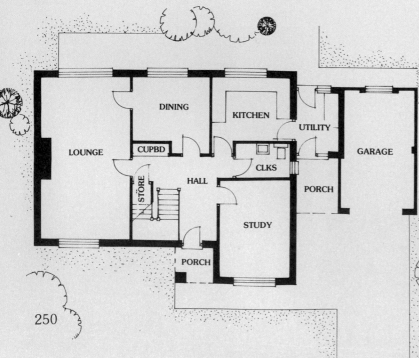

LEAMINGTON

This is the traditional layout for a Tudor home — two gables to the front, an impressive entrance hall lit by a large first floor window, and larger-than-usual bedrooms. The wall between the garage and the house is illustrated with a solid door, and this helps to spread the appearance of the house and garage together, and makes everything seem even larger and more imposing.

Design Number 83251

Floor Area	1570 sq.ft.	146 sq.m.
Overall dimensions	25'3" x 36'6"	7.7 x 11.1
Lounge	23'5" x 12'0"	7.14 x 3.65
Dining	12'0" x 10'0"	3.65 x 3.05
Kitchen	13'1" x 12'0"	3.99 x 3.65
Study	10'0" x 8'10"	3.05 x 2.70
Garage	18'0" x 11'2½"	5.48 x 3.41
Master Bed (overall)	12'0" x 13'1"	3.65 x 3.99
Bed 2	12'0" x 11'0"	3.65 x 3.35
Bed 3	12'0" x 10'0"	3.65 x 3.05
Bed 4	8'0" x 12'1"	2.43 x 3.68

NEWMARKET

The Newmarket design meets the requirements of those who entertain, and who want a large hall and reception rooms. It has often been built as a farmhouse, with an additional door provided to give access to the study from the back door, so that the study can be used as the farm office. The large kitchen also suits rural living.

Upstairs the en suite bathroom is shown with a shower, basin and WC, but it can easily be rearranged to include a bath and a bidet as well. The main bathroom is also unusually large, and there is an enormous walk-in airing cupboard.

The fourth bedroom is small, and if necessary we can rearrange the whole of the first floor to give more room in the bedrooms at the expense of the large bathrooms, the choice lies with our clients.

A ground floor accommodation for an elderly relative can be provided in this design at the expense of the study and utility room. The modified design is called the Chippenham, reference number 82252.

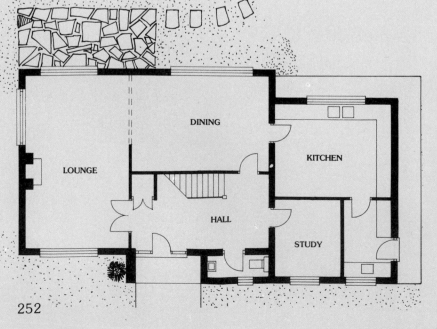

Design Number 83252

Area	1905 sq. ft.	177 sq. m.
Overall	50'2'' x 28'9''	15.29 x 8.76
Lounge	23'5'' x 14'1''	7.14 x 4.30
Dining	17'10'' x 12'11''	5.44 x 3.94
Kitchen	15'5½'' x 13'1½''	4.70 x 4.00
Study	10'0'' x 9'6''	3.04 x 2.90
Hall	17'10'' x 10'2''	5.44 x 3.10
Bed 1	13'1½'' x 12'11''	4.00 x 3.94
Bed 2	12'11'' x 11'0''	3.94 x 3.35
Bed 3	10'2'' x 11'0''	3.10 x 3.35
Bed 4	9'10'' x 7'6''	2.99 x 2.29

WENTBRIDGE

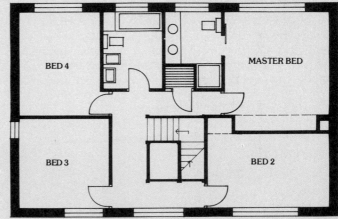

This large 4 bedroomed house was originally designed for a 50 foot wide plot in a very up-market suburb, but it will look equally well on a far larger site which would give an opportunity for some of the windows to be moved into the side walls. The porch roof which continues over the bay window is supported on a gallows bracket: it is always important that these should be really massive and well finished with plenty of detail.

The garage door is a key feature in the appearance of this house, and it is most important that it should be chosen with care. It is illustrated here as a panel door, but there are many other attractive designs available from specialist suppliers, and in most situations one should try to avoid the standard horizontally ribbed doors, which clash with the vertical emphasis of the casement joinery.

The generous hall with its feature staircase is lit by the large first floor landing window, and gives a welcoming feel to the whole house when you step inside the front door.

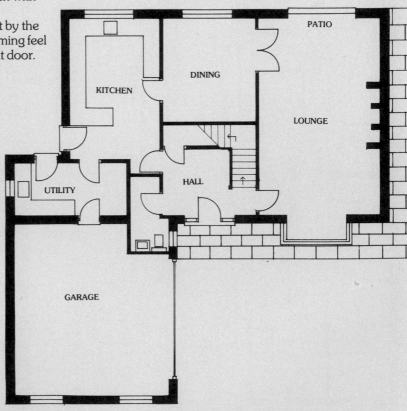

Design Number 83253

Area (exc. garage)	1770 sq.ft.	164 sq.m.
Overall dimensions	46'11'' x 39'0''	14.3 x 11.8
Lounge	23'5'' x 14'6''	7.14 x 4.42
Dining	11'0'' x 12'3''	3.35 x 3.73
Kitchen	11'0'' x 16'9''	3.35 x 5.10
Utility	6'6'' x 13'5''	1.98 x 4.10
Garage	20'9'' x 18'3½''	6.32 x 5.57
Master Bed	12'6'' x 12'1''	3.81 x 3.68
Bed 2	14'6'' x 9'0''	4.42 x 2.75
Bed 3	11'0'' x 11'0''	3.35 x 3.35
Bed 4	10'0'' x 12'1''	3.05 x 3.68

JERSEY

A Granny Flat as an annexe to a large four bedroom home is a design requirement that we meet all the time. The problem comes when the whole lot has to fit on a narrow site: one answer is the Jersey design, which is only 34ft overall and will meet the building regulations requirements to fit on a 40ft wide plot. Possibly the Planners would consider this over development, (ie. too much house on too little plot), but it has proved a very useful design on plots with many different frontages.

Note that the flat has its own separate front door: our experience is that this is something which the occupants value very highly.

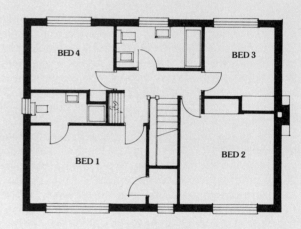

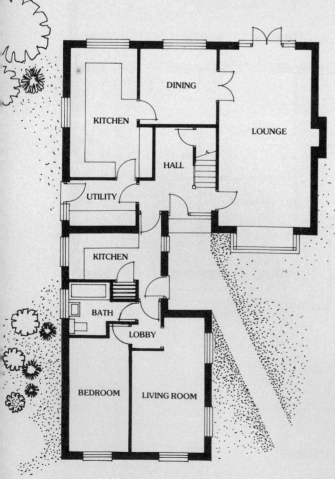

Design Number 83254

Floor Area		
(inc. annexe)	1922 sq. ft.	178 sq.m.
Dimensions overall		
(inc. annexe)	55'7½'' x 34'1½''	16.9 x 10.4
Lounge	23'5'' x 12'4''	7.14 x 3.76
Dining	10'0'' x 10'3½''	3.04 x 3.13
Kitchen	17'3'' x 9'0''	5.26 x 2.74
Utility	9'0'' x 5'10''	2.74 x 1.77
Master Bed	15'6'' x 10'2''	4.72 x 3.10
Bed 2	12'4'' x 11'11½''	3.76 x 3.64
Bed 3	9'3'' x 9'2½''	2.81 x 2.80
Bed 4	10'10½'' x 8'7½''	3.31 x 2.62
Granny Annexe:		
Living Room (overall)	9'8'' x 18'0''	2.95 x 5.48
Bedroom	8'0'' x 15'1''	2.43 x 4.60
Kitchen	6'0'' x 12'3½''	1.83 x 3.75

MANSFIELD

This is one of four designs from the architectural practice of Scattergood & Woodhams of Nottinghamshire. Working from one of the old Dukeries Estate Offices on the edge of Sherwood Forest, they design homes to suit the wooded sites in the local area. The distinctive gable return of the fascia is their unmistakable trademark!

The Mansfield design has an interesting projecting tower which is both distinctive and practical, providing a lobby on the ground floor and an en suite bathroom above.

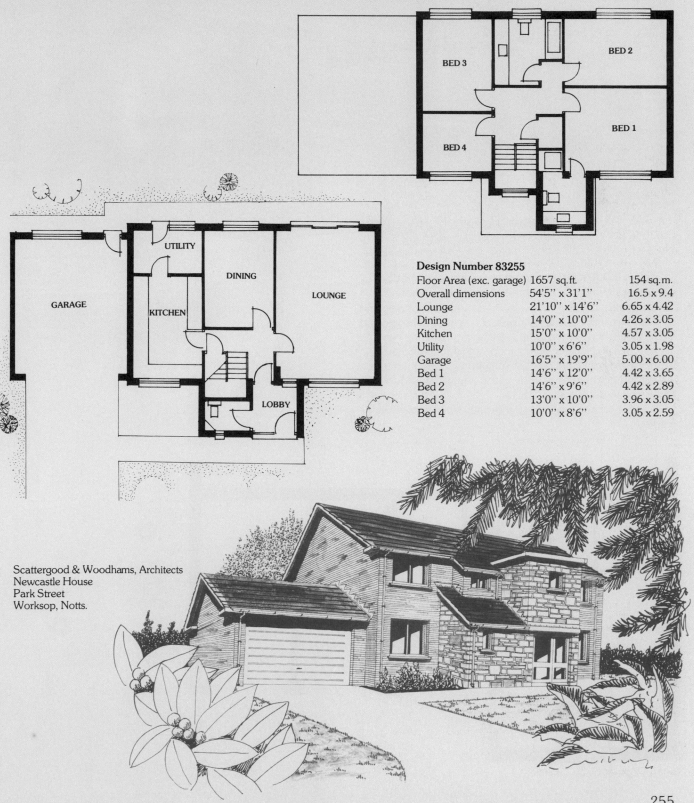

Design Number 83255

Floor Area (exc. garage)	1657 sq. ft.	154 sq. m.
Overall dimensions	54'5'' x 31'1''	16.5 x 9.4
Lounge	21'10'' x 14'6''	6.65 x 4.42
Dining	14'0'' x 10'0''	4.26 x 3.05
Kitchen	15'0'' x 10'0''	4.57 x 3.05
Utility	10'0'' x 6'6''	3.05 x 1.98
Garage	16'5'' x 19'9''	5.00 x 6.00
Bed 1	14'6'' x 12'0''	4.42 x 3.65
Bed 2	14'6'' x 9'6''	4.42 x 2.89
Bed 3	13'0'' x 10'0''	3.96 x 3.05
Bed 4	10'0'' x 8'6''	3.05 x 2.59

Scattergood & Woodhams, Architects
Newcastle House
Park Street
Worksop, Notts.

255

DARTMOUTH

This is an interesting home: we show two sketches to demonstrate how it is designed to be built into a steep bank, so that it is seen to be a bungalow from the back, and a house from the front. Two bedrooms are on the ground floor, which only extends halfway back under the upper floor, which has all the living accommodation and two more bedrooms. This takes some getting used to, but when you get the hang of the plans you will quickly see what a clever arrangment this is.

A most successful design, originally built on a site in Surrey.

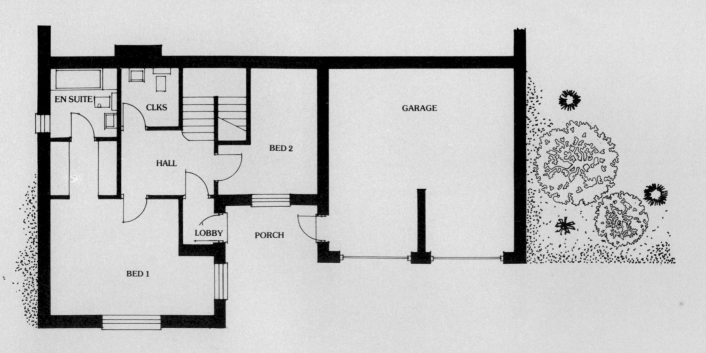

EN SUITE

CLKS

GARAGE

HALL

BED 2

LOBBY   PORCH

BED 1

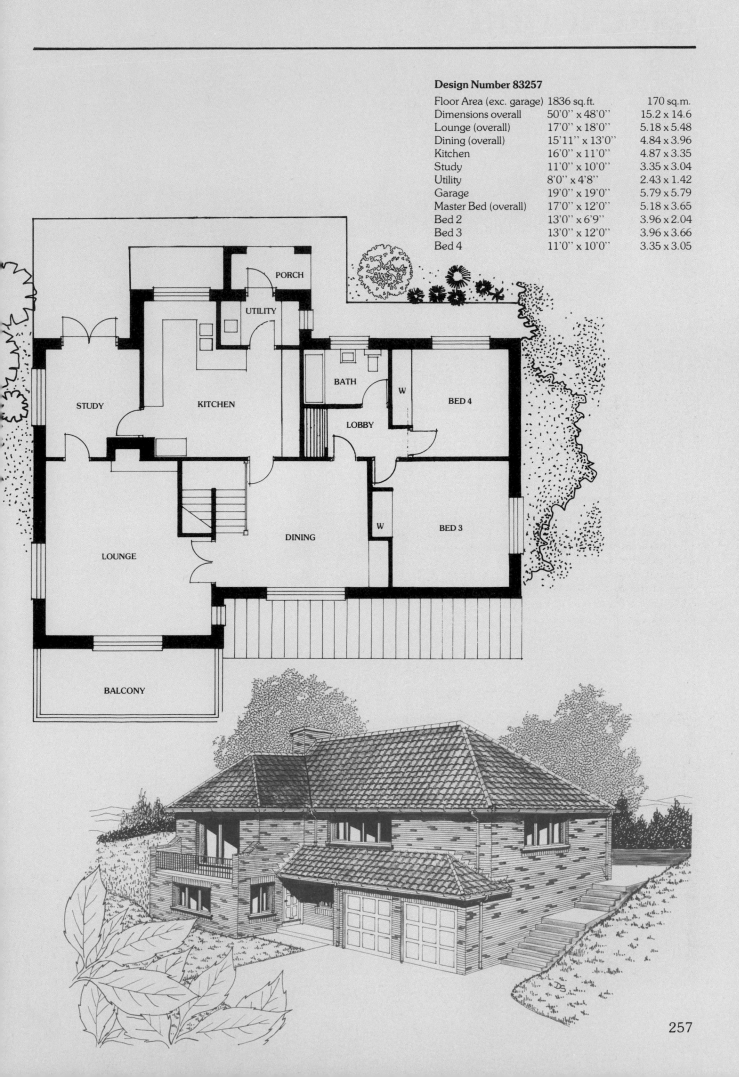

Design Number 83257

Floor Area (exc. garage)	1836 sq. ft.	170 sq.m.
Dimensions overall	50'0'' x 48'0''	15.2 x 14.6
Lounge (overall)	17'0'' x 18'0''	5.18 x 5.48
Dining (overall)	15'11'' x 13'0''	4.84 x 3.96
Kitchen	16'0'' x 11'0''	4.87 x 3.35
Study	11'0'' x 10'0''	3.35 x 3.04
Utility	8'0'' x 4'8''	2.43 x 1.42
Garage	19'0'' x 19'0''	5.79 x 5.79
Master Bed (overall)	17'0'' x 12'0''	5.18 x 3.65
Bed 2	13'0'' x 6'9''	3.96 x 2.04
Bed 3	13'0'' x 12'0''	3.96 x 3.66
Bed 4	11'0'' x 10'0''	3.35 x 3.05

PORCH

UTILITY

STUDY

KITCHEN

BATH

W

BED 4

LOBBY

LOUNGE

DINING

W

BED 3

BALCONY

GREENWOOD

The Greenwood design is the most popular of our genuinely five bedroom designs, having a study as well as the fifth bedroom. It is shown here as it might be built in two different areas — the brick with tile hanging to suit Kent or Sussex, and stone with render above is typical of the houses our clients build in Wales.

Design Number 83258

Floor Area (exc. garage)	2075 sq.ft.	192 sq.m.
Dimensions overall	54'11'' x 31'6½''	16.7 x 9.6
Lounge (overall)	26'9'' x 16'0½''	8.15 x 4.88
Dining	10'0'' x 11'0''	3.05 x 3.35
Kitchen	14'9'' x 11'0''	4.50 x 3.35
Study	9'6'' x 8'0''	2.90 x 2.43
Utility	11'0'' x 8'0''	3.35 x 2.43
Garage	19'10½'' x 18'0''	6.06 x 5.48
Master Bed	11'6'' x 12'6''	3.50 x 3.80
Bed 2	14'5'' x 14'0''	4.39 x 4.26
Bed 3	12'0'' x 13'0''	3.65 x 3.96
Bed 4	11'9'' x 8'10''	3.58 x 2.70
Bed 5	8'0'' x 9'10''	2.43 x 3.00

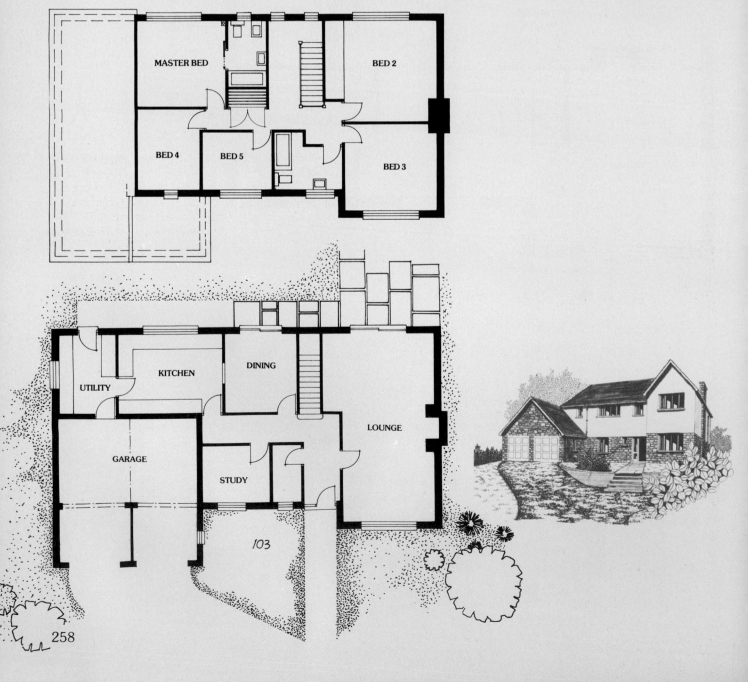

103

FOXWOOD

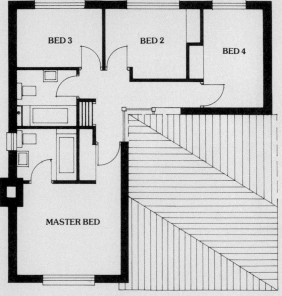

BED 3

BED 2

BED 4

MASTER BED

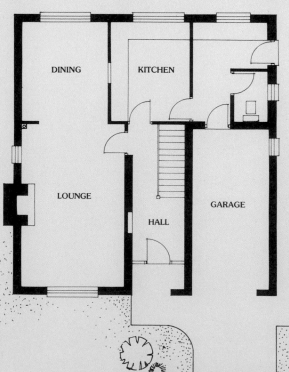

DINING

KITCHEN

LOUNGE

HALL

GARAGE

The complex shape of the roof of this large four bedroom home is typical of Surrey, Kent, and Sussex, where the tile hanging would also be in character. However, it is not an expensive house and can be built on a site of restricted width as none of the side windows are the principal windows of what the Building Regulations call "habitable rooms".

The ground floor layout is straight-forward, while upstairs the master bedroom is well separated from the other three bedrooms. This is always a popular feature.

Design Number 83259

Floor Area (exc. garage)	1614 sq.ft.	150 sq.m.
Dimensions overall	33'0'' x 30'0''	10.0 x 9.1
Lounge	12'0'' x 19'0''	3.65 x 5.75
Dining	10'0'' x 12'0''	3.05 x 3.65
Kitchen	9'0'' x 12'0''	2.74 x 3.65
Utility (overall)	8'6'' x 12'0''	2.59 x 3.65
Garage	18'6'' x 8'10''	5.63 x 2.70
Master Bed	12'0'' x 10'6''	3.65 x 3.20
Bed 2	9'0'' x 8'8''	2.74 x 2.65
Bed 3	10'0'' x 6'9''	3.05 x 2.05
Bed 4	8'2'' x 12'0''	2.49 x 3.65

HORNCASTLE

Three hips and one projecting gable was a feature of homes built in the thirties, and in this design it serves to make a large house look even larger. The storey height window to the stairs serves the same purpose, and the whole feel of this house is of a home that is even larger than its 2100 sq. ft. All the rooms are generous in size, particularly the master bedroom suite. An impressive house for a prestige site.

Design Number 83260

Floor Area (exc. garage)	2109 sq.ft.	196 sq.m.
Overall dimensions	29'3'' x 58'2''	8.9 x 17.7
Lounge	14'0'' x 27'0''	4.26 x 8.24
Dining	11'6'' x 13'0''	3.50 x 3.96
Kitchen	12'0'' x 11'6''	3.65 x 3.50
Breakfast	8'0'' x 9'10''	2.43 x 3.00
Study	8'8½'' x 11'7''	2.65 x 3.53
Garage	17'0'' x 16'4½''	5.18 x 4.98
Utility	7'5'' x 9'10''	2.26 x 3.00
Master Bed	12'0'' x 11'6''	3.65 x 3.50
Bed 2	14'0'' x 15'2''	4.26 x 4.63
Bed 3	11'6'' x 13'0''	3.50 x 3.96
Bed 4	14'0'' x 11'6''	4.26 x 3.50

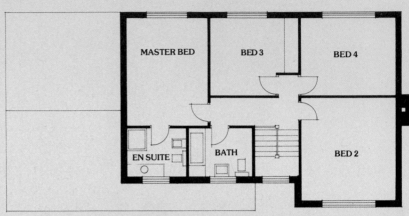

DUNHOLME

This tile hung house in the Essex style will take its character from the tiles that are chosen for it. Whether both walls and roof are clad with plain tiles, as illustrated, or whether the roof tiles should be a contrasting colour and profile, is something to be considered on site. In doing this it is always important to give careful consideration to the style of adjacent properties.

The ground floor guest room is a popular feature, and is put to many other uses besides accommodating visitors.

There are two variants of this design, both with the study used as the dining room. The Somersham design, reference 82261 dispenses with the rear projection, saving 230 sq. ft. in the total area, while the Buckland design, reference 81261, uses this part of the house for a granny flat.

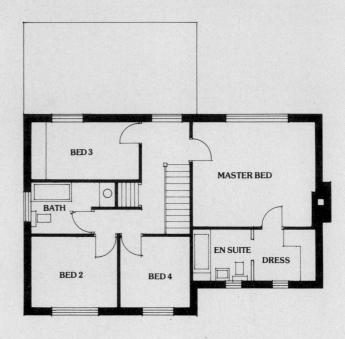

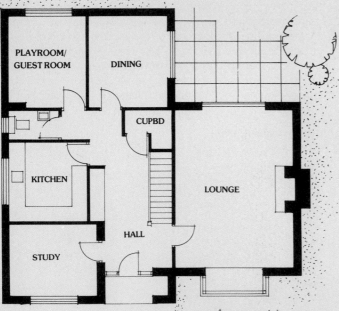

Design Number 83261

Floor Area	1796 sq.ft.	167 sq.m.
Overall size	25'6'' x 39'7''	7.7 x 12.0
Lounge	20'0'' x 15'0''	6.10 x 4.57
Dining	11'6'' x 10'0''	3.50 x 3.05
Kitchen	9'8'' x 10'0''	2.95 x 3.05
Study	11'0'' x 9'0''	3.35 x 2.74
Playroom/		
Guest Room	11'6'' x 9'8''	3.50 x 2.95
Master Bed	15'0'' x 13'2''	4.57 x 4.02
Bed 2	11'0'' x 9'0''	3.35 x 2.74
Bed 3	7'4½'' x 13'7½''	2.25 x 4.15
Bed 4	8'8'' x 9'0''	2.64 x 2.74

261

HOLBROOK

This large detached house with the garage linked to it by the utility room can be built in two stages: house first, the garage and utility room later. The lounge has an unusual shape and the arrangement of the windows in it can be altered as required to suit the views, or your own ideas on the decor that you require. There are five bedrooms and two bathrooms above, and a great deal of cupboard space. A big home that needs to be set in a big garden.

Design Number 83262

Floor Area		
(exc. garage)	2345 sq. ft.	218 sq.m.
Dimensions overall	76'3½'' x 34'1½''	23.2 x 10.4
Lounge	23'5'' x 21'4''	7.14 x 6.50
Dining	12'6'' x 12'0''	3.81 x 3.65
Kitchen	17'5½'' x 12'0''	5.32 x 3.65
Study	12'0'' x 11'1''	3.65 x 3.38
Utility	12'5'' x 10'4''	3.80 x 3.14
Garage	22'1'' x 19'11''	6.74 x 6.06
Master Bed	17'2½'' x 12'0''	5.24 x 3.65
Bed 2	15'5½'' x 12'0''	4.71 x 3.65
Bed 3	14'6'' x 12'0''	4.41 x 3.65
Bed 4	13'5'' x 10'2½''	4.08 x 3.11
Bed 5	11'1'' x 10'8½''	3.38 x 3.26

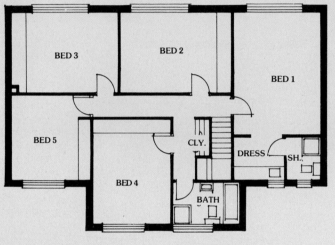

LINCOLN

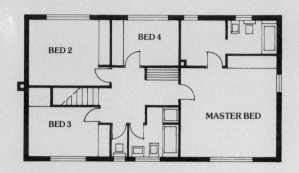

The Lincoln house is a D & M design which has been built in many parts of the country over the last 10 years, and is invariably built at a low unit cost because of the simplicity of the basic shell design. Look how the internal walls to the first floor rise from corresponding walls on the ground floor, at how the drainage is grouped into two soil pipes, and how the two separate parts of the roof are the same span. These are the sort of features which make for cost effective construction.

The Lincoln is illustrated here in a rural setting in an area where traditional stone construction is required, but it looks just as well when built in brick under a pantile roof. The windows in the lounge can be moved around to suit the view, and a great deal of character is given to the room by the load bearing walls which separate it from both the hall and the lounge. Double doors or a feature arch look well when set in a deep reveal, and most clients building the Lincoln house have exploited this potential to the full.

Design Number 83263

Area (inc. garage)	2350 sq. ft.	218 sq.m.
Overall	62'0'' x 27'1''	20.00 x 9.64
Lounge	23'5'' x 16'9''	7.14 x 5.11
Dining	13'11'' x 11'6''	4.25 x 3.50
Study	11'10'' x 8'4''	3.60 x 2.54
Kitchen	14'9'' x 11'10''	4.50 x 3.60
Bed 1	16'2'' x 15'1''	4.94 x 4.60
Bed 2	13'11'' x 11'6''	4.25 x 3.50
Bed 3	13'11'' x 8'6''	4.25 x 2.59
Bed 4	11'10'' x 8'0''	3.60 x 2.44

BAKEWELL

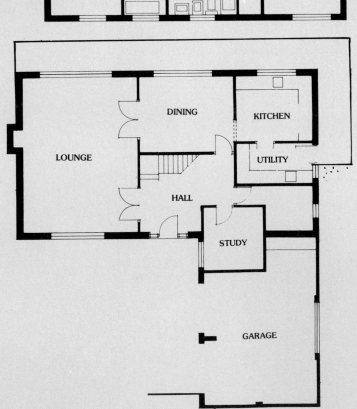

The Bakewell design was first drawn for a client who insisted on a large cloakroom by the front door where he could keep his golf clubs. He also wanted easy access from the hall through the lounge and dining room back to the hall again for the frequent occasions when he was entertaining on some scale. The Bakewell design resulted.

This home is best suited to a large site with views to the rear. It is usually built with patio windows leading outside from both the lounge and the dining room. If this is done, it is essential that the patio on to which they open should be large enough: a generous paved area gives an additional dimension to the feel of any house, while a cramped terrace gives a cramped feel to all about it.

Design Number 83264

Area (inc. garage)	2465 sq.ft.	229 sq.m.
Overall	50'11'' x 45'2½''	15.51 x 13.77
Lounge	23'5'' x 16'11''	7.14 x 5.15
Dining	13'11'' x 11'5½''	4.25 x 3.49
Kitchen	11'10½'' x 10'0''	3.61 x 3.05
Study	9'2'' x 9'0''	2.79 x 2.74
Bed 1	23'5'' x 16'11''	7.14 x 5.15
Bed 2	13'11'' x 8'2''	4.25 x 2.49
Bed 3	11'10½'' x 11'5½''	3.61 x 3.49
Bed 4	11'10½'' x 11'8''	3.61 x 3.55

AVONMERE

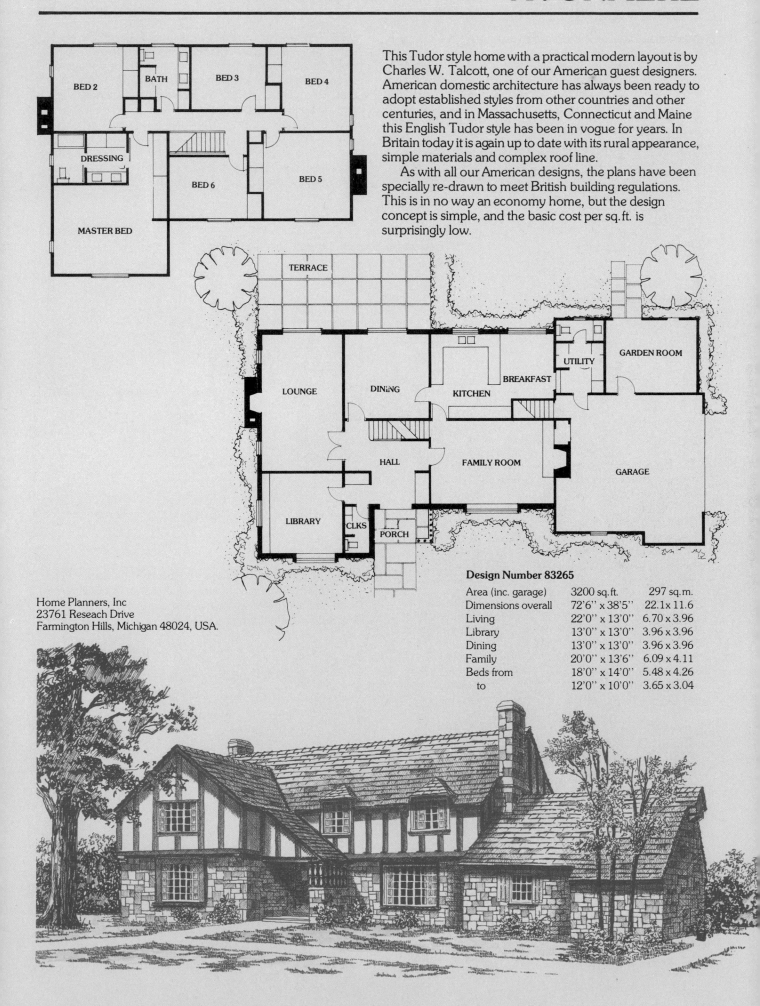

This Tudor style home with a practical modern layout is by Charles W. Talcott, one of our American guest designers. American domestic architecture has always been ready to adopt established styles from other countries and other centuries, and in Massachusetts, Connecticut and Maine this English Tudor style has been in vogue for years. In Britain today it is again up to date with its rural appearance, simple materials and complex roof line.

As with all our American designs, the plans have been specially re-drawn to meet British building regulations. This is in no way an economy home, but the design concept is simple, and the basic cost per sq. ft. is surprisingly low.

Home Planners, Inc
23761 Reseach Drive
Farmington Hills, Michigan 48024, USA.

Design Number 83265

Area (inc. garage)	3200 sq. ft.	297 sq. m.
Dimensions overall	72'6'' x 38'5''	22.1x 11.6
Living	22'0'' x 13'0''	6.70 x 3.96
Library	13'0'' x 13'0''	3.96 x 3.96
Dining	13'0'' x 13'0''	3.96 x 3.96
Family	20'0'' x 13'6''	6.09 x 4.11
Beds from	18'0'' x 14'0''	5.48 x 4.26
to	12'0'' x 10'0''	3.65 x 3.04

CHATSWORTH

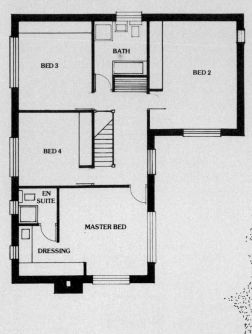

The Chatsworth house suits a site with all-round views, and is a design that affords the housewife the same view from the kitchen sink that she gets from the lounge and dining room. Many clients specifically ask for this, saying that they spend so much of their lives in the kitchen that the view from the kitchen window should be as good as any other.

The arrangement of the master bedroom suite can be changed to give a view to the rear if this is appropriate: if you do this then some re-arrangement of the shower room is necessary so that the windows line up with the lounge windows below.

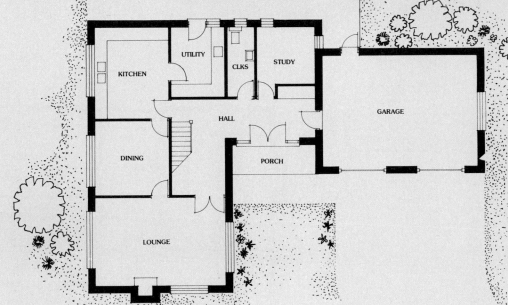

Design Number 83266

Floor Area		
(exc. garage)	2052 sq. ft.	190 sq. m.
Dimensions overall	60'6'' x 41'8½''	18.4 x 12.7
Lounge	20'0'' x 13'5½''	6.10 x 4.10
Dining	11'10'' x 11'2''	3.60 x 3.40
Kitchen	13'7½'' x 11'2''	4.15 x 3.40
Study	9'2'' x 8'10''	2.80 x 2.70
Utility	10'10'' x 8'6½''	3.30 x 2.60
Garage	23'11½'' x 17'1''	7.30 x 5.20
Master Bed	13'9'' x 13'5''	4.20 x 4.10
Bed 2	17'1'' x 11'6''	5.20 x 3.50
Bed 3	12'0'' x 11'2''	3.65 x 3.40
Bed 4	11'10'' x 9'2''	3.60 x 2.80

Drawings are available for a variation of this design with the ground floor layout rearranged so that the utility room is adjacent to the garage, and connects with it. This is the Hardwick design, reference 82266.

MINSTER

The Minster developed from our York design, with the same structure adapted to suit a site where the views are to the rear. One result is to separate the kitchen from the utility room: some housewives find it a disadvantage, but others like the idea.

The garage wing has the same popular garden store as the York, and if required the garage door can be moved into the side wall to suit a different drive layout.

As with all designs where the front entrance is in the angle between two wings of the house, care should be taken to give it appropriate emphasis, with projecting steps and an angled approach path. This is so important.

Design Number 83267

Area (inc. garage)	2600 sq. ft.	240 sq.m.
Overall	53'10'' x 38'4''	16.41 x 11.69
Lounge	23'5'' x 14'1''	7.14 x 4.30
Dining	14'1'' x 11'11''	4.30 x 3.64
Study	11'11'' x 7'10''	3.64 x 2.39
Kitchen	14'5'' x 11'2''	4.40 x 3.40
Bed 1	11'11'' x 11'2''	3.64 x 3.39
Bed 2	12'2'' x 11'11''	3.70 x 3.64
Bed 3	12'2'' x 11'2''	3.70 x 3.40
Bed 4	8'10'' x 8'10''	2.70 x 2.70

REGENCY

This very large five bedroomed house is a splendid design for a prestige site. The key feature — the portico, stairs, and the two huge round bay windows — must be to a very high standard, and we have detailed drawings and specifications for them.

An unusual feature is that the bathroom to the Master Suite is very large with every luxury, at the expense of the bathroom which serves the other bedrooms. And why not — who is paying for it all anyway! Another factor is that there will probably be washbasins in bedrooms 2 and 3 in a house of this size anyway.

The arrangement of stores, workshop and laundry room in the garage wing was drawn to suit the requirements of a client who particularly wanted this layout, and we anticipate that those wanting a home of this size will have the plan modified to suit their own individual requirements.

Design Number 83268

Floor Area (exc. garage) 2484 sq.ft.		230 sq.m.
Dimensions Overall		
(approx.)	84'6½'' x 32'8''	25.77 x 9.95
Drawing Room	16'0'' x 24'0''	4.87 x 7.31
Dining	17'0'' x 11'0''	5.18 x 3.35
Kitchen/		
Breakfast (overall)	23'10'' x 12'8''	7.26 x 3.86
Workshop	11'3'' x 7'6''	3.42 x 2.28
Store	7'6'' x 8'3''	2.28 x 2.51
Garage	18'0'' x 20'0''	5.48 x 6.09
Laundry	8'9'' x 7'3''	2.66 x 2.21
Master Bed	12'8'' x 16'0''	3.86 x 4.87
Bed 2	16'0'' x 11'0''	4.87 x 3.35
Bed 3	11'0'' x 12'8''	3.35 x 3.86
Bed 4	10'0'' x 11'0''	3.05 x 3.35
Bed 5/Study	8'0'' x 9'0''	2.43 x 2.74

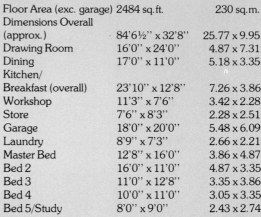

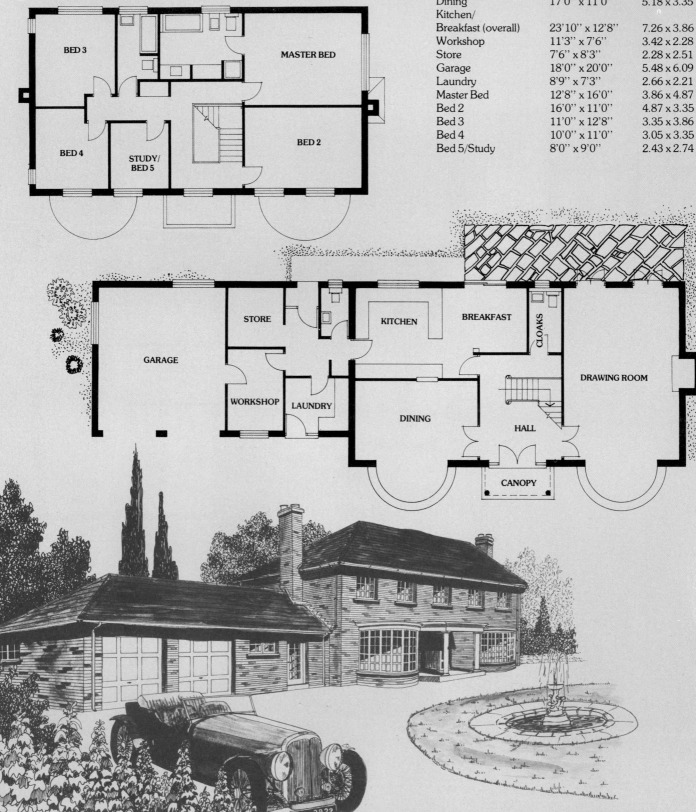

BATHAMPTON

This is a well laid out example of the classic Neo-Georgian house which has always been popular and which can be relied on to appreciate in value ahead of the market. Ideally it should be built with sash windows, but if this is not possible it will still maintain its elegance from the proportions, and from the way in which the front entrance is a focal point.

The choice of walling and roofing material is critical if one is building this house, particularly the balance between the two colours. Often this is a matter of local practice, and before choosing bricks and tiles one has to see whether the original Georgian houses in the area have roofs that are darker than the walls, or lighter — and by how much. You won't want to match the original materials, but stonewold tiles can replace slate, and modern wire-cut bricks will look every bit as well as handmades if the balance between their colours is right.

Design Number 83269

Floor Area		
(exc. garage)	2204 sq.ft.	204 sq.m.
Lounge	25'3'' x 14'0''	7.70 x 4.26
Dining	13'9'' x 14'0''	4.19 x 4.26
Breakfast/Kitchen		
(overall)	15'9'' x 19'0''	4.80 x 5.80
Study	9'0'' x 11'0''	2.74 x 3.35
Utility	8'0'' x 12'3''	2.43 x 3.74
Garage	16'0'' x 18'0''	4.87 x 5.48
Master Bed	12'0'' x 15'3''	3.65 x 4.65
Bed 2	9'8'' x 12'0''	2.95 x 3.65
Bed 3	15'8'' x 10'5''	4.79 x 3.17
Bed 4	9'0'' x 10'5''	2.74 x 3.17

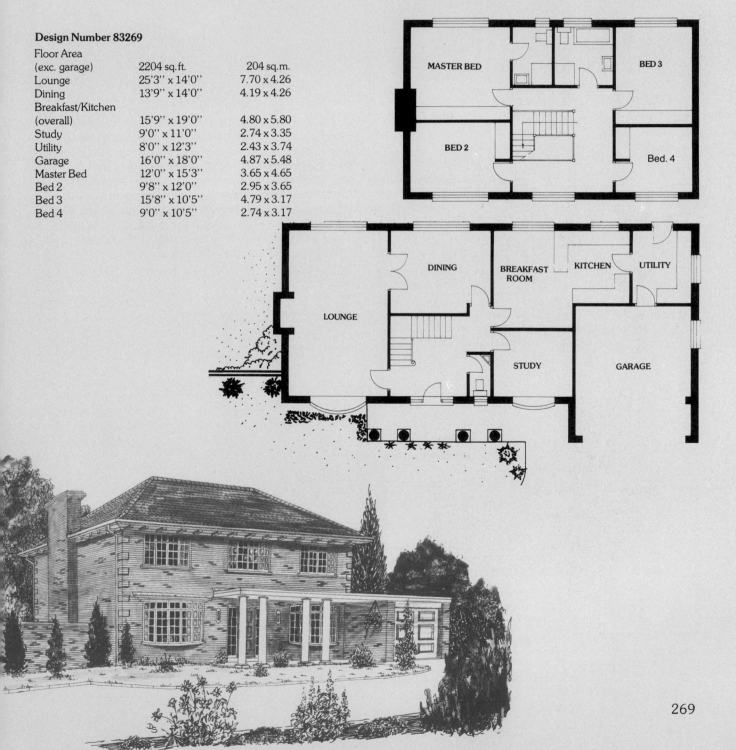

YORK

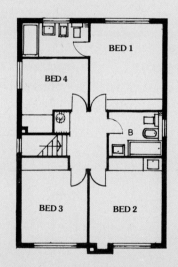

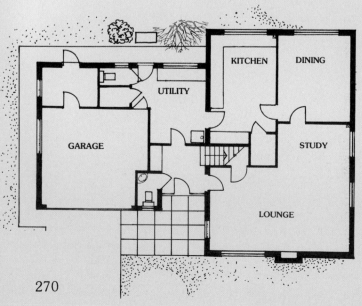

This is a big house, and needs a site with plenty of room. As shown it suits a situation where the main views are to the front. The chimney is a key feature in the building, but if it is not required it can be built internally, giving an opportunity for an angled fireplace at the corner of the inside wall of the lounge. If this alteration is made, the arrangement of windows on the gable end elevation will then have to be considered with care, and the decision must take the landscaping proposals into account.

If the roof pitch has to be increased above 35° to suit the planners, the window to the fourth bedroom may be affected.

The workshop or garden store at the back of the garage is a popular feature of the design.

Design Number 83270

Area (inc. garage)	2600 sq. ft.	240 sq. m.
Overall	53'10'' x 38'4''	16.41 x 11.69
Lounge	23'5'' x 14'1''	7.14 x 4.30
Dining	14'1'' x 11'11''	4.30 x 3.64
Study	11'11'' x 7'10''	3.64 x 2.39
Kitchen	18'5'' x 11'2''	5.60 x 3.40
Bed 1	14'1'' x 11'11''	4.30 x 3.64
Bed 2	12'2'' x 11'11''	3.70 x 3.64
Bed 3	12'2'' x 11'2''	3.70 x 3.40
Bed 4	11'2'' x 9'6''	3.40 x 2.90

A version of this design with a farm office at the rear of the garage (but with its own separate access) is the Pickering, reference 82270.

BUXTON

This large house meets a planning requirement in many rural areas that a building of this size should have a complex roof arrangement. To achieve this with an attractive internal layout while arranging for a loadbearing wall below the point at which a roof changes direction is not easy, but it is essential if costs are to be kept down. We think that we have achieved this very well in this new design, and we are sure it will become justly popular.

The huge lounge/dining/living arrangement can be adapted to suit a clients own requirements — and also to suit the view — and if necessary the kitchen can be extended to take in the living room to give a traditional farmhouse kitchen. The storm porch with its cloakroom between 2 sets of doors is a useful feature.

Design Number 83271

Area	2378 sq.ft.	221 sq.m.
Overall	45'9'' x 44'3''	13.94 x 13.49
Lounge	19'0'' x 18'4½''	5.79 x 5.60
Dining	23'5'' x 14'9''	7.14 x 4.50
Kitchen	15'0'' x 11'8''	4.56 x 3.55
Study	10'10'' x 8'11''	3.30 x 2.72
Bed 1	23'5'' x 14'9''	7.14 x 4.50
Bed 2	15'0'' x 11'8''	4.56 x 3.55
Bed 3	18'4½'' x 9'10''	5.60 x 3.00
Bed 4	14'9'' x 8'10''	4.50 x 2.69

The study/utility room area of the Buxton can be used for a self contained flat. Drawings for this are available as the Matlock design, reference 82271.

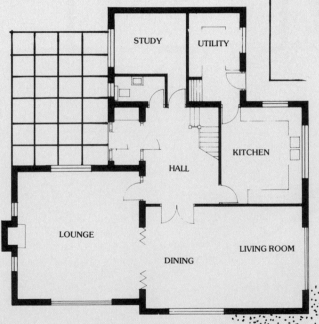

HORNDEAN

This boathouse and holiday home is designed for the familiar situation where a yachtsman wants to let the living accommodation on a commercial basis for part of the year, but does not want the tenants to have the use of his boathouse. To meet this requirement there are no internal stairs, and the two parts of the building are quite separate. The whole structure is designed to be built economically, and the first floor is supported on a prefabricated concrete decking which can be positioned by the crane on the lorry that delivers it. There are further savings to be made if some pillars are acceptable in the boathouse, but a clear span is quite practicable.

Design Number 83272

Floor Area
(exc. boathouse)	840 sq.ft.	79 sq.m.
Lounge	19'0'' x 11'0''	5.79 x 3.36
Dining	12'4'' x 8'2''	3.78 x 2.50
Kitchen	12'0'' x 10'6''	3.68 x 3.19
Bed 1	11'7'' x 10'6''	3.54 x 3.21
Bed 2	10'7'' x 9'0''	3.23 x 2.75

LEANDER

There are still sites for the classic waterside home for the boating enthusiast. Planning considerations will almost certainly require that the design should be traditional, and practical considerations will dictate a generous "wet oil skins" area by the door, a first floor lounge, and a balcony.

This design from the USA is the classic answer to these requirements. The master bedroom suite is on the ground floor with bedroom 2, whilst a further guest room is above. The layout is as practical for the soaking wet crew coming in from a gale as it is for the party they will give when they hear that they have won the race on handicap. Above all the structure is very cost-effective and avoids the money-no-object features often found in this sort of building.

Design Number 83273

Floor Area		
(exc. covered area)	1469 sq. ft.	136 sq.m.
Lounge	15'0'' x 23'4''	4.57 x 7.11
Dining	9'11'' x 9'0''	3.02 x 2.74
Kitchen	9'0'' x 11'1''	2.74 x 3.36
Utility	7'2'' x 7'8''	2.20 x 2.35
Master Bed	14'0'' x 9'0''	4.26 x 2.74
Bed 2	10'9'' x 11'0''	3.26 x 3.35
Bed 3	10'9'' x 13'0''	3.26 x 3.96

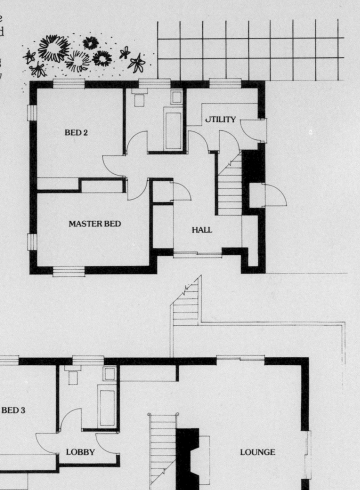

Home Planners, Inc
23761 Reseach Drive
Farmington Hills, Michigan 48024, USA.

273

CARSHOLME

The Carsholme garage/flat was originally built in a Notts orchard where the planners insisted on a 40° pitch roof. It seemed a pity to waste the space in the roof and so provision was made for a small flat above. The whole arrangement works very well, and the design has been used many times. Sometimes the flat has been built as a games room, but usually it is used for overflow accommodation or as a staff flat

This garage can be built without fitting out the first floor, and provided that this space is shown as a loft in the planning application it should escape rating as domestic accommodation. It can always be completed as a flat at a later date.

The two illustrations shew alternative arrangements for the side windows in the flat.

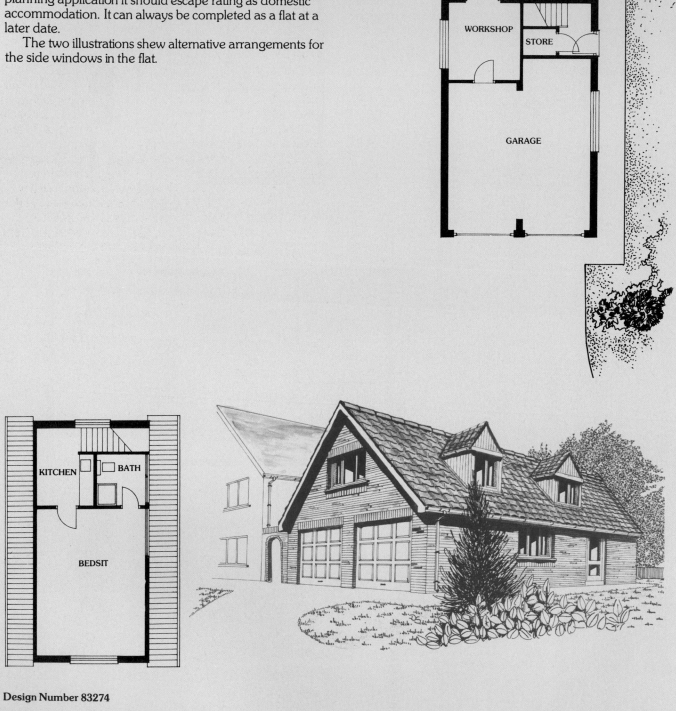

Design Number 83274

274

GARAGE G.21

This large double garage has two separate doors in a gable end, with a garden store and optional W.C. behind. The doors are deeply set in the brick reveals, which gives a very substantial feel to the building. It is important that the roof pitch should match the pitch of the roof to the house or bungalow — the two illustrations show how important this is.

Floor Area (total)	460 sq. ft.	42.7 sq.m.
Overall external	21'6'' x 23'5''	6.5 x 7.1
Garage	18'0'' x 20'10½''	5.48 x 6.36
Store	4'0'' x 14'6½''	1.22 x 4.43
W.C.	4'0'' x 6'0''	1.22 x 1.83

Every garage for a new home should be considered in relation to the house or bungalow itself, so that the smaller building enhances the appearance of the larger, and is related to it in a way which is both practical and attractive. The garage may not be built until a later stage, but the planning application for a new home invariably shows it on the site plan. Remember that the Local Authority may insist on the garage being sited where there is room for a vehicle to turn round on the plot, without having to back out into the road.

All the garages shown are intended to illustrate styles, and practicable sizes. Drawings are available for all of them with garage doors in any style and with any arrangement of side doors, garden stores, workshops or outside W.C.'s that may be required. The dimensions can also be varied within fairly wide limits, but remember that the minimum internal width for a single garage is eight feet, for a double garage with double door is sixteen feet, and for a double garage with twin doors is seventeen feet six.

Standard garage doors are either 6ft. 6'' or 7ft. high. We are often asked for drawings for garages with increased headroom for caravans. This can be arranged, but it is rarely a success. A high garage usually manages to make the adjacent house or bungalow look small, and it is difficult to get the proportions right. If this is what you want please discuss the problem with us — there are ways around it.

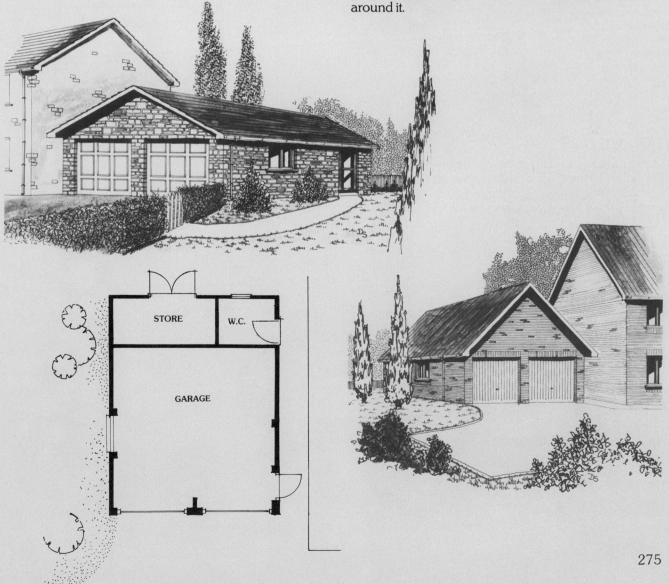

GARAGES

GARAGE G.22

This unusual roof arrangement keeps down the overall height to the building while retaining a tiled front elevation. It also keeps down construction costs. Drawings are available for a version of this garage with two separate 7ft. doors.

Total Floor Area	387 sq.ft.	36 sq.m.
Overall external dimensions	22'11'' x 18'10''	6.9 x 5.7
Garage (internal)	18'2½'' x 18'0''	5.55 x 5.48
W.C. (internal)	8'11'' x 3'6''	2.72 x 1.06
Store	8'11'' x 3'6''	2.72 x 1.06

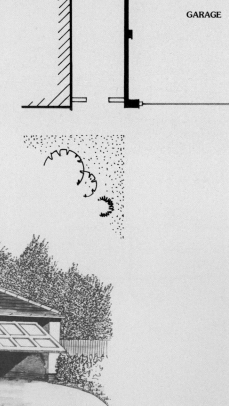

GARAGE G.23

A hip roof may be appropriate to a garage built beside a new house where this roof style is a feature. It is shown here with a double door, but drawings are available for this garage with two doors separated by a substantial pillar.

GARAGE G.24

This flat roofed garage has room for a workbench in front of one car, and a garden store in front of the other. The double doors into the store are necessary if a ride-on mower has to be garaged as well as the cars: few of these will go through a standard doorway.

Total Floor Area	396 sq. ft.	36.8 sq.m.
Overall dimensions	21'6½'' x 20'1''	6.5 x 6.1
Garage (internal overall)	19'0'' x 20'10½''	5.79 x 6.36
Garden Store	10'4'' x 5'0''	3.13 x 1.52

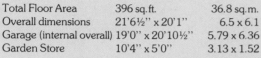

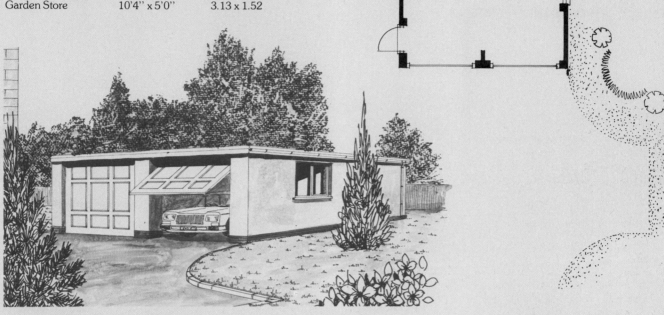

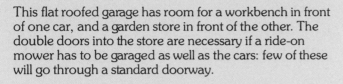

GARAGE G.25

When choosing a design for a garage it is important to consider how it will look in relation to the house which it serves. Sometimes this means that the doors of the garage should be under the eaves and not in the gable end, and this design meets this requirement. Drawings are available for a version with two separate doors.

Floor Area	327 sq. ft.	30.4 sq.m.
Internal dimensions	18'0'' x 18'2½''	5.4 x 5.5
External dimensions	18'10'' x 19'0''	5.7 x 5.8

GARAGES

GARAGE G.26

This garage has a parapet roof with a coping. It is an extremely useful design in some areas, particularly when built in stone to match existing stone buildings.

Floor Area	392 sq. ft.	36.4 sq.m.
Internal	18'0'' x 21'9''	5.4 x 6.6
Overall dimensions	23'9'' x 20'0''	7.2 x 6.0

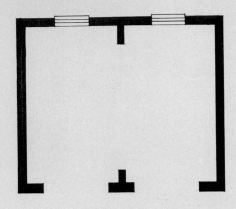

GARAGE G.27

This straight-forward single garage with a pitched roof is shown with traditional side-hung doors. In spite of the convenience of up-and-over doors there are many who like wooden doors of this sort, and all our garage drawings can be altered to show this feature.

Floor Area	207 sq. ft.	19.2 sq.m.
Internal dimensions	11'2'' x 18'0''	3.4 x 5.4
External dimensions	11'10'' x 19'0''	3.6 x 5.8

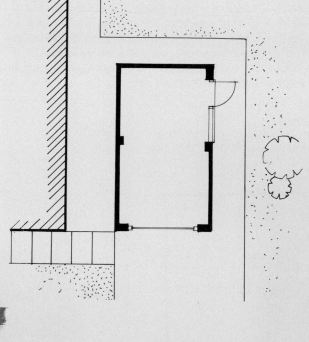

GARAGE G.28

This is a very useful design for a village site where small outbuildings are the rule, and a rectangular garage would seem too modern. The workshop is a useful size, and can, of course, be used for many other purposes, including being a farm office.

Overall dimensions	17'2½" x 17'8"	5.2 x 5.3
Workshop Floor Area	84 sq. ft.	7.8 sq.m.
Workshop Internal	7'0" x 12'0"	2.13 x 3.66
Garage Floor Area	150 sq. ft.	14 sq.m.
Garage Internal	9'0" x 16'8"	2.74 x 5.07

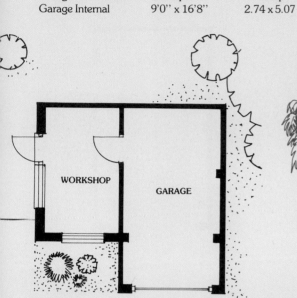

GARAGE G.29

A simple straight-forward garage of the minimum width for a modern car, making it suitable for sites where space is at a premium.

Floor Area	140 sq. ft.	13.0 sq.m.
Overall dimensions	9'9" x 18'6"	2.9 x 5.6
Internal dimensions	8'3" x 17'0"	2.5 x 5.1

GARAGES

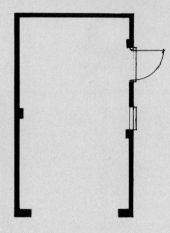

GARAGE G.30

A single garage with the up-and-over door under the eaves. This is the minimum size for a modern car, but of course, it can be extended to your own requirements.

Floor Area	140 sq. ft.	13 sq. m.
Overall dimensions	9'9" x 18'6"	2.9 x 5.6
Internal dimensions	8'3" x 17'0"	2.5 x 5.1

GARAGE G.31

This flat roofed garage attached to one wall of a bungalow requires very careful consideration of floor heights if it is to look right. It is important that the fascia continues from the bungalow right around the garage at the same depth.

Floor Area	333 sq. ft.	31 sq. m.
Internal dimensions	18'6" x 18'0"	5.6 x 5.4
Overall dimensions	18'4" x 19'0"	5.7 x 5.8

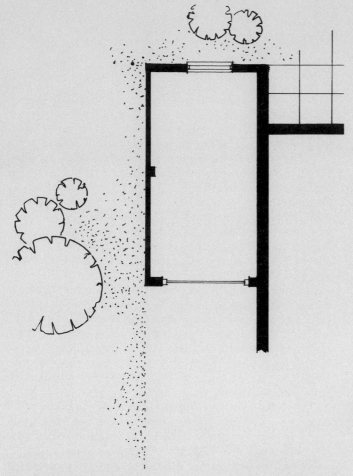

GARAGE G.32

This is a single garage version of Garage G.31 showing it projecting behind the rear wall of the bungalow. This is often arranged to give a sheltered patio area.

Floor Area	207 sq. ft.	19.2 sq.m.
Internal dimensions	11'6'' x 18'0''	3.5 x 5.4
External dimensions	11'10'' x 19'0''	3.6 x 5.8

GARAGE G.33

It is far easier to build a garage against the side of a house than against the side of a bungalow, as the relationship between the floor levels is not critical.

Floor Area	207 sq. ft.	19.2 sq.m.
Internal dimensions	11'6'' x 18'0''	3.5 x 5.4
External dimensions	11'10'' x 19'0''	3.6 x 5.8

P.S.S. service

P.S.S. PLANS

Plan Sales Services Ltd is a specialist company within the D. & M. group which was formed to handle sales of plans for the designs in this book. The service which is offered covers the supply of

* 12 copies of 1:50 floor plans, 1:100 elevations and 1:20 sections with full notes indicating compliance with Building Regulation Standards.
* 10 copies of a roof drawing.
* 4 copies of a foundation plan.
* 4 copies of a floor joist plan.
* 12 copies of a site plan and location plan. Notes on submitting planning applications using P.S.S. drawings.
* 3 copies of a bound short form of specification for the building, without quantities, in the general style of the specification on pages 76 and 77 of this book, but expanded and specifically related to the design to which it refers.
* Notes on placing contracts with builders and copies of the N.H.B.C. hand books for those using the services of N.H.B.C. registered builders.
* A copy of *Building Your Own Home*, the standard hand book for those who build using sub-contractors.

To provide these plans and documents P.S.S. require specific information regarding the site and other details for the proposed building, and this is most conveniently provided by completing the order form on page 285.

ALTERATIONS TO PLANS

Standard plans can be altered provided that the design concept is not changed. The cost of such alterations is quoted as an extra to the basic cost of the plans, and the procedure for preparing altered plans is for an order form to be sent to P.S.S. with the appropriate remittance for the cost of the standard plans. Two prints of the floor plans and elevation for the standard plans will be sent to the client with notes for guidance in considering alterations. One copy of the plans should be returned marked up with the alterations required.

If they are practicable the extra fee required for the altered drawings will be quoted, and if accepted the special drawings will be prepared and despatched within ten working days. If the quotation is not acceptable then the fee already paid will be returned less a handling charge of £5. Fees for alterations will never exceed 50% of the basic cost of the plans.

If the alterations required are not practicable we will discuss the problem by telephone, or will explain the difficulty in a letter, and are usually able to suggest another way of meeting the client's requirements. If it is not possible to make the alterations required, the original fee paid is returned less a handling charge of £5.

SITE PLANS AND LOCATION PLANS

Planning applications require a site plan and a location plan. These are normally reproduced on a single sheet. The standard P.S.S. service includes drawing these plans from data supplied by clients, and responsibility for the accuracy of this data rests with the client.

Location plans are prepared from either any location plan which accompanied an application for an exisiting outline consent, or from a 1:2500 or similar large scale Ordnance Survey map, or from a deed plan or other map available. The original or photostats of such plan should be sent with the order and should have the boundary of the client's land clearly marked. The company holds a licence to reproduce Ordnance Survey plans in this way.

Site plans are best drawn from sketches prepared by clients. An example is shown on page 284, together with a check list of the information which is required.

P.S.S. cannot visit sites to prepare site plans except by special arrangement. Any additional information required by the local authority will be added to a site plan by P.S.S. but the responsiblity for obtaining this information rests with the client.

Clients who wish to prepare their own site plans or to engage a local surveyor to do this for them are welcome to do so, and a reduction of £15 is made to standard fees when site and location plans are not required.

When a client sends an order for a set of plans together with details for his site plan, and our technical staff find that the design of home required cannot be fitted on the site in accordance with building regulations, the fee will be returned less a handling charge of £5. More usually we advise the client of other designs which will meet the requirements of the regulations.

Plans are individually prepared from master data, and are normally captioned with a general description such as "Proposed bungalow for Mr H. Smith at High Lane, Sutton". They carry the client's name and address in the bottom right-hand corner. Except for a reference number they do not carry a P.S.S. or any other logo or name, except when they are timber frame plans for which the design calculations are available from Prestoplan Ltd.

Purchase of the plans conveys an automatic licence to build the dwelling to which they refer. They may not be used for the construction of further dwellings unless arrangements for this have been specially negotiated and confirmed in correspondence. Enquiries from builders and others for the use of our designs on a repeat basis are welcomed.

ALTERATIONS TO PLANS FOLLOWING NEGOTIATIONS WITH PLANNING AUTHORITIES

Negotiations with planners sometimes result in a request from the local authority for a new set of plans incorporating design changes. In this case the planning officer concerned should be invited to overdraw one of the original prints with his required alterations, and this should be sent to us. We will quote for preparing the revised drawings and supplying prints as appropriate.

Such quotations will not exceed 50% of the original cost of the drawing. In exceptional cases the complexity of the planners requirements may lead us to advise clients that we recommend that they seek the assistance of a local architect, and that we withdraw from the matter. This situation arises only very rarely. P.S.S. are unable to represent clients in meetings with planners, or to prepare revised plans except where planners have detailed their requirements in a direct fashion.

All alterations to drawings required by planners are given absolute priority in the P.S.S. drawing office, so there is rarely any delay in providing Planning Authorities with the revised drawings.

QUERIES RAISED IN CONNECTION WITH BUILDING REGULATION APPLICATIONS

Queries relating to site conditions must be dealt with by the client. P.S.S. will deal with all queries *which relate to the structure to the building* raised by the local authority arising from building regulation applications. This is handled by sending P.S.S. the original or a photostat of the letter setting out the additional information required, and P.S.S. will return to the client two copies of a plain sheet providing the relevant information or calculations — one for the client to retain and one to be sent to the authority. There is no charge for this if standard designs are involved, and if the local authority insist on having alterations shown on drawings, the revised prints required will be supplied free of charge.

If building regulation queries relate to an altered design, and arise from the alteration to the design, as when roof design calculations are required after the span of a standard design has been increased, the cost of providing this information and any revised drawing will be quoted. In no case will this exceed 20% of the fees already paid.

For obvious reasons it is preferable that clients check that no alterations are required by planning officers before dealing with building regulation queries. This may result in a statutory refusal being issued on the building regulation application. This is no bar to re-opening the matter, and no further fees are payable. (See page 67).

Additional copies of plans required are available at a nominal charge to cover printing and postage.

A very few local authorities still require a linen print of plans. If clients are asked for this by the local authority we will supply the special prints free of charge.

P.S.S. are able to handle a limited number of planning and building regulation applications on behalf of clients. Fees for this are quoted individually. This work may be carried out by other companies within the D. & M. group, or by associates. The number of applications handled in this way is limited as all are given individual attention. This service is best discussed by telephone — see the order form on page 285.

TIMBER FRAME CONSTRUCTION

Clients wishing to build using a timber frame system will have to have supplementary drawings prepared by the timber frame manufacturer, who will also have to provide design calculations for the structure. The drawings supplied by P.S.S. Ltd are not suitable for this

purpose, nor is the specification supplied relevant to timber frame construction.

The Prestoplan designs on pages 171 to 190 are specifically for timber frame construction, and drawings and design calculations are immediately available for them from Prestoplan, who will also discuss providing their service for most other designs in this book.

Clients who have purchased plans from P.S.S. Ltd and who build with Prestoplan will have the cost of the plans set against their account for the timber frame. Prestoplan Ltd., Stanley Street, Preston PR1 4AT, Lancs. Phone 0772 51628.

DESIGN AND MATERIALS LTD

P.S.S. Ltd is a subsidiary of Design and Materials Ltd, who will provide a package of architectural and material supply services for most designs in the book. They handle planning and building regulation applications for clients who use their service, help them to obtain quotations and to place contracts with builders, and offer a whole range of special services. Their clients who build using sub-contractors are helped with insurances, VAT claims and much else.

The cost of P.S.S. plans is allowed against the cost of the full D. and M. service.

Design & Materials Ltd, Carlton Industrial Estate, Worksop, Notts. Phone 0909 730333.

SITE PLANS

If you wish us to prepare site and location plans for you, please send us a sketch. Something like the example on the right is perfectly adequate for a start. Please show:

The boundaries
Dimensions where these are relevant
Hedges/Walls/Fences
Ditches and direction of flow
Trees if significant
Drainage proposals
Any services or cables on the site
Any existing entrances
Indicate levels and slopes
Mark road and footpath widths
Indicate North point
Indicate scale, or note
 plan *not* to scale
Proposed access
Proposed site and front door
 position of the dwelling
Proposed garage position

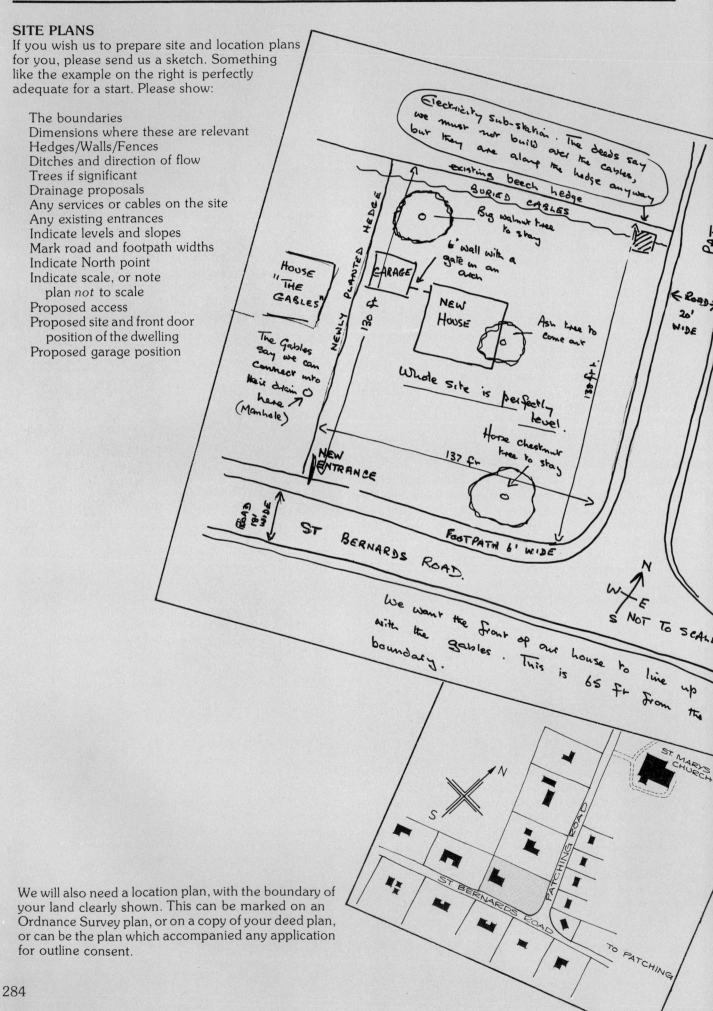

We will also need a location plan, with the boundary of your land clearly shown. This can be marked on an Ordnance Survey plan, or on a copy of your deed plan, or can be the plan which accompanied any application for outline consent.

PLANS ORDER FORM

What design is required? — Name and reference number

To which hand is the design required — as shown in the book, or in mirror image of the illustration in the book?

Do you want any alterations made?

What walling material is proposed? This will be shown schematically on the front elevation. Advise whether brick, random stone, coursed stone, render — please be as specific as possible.

Please indicate roof pitch, ticking the appropriate illustration.

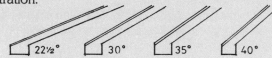

Is the roof to be shown with barge boards and fascia, or with a pointed verge and corbells? Please tick the style required.

BARGE BOARD AND FASCIA   POINTED VERGE AND CORBELLS

Advise whether any french windows or patio doors shown in our design should be shown as french windows or as sliding patio doors (this does not count as an alteration to a standard design).

Should any fireplace and chimney shown in the drawings be retained or deleted? This does not count as an alteration.

Advise which style of external doors should be shown on the drawing — mark "F" for front door, "S" for side door, "B" for back door.

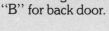

SOLID DOORS   GLAZED DOORS

Do you wish us to prepare a site plan? If so please answer the questions below:

Is a location plan enclosed, or is it to follow?

Is a site plan enclosed, or is it to follow?
(Site plans must give the information shown on the specimen site plan opposite.)

If a full set of standard plans are required please complete this form and send with your remittance.

If you wish P.S.S. to alter standard plans to your own requirements in accordance with the arrangements set out on the preceding pages please complete the form and send with your remittance. We will then send you two standard drawings for you to mark up with your alterations.

If you wish to discuss P.S.S. making a planning application on your behalf please tick this box. ☐

P.S.S. Ltd

Please supply a set of plans and specification as above. A cheque to cover fees is enclosed.

Plans for homes to 1001 sq. ft. —
£120 + £18 VAT = £138

Plans for homes to 1501 sq. ft. —
£160 + £24 VAT = £184

Plans for homes over 1501 sq. ft. —
£190 + £28.50 VAT = £218.50

I understand the basis on which plans are supplied, and am available to deal with queries by phone at the numbers below, when the most convenient time to ring is

................a.m. / p.m.

Date .... Signed ....

Name ....

Address ....

....

....

Daytime phone number ....

Evening phone number ....

Site address ....

....

....

Plan Sales Services Ltd.
Fourways
Blyth
Worksop
Notts S81 8EW.
Phone Blyth (0909 76) 225

Co. Reg. No. 1625297

Orders for plans for S. Ireland to:
P.S.S., Moatland, Navan, Co. Meath.

TERMS AND CONDITIONS OF SALE

1. These terms and conditions are concerned with the sale by Plan Sales Services Ltd, of plans as advertised in the book *Home Plans for the Eighties.* All sales of plans by the company unless expressly stated otherwise are in accordance with these terms and conditions of sale, and clients placing an order for these plans are deemed to do so on these conditions.

2. All contracts are for the sale of plans only, and do not imply the provision of an architectural service, advice on the use of plans or the construction of buildings or other services of any sort except where specifically arranged in writing.

3. All plans offered are drawn to meet the specifications which they are stated to meet, but no liability is accepted for any loss of any sort or additional expense incurred consequent on any failure, real or alleged, of the plans to meet the requirements of any body, statutory or otherwise, or of any loss of any sort or additional expense incurred due to any failure by the purchaser to submit the plans as and when required to any body, statutory or otherwise. All dimensions on drawings which relate to site dimensions, drainage, access, or other features of a development are deemed to have been checked and approved by clients. Clients purchasing plans are advised in writing to check all dimensions shown on drawings and to satisfy themselves that they meet their requirements. No responsibility can be accepted for any loss consequent on failure to do this.

4. All plans are supplied as being adequate to enable competent craftsmen, properly directed and working to the published recommendations of the National Housebuilders Registration Council to erect the building to which they relate, but no liability whatsoever is accepted for the building so erected. Contracts are established the understanding that all plans and drawings supplied will be used by persons competent and experienced in the use of building plans and drawings, and no liability will be accepted for any expense incurred due to the failure of such persons to relate plans and drawings to site conditions, materials delivered, or other circumstances.

5. The company will alter drawings as detailed in the book *Home Plans for the Eighties*, and in other advertising literature, but such alterations will only be made in accordance with specific and precise instructions.

6. The company will deal with technical queries dealing with the application of the Building Regulations and N.H.B.C. requirements to the structures shown in the drawings, but can only do this if provided with the original or a photostat of the query on the letter-head of the authority requiring this information.

7. The company is unable to deal with queries from statutory authorities relating to site conditions.

8. All order for plans are dealt with immediately they are received. If plans are required urgently, as when drawings have to be submitted to a planning authority within a deadline, this should be advised to the company in writing and the work will be given every priority, However, no responsibility can be accepted for the consequences of any delay in delivery of plans.

9. Proof of posting of plans shall be proof of delivery. Any plans lost in the post will be replaced at "copy plan" cost.

10. Master negatives of plans supplied will be kept for a period of three years only.

11. No refunds can be made in respect of plans returned as no longer required, whether or not they have received Planning Consent or Building Regulation Approval.

12. Where clients are referred to Design & Materials Ltd, or any other company for special services beyond the scope of the P.S.S. service, any new contract is between the client and the company concerned, and P.S.S. Ltd will not be a party to any such contract.

13. The copyright of all plans is held by the company, and remains with the company on the supply of plans. The supply of a set of plans as advertised conveys a licence to build one dwelling to the plans supplied, and the erection of further dwellings is a breach of copyright unless this has been the subject of a separate written contract.

14. These terms and conditions define the nature of the contract, and attention is drawn to them in the book *Home Plans for the Eighties* and other publications. They do not detract from the statutory rights of the client in the contract.

Addresses

Plans for designs in this book.
Plan Sales Services Limited, Fourways, Blyth, Worksop, Notts. Tel: 090976 225.

A special service for building designs in this book using traditional construction.
Design and Materials Limited, Carlton Industrial Estate, Worksop, Notts. Tel: 0909 730333.

A service for timber frame construction.
Prestoplan Limited, Stanley Street, Preston, Lancs. Tel: 0772 51628.

Choosing bricks.
Butterley Building Materials, Wellington Street, Ripley, Derby. Tel: 0773 43661.

Choosing stone.
Bradstone — E.H. Bradley Limited, Okus, Swindon, Wilts. Tel: 0793 28131.

Choosing tiles.
Redland Roof Tiles Limited, Redland House, Reigate, Surrey. Tel: 07372 42488.

Choosing joinery.
Bowater Ripper Limited, Castle Hedingham, Halstead, Essex. Tel: 0787 60391.

Choosing a bathroom.
Ideal Standard Limited, P.O. Box 60, Hull HU 5 4JE.

Choosing a kitchen.
Moores International Limited, Aycliffe Industrial Estate, Newton Aycliffe, Co. Durham.

Advice on heat pumps.
Eastwood Heat Pumps, Portland Road, Shirebrook, Mansfield, Notts. Tel:0623 858484.

NHBC publications are available to non-members from:
NHBC, 58 Portland Place, London W1.

Building on your own, using sub-contractors or your own labour?
Read *Building Your Own Home*, £5 post paid from Ryton Books, Worksop, Notts, who send it with the current month's list of councils with plots for sale to self builders.

Self build groups.
General leaflets from the National Federation of Housing Associations, 30/32 Southampton St., London WC2 7AE

Details of professional management services from Wadsworth and Company, Northfield, Snelsins Road, Cleckheaton, W. Yorks.

N.S.S.B.C., 104 Leiden Road, Headington, Oxford OU3 3QU

Insurances for those building on their own
Design and Materials Limited, Carlton Industrial Estate, Worksop, Notts.

Bibliography

The book list below has been produced for us by The Building Bookshop, 39 Store Street, London WC1. They specialise in books on all aspects of building and run an excellent postal service.

Bricklaying
Brickwork Bonding: Problems and Solutions. W.G. Nash.
Brickwork for Apprentices. J.C Hodge.
Initial Skills in Bricklaying. P.J. Tempest.

Carpentry and Joinery
Carpentry and Joinery. R. Bayliss.
Framing, Sheathing and Insulation. Delmar.
Working in Wood. Readers Digest Basic Guide.

Central Heating
Beginners Guide to Central Heating. W.H. Johnson.
Central Heating. Consumers Association.
Central Heating for the Handyman. D.B. York.
Design of Domestic Central Heating. Solid Fuel Advisory Service.
Do Your Own Central Heating Controls. T. Crabtree.
Do Your Own Central Heating Installation. D.B. York.
Microbore Central Heating Systems. Wednesbury Tube Company.

Decorating
Decorating Book. M. Gilliatt.
Home Decorating. Readers Digest Basic Guide.
Laura Ashley Book of Home Decorating.

Drainage
Drainage Details. L. Woolley.

Electricity
Home Electrics. G. Burdett
Home Electrics. J. Worthington.
Householders Electrical Guide. G. Burdett.
Understanding Practical Electrics. Readers Digest Basic Guide.

Exterior Design
Concrete Around Your Garden. C. & C.A.
Constructing Walls, Paths and Outbuildings. A.C. Limon.
Garden and Patio Building Book. Sunset.
How to Build Walls, Walks and Patio Floors. Sunset.
Working with Bricks, Concrete and Stone. Readers Digest Basic Guide.

Heating and Insulation
Domestic Heat Pumps. J. Sumner.
Heat Pumps and Houses. M. Armor.
Keeping Warm for Half the Cost. J. Colesby and P. Townsend.

House Construction
Building Your Own Home. M. Armor.
Build Your Own House. S. Martin.
Construction of Buildings. Barry.

Interior Design
Bed and Bathroom Book. T. Conran.
Home Design. L. Mack & J. Manser.
Homeowners Guide to Fireplaces. R.J. & M.J. Lytle.
How to Plan and Build Fireplaces. Sunset.
House Book. T. Conran.
Kitchen Book. T. Conran.

Legal
Building Regulations. HMSO.
Bradshaws Guide to D.I.Y. House Buying, Selling and Conveyancing.
Conveyancing Fraud, The. M. Joseph.
Legal Side of Buying a House. Consumers Association.
Setting Up Home. S. King & J. Lowrie.

Maintenance
Book of D.I.Y. Skills and Techniques. Readers Digest.
Complete D.I.Y. Manual. Readers Digest.
Concise Repair Manual. Readers Digest.
Home Handyman Encyclopedia. H. King.
Repair Manual. Readers Digest.
Weekend Builder. ed J. Worthington.

Miscellaneous
Concrete Around the House. D. Beadle.
D.I.Y. Tool Guide. ed R. Ball.

Plumbing
Beginners Guide to Domestic Plumbing. E. Hall.
David and Charles Manual of Home Plumbing. E. Hall.
D.I.Y. Home Plumbing. E. Hall.
Home Plumbing Manual. ed D. Thomas.
Home Plumbing. Readers Digest Basic Guide.
Householders Guide to Plumbing. J.M. Haig.

If you have any interest in building for yourself using sub-contractors or perhaps doing some of the work yourself, then the essential book is *Building Your Own Home*. It is not concerned with laying brick on brick, but with *every* aspect of managing the job. It is published by Prism Press and can be obtained by mail for £5 (p. & p. inc.) from Ryton Books, Worksop, Notts who also send a monthly list of local authorities with land for sale to self builders. It is also available from any bookseller.